HOW TO STOP THE PORN PLAGUE

HOW TO STOP THE PORN PLAGUE

071323

A simple, straightforward action plan that can work in your community.

Neil Gallagher

BETHANY FELLOWSHIP, INC.
Minneapolis, Minnesota

Scripture quotations are from the King James Version, The Living Bible, and The Revised Standard Version.

Published by Bethany Fellowship, Inc.
6820 Auto Club Road, Minneapolis, Minnesota 55438

Printed in the United States of America

Library of Congress Cataloging in Publication Data:

Gallagher, Neil, 1941-
    How to stop the porno plague.

    1. Obscenity (Law)—United States.   2. Literature, Immoral. I. Title.
KF9444.G34   345'.73'0274   77-21992
ISBN 0-87123-231-6

Dedication

To Gail, prayer partner and wife,
continuing to trust,
though the money was gone
and threats of harassment grew.
And in whose embrace the ecstacy
of sexual love unfolds.

And to Mr. and Mrs. Charles H. Keating, Jr.,
for twenty-five years of sacrificing
life, fortune, and sacred honor.

Comments

You have done a great organizational job in cleaning up smut. I wish we had a Neil Gallagher in every state.

Morton Hill, S.J.
President, Morality in Media
Commissioner, Presidential
Commission on Obscenity &
Pornography

Neil Gallagher and colleagues have won spectacular skirmishes against pornography, but not without wounds. The campaign in this warfare is always vulnerable; but wounds suffered with honor are reflected in scars endured with pride.

Most evident immediately is the social and economic risk by Mr. Gallagher who sacrificed time, income, and personal comfort when he became involved in smut-removal. It is obviously not an exercise for fainthearted, squeamish, or thin-skinned folk.

Edwin Hayden, Ed.
The Christian Standard

We at CDL appreciate the inspirational work you are doing for the cause of decency in this nation.

Charles H. Keating, Jr.
President, Citizens for Decency
Through Law
Commissioner, Presidential
Commission on Obscenity &
Pornography

I have had the privilege of knowing Mr. Gallagher personally and working with him in efforts for decency and of sharing on an inter-faith level his deep convictions.

I heartily endorse his book for the promotion of human values in the truest Christian sense.

Mother M. Perpetua Hawes
Superioress General,
Diocese of San Antonio

Unfortunately, by default, most communities let a minority set the moral standard, but this evangelical mobilized a campaign which succeeded in removing *Playboy* and a number of offensive magazines.

Editorial
Moody Monthly

Foreword

The good that men do is always in the realm of the uncertain and of the fluid, because the needs and sufferings of men, the sins and failures of men, are constant, and *love triumphs, at least in this life, not by eliminating evil once for all but by resisting and overcoming it anew every day. The good is not assured once for all by one heroic act. It must be recaptured over and over again.*

—Thomas Merton

Forewarning

You are reading dangerous words on sex—the second-most dangerous words on sex written in the past twenty years. The first were written in a magazine, *Playboy*. It opened the door for savage sex. This book closes it.

Reading and acting on *How to Stop the Porno Plague*, you will be misunderstood, gossiped about, insulted, and laughed at. You will receive obscene phone calls and obscene letters. You may be beaten up as Harold Doran was. You may receive a bomb threat as I did.

Pornographers—the people who produce, sell, and buy *Adam, Adam Film World, All Man, Bachelor, Best for Men, Cabaret, Cavalier, Daring Special, Escapade, Fling, Gala, Gallery, Gem, Hustler, Jaguar, Knight, Male, Man's Pleasure, Man to Man, Man's Digest, Modern Man Deluxe, Mr., Night and Day, Oui, Penthouse, Playboy, Playboy Holiday Album, Playgirl, Rampage, Rascal, Rogue, Sir, Swank, Tab, The Swinger, Tiger, Venus, Viva, Vue, Wildcat*—have the hypocrisy of Pharisees, the savagery of piranha, the lust of a stallion sniffing a mare, and the despair of a suicidal. They are full of hate, greed, and fear. They don't know love.

You must love them, pray for them, and fast for them. You must hate what they produce, sell, and buy. Hate it! Jesus hates sin. For that hate, He was killed.

If you're not willing to die for your hatred of pornography, stop.

NEIL GALLAGHER was born in New York and educated in Massachusetts and Rhode Island. From 1963-1965, he served as a Peace Corps teacher and medic in leper colonies in Northern Thailand, receiving the *Foreign Service Award* from the government of Thailand.

He has been a high school teacher, college instructor, university adminstrator, minister and United States Senate political intern. He was elected to *Outstanding Young Men of America* in 1966.

He holds the B.Ed. (History); M.A. (Religion) and M.A. (Philosophy). In 1972, following doctoral studies in Philosophy and Psychiatry at the University of Cincinnati Graduate School and College of Medicine, he returned to college teaching, leaving more time to devote to writing.

He has written thirty articles for popular and professional periodicals, including *The Christian Science Monitor, The Journal of Psychology and Theology, Tall Windows: National Library Literary Review,* and *World Vision.*

Table of Contents

CHAPTER 1

The Descent into Hell

The Gallup and Harris polls say that 79-80 percent of Americans oppose pornography. Why, then, does it stay?

(1) Because citizens are ignorant. They know neither the terror of pornography nor the civic and legal tools to get rid of it. (2) They know little about the answers to basic questions distorted by the pornographers; i.e., what about "censorship"? What about the right to read? What about nudity in museums? Etc., etc.

Short of reprinting actual pornography, I'm telling you the ugly, sick, maniacal, savage, lust-addicted nature of pornography. If you don't want to know, forget it. Drop the book and leave. Don't even pretend you oppose pornography.

Pornography is *not* "just a few naked women." Pornography is sex-torture of children, intercourse between a horse and a woman on a public screen, tying up women and whipping them before and after sex acts—all wrapped up in glossy magazines and sold in your drugstore, drive-in store, and local airport, and shown at the adult theaters in your town.

I am not exaggerating. I am telling you the truth. And I beg you to look for yourself.

I'm telling you how to get rid of it. I'm telling you how to petition, boycott, pass laws, and complain, complain, complain. I'm telling you how to organize complaints, shoving them before city councilmen, state legislators, and governors who, because of the force of your rage, *will act.* Otherwise (they fear) you'd probably lynch them. Some legislators and city councilmen are deeply moral and will, on their own, introduce and press for legislation protecting the beauty and privacy of sex. But some aren't deeply moral. They will pass good, moral legislation only because of public fury.[1]

And the public feels fury only when they *know* the terror of pornography.

The aggressive, open marketing of abusive sex began about 1955 with the limited circulation of a then-unknown magazine called *Playboy.* During the next twenty years, one hundred competitors followed, crowding good magazines off the newsstands. No one dreamed the competition in filth would eventually excrete a magazine like *Hustler*—sold everywhere—peaking 1,500,000 circulation, and boasting a serious challenge to *Playboy's* market.

In the Bicentennial issue of *Hustler,* one finds (July, 1976): a vagina wrapped in a small American flag (on the magazine's cover); a full page color-cartoon, "Chester the Molester," showing a man seducing a doll-clutching, pig-tailed girl; a centerfold showing caricatures of Jerry Ford, Henry Kissinger, and Nelson Rockefeller involved in sexual acts with an animated Statue of Liberty; and caricatures of George Washington, Paul Revere, and Ben Franklin involved in a variety of sex acts with prostitutes.

I cannot tell you the other pictures in *Hustler.* No reputable publisher would accept this book if I did. *Hustler* is sold alongside *Reader's Digest, Time,* and coloring books. Children see the covers. And, flipping through the pages out of curiosity or the attraction of lust (which they don't yet understand), they see what I described.

Two years ago, *Screw* magazine ran a centerfold feature, "Holy Sh—." The trick photos in that feature included: Caption A: a naked Jesus Christ hanging from a cross. Transfixed between His legs was a huge grotesque penis. Caption B: a Roman soldier steps forward and performs oral sex on the dying Jesus Christ. Caption C: a naked nun and Pope embracing and fondling each other.

Screw magazine is sold in street-corner vending machines, accessible for anyone strong enough to lift a quarter.

A 1976 popular porno monthly ran a series on sex-torture and sadomasochism, including a photo showing one sex partner driving a spiked heel into the eye of her lover.

Currently showing in New York and headed for a nation-wide tour is *Let My People Come,* a live drama of the alleged sexual escapades of the children of Israel while wandering in the wilderness.

The next-to-biggest kick in porno movies is bestiality. Currently making the rounds is the movie *Animal Farm,*[2] showing a feebleminded woman having intercourse with a giant hog.

The *biggest* kick in porno movies is live murder. By "live murder" I mean the real thing. The UPI release in October 1975 told the story:

LATEST PORNO: ACTUAL MURDER

NEW YORK (UPI)—Police are investigating the circulation of a bizarre brand of pornographic movies which show the actual murder and dismemberment of an actress on screen.

Viewers at private screenings reportedly pay up to $200 to witness the filmed killings, Detective Joseph Horman of the Police Department's Organized Crime Control Bureau said Wednesday.

Horman said very reliable sources say there are eight movies—called "snuff" or "slasher" films—being circulated.

"I had first heard about them from a reporter," Horman continued. "As a result of that initial inquiry I sought out my sources in the underworld, sources who have proven to be very reliable in the past. They said that in the end, the climax depicts the actual murder of the female."

He indicated the films begin with an actress and several actors engaging in a variety of sex acts. Soon, however, a knife appears, and the actress—obviously unaware of the nature of the film—is stabbed to death and dismembered.

He said a number of films simulate death, but the eight he is after show real killings.

"We came closest in Miami. This was where we actually pinpointed them as recently as seven days ago," said the detective, who is working on the case with four other members of the bureau. "It's such a secret operation, that these things are well guarded. In Miami I had a source who had access to it, but apparently the FBI is putting quite a bit of pressure on in southern Florida and that killed it."

In Washington, an FBI spokesman said they were aware of allegations the movies may be in the United States.

"The thing that is really astonishing," Horman said, "is that there is such a market. That's almost as astonishing as the fact that somebody would actually commit a murder for the purpose of making a film. Based on the price, I would imagine the people who purchase these things are from affluent backgrounds."

Horman said persons showing such films could only be prosecuted under obscenity laws.

The FBI said any prosecution would involve transportation of pornographic material across state lines.

"The murder is in another jurisdiction," Horman said.[3]

Long before the "snuff" films, however, pornography and murder (and other crimes) went hand in hand.

In the summer of 1973, the attention of the world turned to Houston where police dug up the bodies of twenty-two teenage boys. They had been sexually abused and murdered by Elmer Wayne Henley and Dean Corll. Police found in their apartment sex-torture devices sold in pornography shops.

The Deepest Pit in Hell

Dante said the deepest pit in hell was for Judas.

He was wrong. If there are deeper and deeper pits, the deepest is for child-rapists.

Judas had an active conscience. It whipped him so badly, he grabbed a noose rather than forgiveness. Those who stalk children for sex and money have dead consciences.

"America's runaway-child population," the *New York Post* said,—"estimated at over one million by Senator Birch Bayh's subcommittee on juvenile delinquency— provides smut merchants with a rich source of talent.

"There are very few choices open to a 12-year-old runaway seeking means of support. The girls are particularly easy prey for the bus-terminal pimps.

"Boys are vulnerable to an even wider assortment of predators: 'Chicken anyone?' offers the ad in the underground publication. 'Send for our latest brochures on young goodies for your library and home cinema.'

"In pederast parlance, a 'chicken' means a boy. Through mail-order houses, underground magazines and private clubs, certain men swap pictures of nude boys the way lads trade baseball cards." [4]

It's not just runaways. Some wish they could run away. But how does an *8-month-old baby gagging with gonorrhea of the throat* run from its perverse parents? How do four-year-olds and six-year-olds run from sick parents seducing them for sex acts, filmed at home and sold for $60 a reel or $10 a magazine?

Madness—demonic madness.

Pornographers never know where to stop. *Time* said:

"*Lollitots* magazine is one of the milder examples. It features preteen girls showing off their genitals in the gynecological style popularized by *Penthouse* and *Playboy*. Other periodicals with names such as *Naughty Horny Imps, Children—Love and Child Discipline*, portray moppets in sex acts with adults or other kids. The films are even raunchier.

"I just found out about these magazines and films this summer, and I've become a raving banshee over it," says Dr. Judianne Densen-Gerber, a Manhattan psychiatrist who has been barnstorming around the country in a crusade against this abuse of minors.

Child porn is hardly new, but according to police in

Los Angeles, New York and Chicago, sales began to surge a year ago and are still climbing. Years ago much child pornography was fake—young-looking women dressed as Lolitas. Now the use of real children is startlingly common. Cook County State's Attorney Bernard Carey says porno pictures of children as young as five and six are now generally available throughout Chicago. Adds Richard Kopeikin, a state's attorney investigator: "They are even spreading to the suburbs, where they are now considered rare items, delicacies."

Until recently, much child porn sold in America was smuggled in from abroad. Now most of it appears to be home grown, with the steady stream of bewildered, broke runaways serving as a ready pool of "acting talent" for photographers. Pornographers who stalk children at big-city bus stations find many victims eager to pose for $5 or $10—or simply for a meal and a friendly word. Says Lloyd Martin, head of the Los Angeles police department's sexually abused child unit. "Sometimes for the price of an ice-cream cone a kid of eight will pose for a producer. He usually trusts the guy because he's getting from him what he can't get from his parents—love." In many cases, the porn is a by-product of child prostitution. Pimps invite children to parties, photograph them in sex acts, and circulate the pictures as advertisements to men seeking young sex partners. Frequently, the pictures are then sold to porn magazines.

Even worse, some parents are volunteering their own children to pornographers, or producing the sex pictures themselves. Last year a Rockford, Ill., social worker was sent to jail for allowing his three foster sons to perform sex acts before a camera for $150 each. In January, a couple in Security, Colo., was charged with selling their twelve-year-old son for sexual purposes to a Texas man for $3,000.

Some children in porn photos are victims of incest. Parents will have intercourse with a son or daughter, then swap pictures with other incestuous parents, or send the photos to a sex publisher. Sex periodicals, particularly on the West Coast, publish graphic letters on parents' sexual exploits with their own children. Says Los Angeles Martin: "We had one kid in here the other day who is eleven years old. His father started on him when he was six, then sold him twice as a sex slave. The kid had been in movies, pictures, magazines and swap clubs. After a while, he broke down and cried and said how grateful he was to have been pulled out of it."

Such experiences can, of course, scar a child for life. Warns New York Psychoanalyst Herbert Freudenberger: "Children who pose for pictures begin to see themselves as objects to be sold. They cut off their feelings of affection, finally responding like objects rather than people." Some psychiatrists believe that children who pose in porn pictures are often unable to find sexual fulfillment as adults. Another danger, says Los Angeles Psychiatrist Roland Summit, "is that sexually abused children may become sexually abusing adults." [5]

Robin Lloyd, a television newsman in Los Angeles wrote a book on child porn. He collected 264 *different* child-porn magazines, each costing $7 on the average. The magazines included the *Lollitot* type (young girls aping the sex abuse of their big sisters in *Playboy* and *Penthouse*) to ugly, explicit displays, like *How to Deflower a Virgin*. He says that:

...there are even several organized groups in the United States dedicated to the proposition that sex between adults and children "is not only desirable but necessary for the mental well-being of the child."

One such group is the Rene Guyon Society headquartered at a post office box number in Alhambra, California. It claims a membership of *2,000 families.* (Emphasis mine.)

The society one time sported a slogan on its letterhead that read: "Sex before 8 or it's too late."

The members of the society swear that each has deflowered a girl before her eighth birthday. It's likely they read the child-porn manual (which I personally saw, else I would not have believed it), *Lust for Fun* (sold in adult bookstores). A child seducer's manual, it shows in detail how to pick up a little girl from a school yard or playground; how to entice her home; how to lead her to undress and have sex, without her being frightened; and how to hide the traces that you— or anyone—had sex with her.

Investigating child-porn, Dr. Judianne Densen-

Gerber and Stephen F. Hutchinson, president and directors, Odyssee Institute, New York, discovered *Lust for
Fun*—and more:

> Recently, at the Crossroads Store in New York's Times
> Square, we purchased playing cards which pictured
> naked, spread-eagled children. We also looked at a film
> depicting white-gowned children violently and bloodily
> deflowered on their First Communion day by a motor-
> cycle gang after they "freshly crucified" a priest re-
> placing Jesus on the cross. Next, we saw a film showing
> an alleged father engaged in fellatio with his four-
> year-old daughter.[6]

There would be no child-porn had there not been
Playboy twenty years earlier. Pornography—like the
barn-size tarantula of science fiction—demands more
victims in order to grow.

Twenty years hence (if there is still a civilization
in America) there will be sex-acts between children
and animals, and the butchering and burning of children as the climaxes of sex acts (like the current
"snuff" films involving adults). Pornographers do not
stop.

Unless . . . unless angry fathers and angry mothers
and angry singles stop them. Unless they are angry
enough to lose face, money and sleep in order to fight.
Unless they are angry enough to persist—hang the cost.

Those unwilling to express and channel righteous
anger may leave. Now.

Pornography and Violence

Years ago, J. Edgar Hoover, writing in *This Week*
magazine, scored porno's influence on sex crimes:

> What we do know is that in an overwhelmingly large
> number of cases sex crime is associated with pornography.
> We know that sex criminals read it and are clearly in-
> fluenced by it. . . . I believe pornography is a major
> source of sex violence. I believe that if we eliminate the
> distribution of such items, we shall greatly reduce our
> frightening crime rate.

The Report of the Commission on Obscenity and

Pornography[7] includes extensive police files showing that Hoover was, unfortunately, right:

1. *Murder—Sexual Perversion.* Male, aged 27, and female, aged 23, murder a girl, aged 10, and boys, ages 12 and 17. Prior to their death murderers employed torture and sexual perversion and tape recorded the events. Lewd photographs of young girls in pornographic poses and a library of pornographic and sadistic literature (De-Sade) were found in the male's possession. Lee Ian Brady/Myra Hingley Moors case, December 9, 1965, and Lady Snow's book, *On Iniquity* by Scribner, discussing this famous Moors case.

2. *Rape Case.* Seven Oklahoma teenage male youths gang attack a 15-year-old female from Texas, raping her and forcing her to commit unnatural acts with them. Four of the youths, two the sons of attorneys, admit being incited to commit the act by reading obscene magazines and looking at lewd photographs. See Fellers case, Oklahoma City, Feb. 1, 1966.

3. *Assault.* Male youth, aged 13, admits attack on a young girl in a downtown office was stimulated by sexual arousal from a stag magazine article he had previously read in a public drugstore, which showed naked women and an article on "How to Strip a Woman." See affidavit of youth, dated June 30, 1965.

4. *Attempted Rape—Juvenile Delinquency.* A 15-year-old boy grabbed a 9-year-old girl, dragged her into the brush and was ripping off her clothes. The girl screamed and the youth fled. The next day he was picked up by police. He admitted that he had done the same thing in Houston, Galveston, and now in San Antonio. He said that his father kept pornographic pictures in his top dresser drawer and that each time he pored over them the urge would come over him. See Report of Capt. G. E. Matheny, Juv. Off., San Antonio, Texas, Police.

5. *Rape Case.* Woman is raped on the way to church one morning. Just prior to the attack the man was reading obscenity in his panel truck. Cleveland, Ohio. See County Prosecutor Corrigan's story in Universe Bulletin, April 14, 1967.

6. *Rape Case.* Santa Clara County District Attorney Louis Bergna reports, as printed in San Jose, Calif., Mercury, Nov. 23, 1966: "Santa Clara County Crime File

documents cases where teenage boys have attacked, and killed, women after their sex drives were ignited by lewd photos from readily available men's magazines. One youth after seeing a beautiful young girl kidnapped and held prisoner in the British movie, 'The Collector,' carted off a girl and held her for 18 hours while he forced her to commit every act you can possibly imagine. In his home we found nothing but this type of magazine. . . . The adult bookstores are loaded with books on sadism and masochism—sexual satisfaction through the infliction or receiving of pain." Showing the thin book, he said it contained photos of women tied up or being beaten up by other women and it sells for $5.20. "In Santa Clara County we used to think these things were academic," Bergna said, "but a year or so ago police discovered in Sunnyvale a torture chamber where a young professional man beat other men and committed unnatural sex acts. We just completed another case in the Gilroy area in which a young sailor was bound and beaten by another man bent on fulfilling his sexual hunger. *It just might be we have more of this type of thing in this country than we suspect.*"

7. *Juvenile Delinquency—Sex Perversion.* Police officer making rounds in city park discovers minor boy committing act of sodomy on another minor boy. Center spread of *Playboy* was being used as means of excitation. See Juvenile Police Officer Frank Meehan, West Covina, Calif., 1964.

8. *Juvenile Delinquency—Child Molestation.* First Ass't State's Attorney Edward M. Booth, Jacksonville, Fla., writes in his letter of May 27, 1966, "We have four felony charges pending in our criminal courts at this time wherein adults are charged with various sexual offenses involving minor children. In each of these four cases, we have found that obscene literature and other pornographic materials were used to entice minor children ranging in age from 8 to 16 years, including both boys and girls, into indulging in various lewd and lascivious sexual acts with the adults involved. . . . I have found that most cases involving sexual activities with minor children have obscene and pornographic literature and materials involved, and, *perhaps, this is true throughout the country.* . . .

9. *Juvenile Delinquency.* A 17-year-old youth was

picked up for writing a most obscene and suggestive letter to a 14-year-old girl. The youth took the officer to the neighborhood drugstore and showed him the books he had been reading: "Vengeful Virgin," "Sex Appeal," "How to Make Love," all available at 35¢ to a dollar on numerous newsstands. See Report of Capt. G. E. Mathony, Juv. Off., San Antonio, Texas, Police.

10. *Juvenile Delinquency.* A 14-year-old boy on the north side was arrested for making obscene telephone calls. He admitted that he had called over 200 women and girls. He had in his home a huge manila envelope stuffed with filthy pictures. These he had traced from pictures in such magazines as "Sun Bathing," "Nudist," etc., because he had looked them over many times but did not have the money to buy them. He further admitted that while talking to the women he had the urge to hurt them. See Report of Capt. G. E. Mathony, Juv. Off., San Antonio, Texas, Police.

The survey conducted within the Burbank Police Department produced these case histories:

Lt. Warren King, Vice: Sex Perversion—Glendale case. "A 50-year-old man and an 8- and 11-year-old girl were involved. The girls reported to the parents who reported to the police. The defendant came over with some lewd pictures and showed them to the girls. He worked for the family. He showed the pictures, had them pull down their pants and then they played games—ball in the pants, etc. He eventually committed 288 (oral copulation) on the children at their home."

Lt. Ernest J. Vandergrift: Sex Perversion. W——Case—D.R. 67-8108. "A 17-year-old boy had access to a vehicle. He picked up a 5-year and 7-year-old boy and, after showing them a cutout from a nudist magazine behind a building, took them to a park in Glendale. He copulated the 5-year-old boy and forced the 5-year-old boy to copulate him. His record shows he has used a knife. In Burbank he had a prior—he was excluded from Hawaii on the same activity."

Sex Perversion—G——Case. "It was more than 10 years ago. Suspect lived alone. He got himself made Scout Master of the Sea Scouts and took young boys to his hotel. He would talk to them, then give them something to read. In the book it would say, 'Is this making you excited, are you getting a ___ ___? Do you want me to __ ___ ?' He had all kinds of pictures of lewd acts, homosexual acts, etc. He was given psychiatric treatment."

And, since the release of the *Commission Report,* more cases have been reported:

SUSPECT IN COURT, DENIES KILLING GIRL

John Albert Johnson, 24, stood emotionless yesterday as Municipal Judge Richard F. Matia read charges of rape, kidnapping and murder against him in the death of 8-year-old Melissa Desiree Hinke.

Judge Matia read each charge, explaining each time Johnson's constitutional rights. Three times Johnson said, "Not guilty."

He had been in custody since Friday night, about 12 hours before a 16-year-old boy found Melissa's battered corpse in a wooded ravine in Cleveland Metroparks Rocky River Reservation.

Deputy Coroner Lester Adelson said yesterday he could not isolate the exact cause of the child's death. She had been beaten, stabbed repeatedly, choked and raped before she died, he said. The coroner's office is trying to determine the time of death.

Melissa was last seen alive Thursday at 3:30 p.m. when she left her home at 2245 W. 67th St. on her way to a store for two quarts of milk. Her mother, Janice, 33, reported her missing when she had not returned an hour and a half later.

Johnson became a suspect, *The Plain Dealer* learned, after the father of another girl in the neighborhood reported Thursday that a man had tried to entice his daughter into his car.

The father made his call to the 2nd District police station, giving them the license number of the car.

The next day, when he heard of Melissa's disappearance in the 1st District, he called there and repeated the information. Police said the license was traced to Johnson.

Police searched his apartment and impounded his car. Among items they said they found were a pair of blood-spotted undershorts in the apartment, blood and a semen-stained towel in the car.

> *During a lie-detector test Saturday, Johnson reported-*
> *ly told police he had been in a Lorain Ave. adult book-*
> *store earlier Thursday. Police said he had magazines*
> *portraying nude children in his possession.*
>
> Services for Melissa will be tomorrow at 10 a.m.
> in the Bodnar funeral home, 3929 Lorain Ave.[8]

Somewhat earlier, police in Duluth, Minnesota, discovered two cases, one involving the sexual assault
of a baby-sitter by a man obsessed after seeing an
X-rated movie which included a rape scene, the other
involving the attempted rape of three girl hitchhikers
by a man who admitted to being goaded by pornography
viewed in an "adult" bookstore. They also reported
an increase in juvenile sex crimes in which pornography
served as a model. A 12-year-old boy was caught ex-
perimenting sexually with two 6-year-old girls with the
pages of a porno magazine (belonging to the girls' father) opened to color photos depicting sexual activities
among adults. And editors of *Screw* magazine were
recently arrested for their (successful) attempts to
"buy" from parents the sexual services of their children aged 3 1/2 to 11 for photographing. *Newsweek* (Feb.
28, 1977) said that in one year *alone* 30,000 children—
below 17—were sexually exploited for porno magazines or films.

The problem has not been confined to America (although Americans have been the most fecund producers
of porno). British police finally captured the Cambridge
rapist:

BRITISH RAPIST BLAMES PORNO
FOR ABERRATION (AP)

Norwich, England—Sentenced to life imprisonment
Friday, the hooded rapist of Cambridge said pornographic
films drove him to commit the crimes. "It was like living in hell; in other words, I just had to do something."

Peter Samuel Cook was given seven concurrent sen-
tences of life imprisonment at Norwich Crown Court.

Cook, 47, a truck driver who is 5 feet, 4 inches tall,
admitted raping six girls and committing sodomy against
a seventh in the university city of Cambridge.

He was arrested June 8 while bicycling disguised in women's clothing. A bag he carried contained a hood with the word "rapist" stitched on it, skeleton keys to enter homes and rooms, wigs and various disguises, and a knife.[9]

Police say porno ignites sex crimes. Criminals say porno ignites sex crime. Psychiatrists say porno ignites sex crimes.

Pornographers, protecting $2 billion a year, Mafia-enriched war-chest, deny it.

Lust for Profit

In his *Reader's Digest* article, "Sultan of Smut," George Denison said:

The pornography trade has been marked consistently by gangland-style violence. Police records in several states reveal a chilling pattern of strong-arm tactics, even murder, directed at those connected with smut. While authorities cannot say just how directly Thevis (*the "Sultan of Smut"*) is tied to such crimes, consider what has happened to these people known to have associated with him in pornography traffic:

Kenneth "Jap" Hanna left Thevis' smut operations in 1969 and went into business with a New York Mafia pornographer. Their specialty was plagiarizing sex magazines, films and photographs produced by others. Early on the morning of November 13, 1970, Hanna attended what his wife later described as an "urgent" meeting with Thevis. Two hours later, someone drove Hanna's gold-colored Cadillac into the parking lot of the Atlanta airport. Stuffed in the car's trunk was Hanna, shot four times at point-blank range. The case remains unsolved.

In September, 1973, James A. Mayes, Jr., a former Thevis bodyguard who had gone into the pornography business for himself, walked out of his peep-show shop on Atlanta's Peachtree Street and switched on the ignition of his truck. A dynamite blast blew the 40-year-old Mayes through the roof.[10]

In the fall of 1975 (same time as the exposé of "snuff" films), the *New York Times* documented the gangland-porno link:

Mafia Reaps Profits

CRIME TIE FOUND IN PORNO FILMS

NEW YORK—Organized crime has heavily infiltrated the pornographic film business and is reaping huge profits from such successes as "Deep Throat," "The Devil in Miss Jones" and "Wet Rainbow."

An investigation by the *New York Times* has found that Mafia money and Mafia members are involved in many aspects of the business, including the financing and distribution of films and the ownership of some theaters.

In instances where they do not have a direct financial share in the film—for example, "Behind the Green Door" and "The Life and Times of Xaviera Hollander"— organized crime figures have simply pirated copies of the films and distributed them illegally, earning millions of dollars without any investment.

The popularity of such films has provided a tremendous new source of revenue for organized crime. Hard-core films are playing in hundreds of theaters across the country, not only in major cities, but also in suburban communities and shopping centers.

Moreover, the great success of these pornographic films—"Deep Throat" has, to date, made an estimated $25 million—has given several porno movie-makers with Mafia connections the money to go into the production and distribution of legitimate films.

"If the trend continues, these people are going to become a major force in the movie industry within a few years," said Capt. Lawrence Hepburn of the New York Police Department's organized crime division. "The movie business is going to be like the garment business, riddled with Mafia influence."

James Buckley, a cofounder of the porno newspaper *Screw*, has formed a company with his brothers, David and Frederick, to produce . . . films.

So far they have grossed $14 million.

"Mafia guys keep their word," James Buckley said. "When they make a deal, they stick to it and they pay you up front. We've been waiting eight months for $10,000 that a major theater chain owes us. Every time we call them we get a runaround, but nobody in the Mafia owes us money."

Despite the Buckleys' enthusiasm for the Mafia, some members of the porno industry who have been involved with organized crime have found themselves threatened or even murdered.

Jack Molinas, a former Columbia University basketball star, was shot to death in the backyard of his Hollywood Hills home on Aug. 3 and a woman friend with him was wounded. Law-enforcement officials said Molinas, who had served five years in prison for fixing basketball games, was involved with Mafia members in the distribution and production of pornographic films both in Los Angeles and New York.

Last October a man named Philip Mainer disappeared in Youngstown, Oh., and later his car was discovered with bloodstains on the seat. He has never been found. Mainer had been involved with several Mafia-connected distributors of pornographic films and, according to a police report, was believed to have been killed because his associates thought he was informing on them.

The *Times'* independent inquiry came three years after a landmark bust:

The police and District Attorney Frank S. Hogan announced the completion yesterday of a coordinated investigation into major pornography suppliers in the city.

The investigation, lasting more than four months, resulted in the indictment of 12 men and six corporations of 540 counts of wholesale promotion of obscene material. Each count of the felony is punishable by up to seven years in jail or, for corporations, a fine of $10,000.

"I'm absolutely convinced that we have covered every major distributor of obscene materials in the New York City area," said Assistant District Attorney John H. Jacobs, who coordinated the work for the prosecutor's office. "We also learned the whole nature of the wholesale obscenity business, from how the stuff is ordered to when it is delivered."

William P. McCarthy, deputy police commissioner for organized crime control, said the investigation had shown "to our satisfaction" that there were links between some of the indicted distributors and three Mafia families—those of Joseph A. Colombo, Sr., in Brooklyn, Carmine Tramunti in the Bronx and Manhattan, and Simone Rizzo DeCavalcante in New Jersey.

The names, ages, addresses and occupations of those indicted, along with the number of counts in the indictments, were given as follows by Mr. Hogan:

Edward Mishkin, 57, 53 Algonquin Road, Tuckahoe, N.Y. Proprietor of Wholesale Book Corporation, 48 East 21st Street, 56 counts. He has been described by various prosecutors since at least 1955 as a "kingpin" in the pornography business, and has been arrested many times.

Joseph Brocchini, 39, Poly Park Road, Harrison, N.Y. Proprietor of Jo-Mar Card Company, 150 West 42d Street, 20 counts. He has been identified by the Justice Department as an "associate" in the Mafia family of Gaetano Lucchese, now run by Carmine Tramunti. The State Investigation Commission charged in 1970 that his pornography businesses had grossed $1.5 million a year.

One of Mr. Brocchini's companies is Bark Book Distributing, Inc. Blank checks from the company were found in the room of Jerome A. Johnson last year after he allegedly shot and seriously wounded Joseph A. Colombo, Sr., the reputed Mafia chieftain.[11]

While New Yorkers were finding out that dirty money excreted dirty books in Times Square, Southerners were finding out that the Mafia were hustling for profits south of the Mason-Dixon line. Attempting to belt its way into the Bible belt, Mafia-backed porno smacked into bull-dog John W. Quinlan III, Criminal District Attorney, San Antonio, and member of the Governor's Special Crimes Division. Conducting an intensive investigation into the infiltration of pornography through the South, Quinlan's department and a Special Grand Jury submitted a blockbuster report:

The members of the Special Grand Jury wish to submit this report as a result of our investigation of pornography and organized crime in southwestern and southeastern states. Last week we returned thirty-four indictments as a result of this investigation. Each of us trusts that our findings as presented herein will receive your and the community's most serious attention because of the vitally important nature of this matter.

We believe that the facts found by the Special Grand Jury are hard and convincing and they place beyond dispute, the viciousness and unconscionability of those dealing in pornography. We also believe that there is good reason to believe that organized crime exists in the sale, distribution and exhibition of pornography in most metropolitan cities of Texas and throughout the southwest and southeastern part of the United States.

We believe that eleven of the thirteen "adult" or pornographic movie houses and all the adult bookstores in Bexar County are controlled by either intrastate or interstate crime syndicates; one group of which appears to have definite Mafia connections while another group is strongly suspected of organized mob connections.

We found, as an example, that the type of people associated with these operations, a vice president and general manager of one of these groups, and his assistant who were apprehended were found to be in possession of a bomb, a sawed-off shotgun along with two pistols and further evidence indicated they intended to use these weapons to assassinate one of their local competitors. Such violence we found is common in organized pornography operations. We believe that pornography is one of the most evil, immoral and degrading social problems of our times. The peep shows, dirty books and magazines, plastic and rubber sex "aids" and paraphernalia along with the pornographic movies are especially damaging to the bodies, minds and spirits of our youth and young people. We found that juveniles are commonly noted in the audiences of adult theaters. Pornography develops perverted attitudes—among young and old—toward love, marriage, and morals. It corrupts the young and sickens the old.

While it is not our intention to moralize or preach about the evils of pornography, we feel it is important to say first what pornography is *not*.

The film shown in today's "adult" theater is *not* the old "stag" or "party" film showing intercourse between male and female. "Adult" films in San Antonio now show all varieties of oral and anal sodomy, male adults sexually abusing young children, intercourse and oral sodomy with animals, homosexuality in unbelievable manners, sadism, masochism, adults urinating on each other and including every form of moral depravity the human mind is capable of except cannibalism. We have found also that these theaters are not only used as bordellos, bawdy houses and places of human depravity, but are health and fire hazards as well. From personal observation, we have found contrary to other published reports that the average patrons of these places is *not* a 33-year-old, professional, white Anglo businessman, but many of the patrons as well as the management and employees appear to us as the dregs of society.

During the course of our investigation, we discovered coin-operated machines designed to exhibit 8-millimeter film and commonly known as "peep shows" were located at three of the local theaters. These "peep shows" are owned and operated by a West Coast pornography king pin who was recently convicted on several counts of interstate transportation of pornography. We also found that . . . the manager of this operation is a two-time convicted felon. [He] received vending-machine licenses for the operation of these machines which were [then] used for the sole purpose of exhibiting sodomy, bestiality, homosexuality and child molestation.

There exists, we find, a number of respectable members of our community who profit from this destructive activity, with full knowledge thereof, yet claim innocence of wrong-doing because they remove themselves three or fourfold from the license-operators. These respectable members of our community are the landlords of "adult" theaters and bookstores.

The Grand Jury has discovered from expert testimony that approximately 90% of the pornography in the United States appears to be controlled by three groups, all operating within the blessing and cooperation in the national crime syndicate.

Further, the peep shows found in these bookstores are manufactured and operated by a subsidiary corporation of this group. In addition to obscene books and materials, these bookstores also sell 8-millimeter film and paraphernalia[12] designed for perverted sexual use.

In addition, testimony has shown that these locations are among favorite meeting places for various deviate groups.

A Memphis base operation owns three movie houses in Bexar County at the present time. During the course of this investigation, it was found that these theaters have shown exclusively 16-millimeter pornographic films. Inspection of these theaters by police officers and a visit by members of the Grand Jury to one of the theaters have shown violations of the Fire and Health Codes, including nonexistence of fire and exit lights, no locked fire doors, empty cigarette packs and cigarette butts on the floor of the theater, male sperm on the seats, floors and walls of the theaters, and used prophylactics on the floor of the interior of the theater. Evidence that the management encourages homosexual and heterosexual rendezvous in this theater is noted by the prophylactics machines in the restrooms, used prophylactics on the floor, and complete darkness in the theater.

The Grand Jury has found no evidence that teenagers and persons under twenty-one years of age are excluded from these theaters. To the contrary, a seventeen-year-old boy has testified that he has frequented at least three of these adult theaters since he was fifteen and has had both sodomy and masturbation performed on him by adult males. Further testimony of an ex-employee of one theater close to San Antonio College showed that teenage prostitutes applied their trade at his establishment providing patrons with acts of sodomy and intercourse for a price within the theater. Furthermore, another ex-employee of yet another theater testified that male prostitutes in number "cruise through his theater soliciting male patrons at $10 a trick." The same person testified that a fellow employee was himself a male prostitute and made extra money by soliciting patrons. A former female of one of these institutions who had provided live entertainment, told the Grand Jury that she allowed male patrons, at a price, to engage in oral sodomy with her on the stage before the other patrons. This was further corroborated by police officers who witnessed the act.

The Grand Jury has further found that persons involved in the sale and distribution of pornography hide behind dummy corporations and false names. On many occasions they have failed to withhold income tax from employees and pay Social Security Tax, Franchise Tax, and Admission Tax to the State government. And further that due to the use of dummy corporations, false names and false addresses, it is very difficult for law enforcement officers to ferret out the kingpin of these porno operations.

CONCLUSION

After three months of intensive investigation into all aspects of pornography, we are unanimously and unalterably in favor of closing the "adult" bookstores, peep shows and movie houses not only because of their affront to simple public decency but because of their corruption of public morals. These establishments violate every form of moral decency, social acceptability and attack the very heart and fiber of traditional values.

As a group of twelve citizens with widely differing backgrounds and business interests, we solidly appeal to our friends, neighbors and other citizens to ask the members of the City Council and state legislature to enact local ordinances and state laws prohibiting the display and sale of pornographic material in San Antonio and the State of Texas.

We urge Benavides and other members of the District and County Court Judiciary to expedite the trials of those charged with violations of the obscenity laws. . . .

Respectfully submitted,

M. O. Turner
(Foreman of the Bexar County
Special Grand Jury)
Hugh H. Sello
Roy F. Pina
Waddell E. Bohman
James A. Bryant

Graham Lee Burris
Roy E. Cosgrove
Richard E. Eddleman
Arnold T. Garza
Leroy Kirkland Grimes
Chester Huskey
Mrs. Hiram B. Johnson

Meanwhile in the Midwest, Minneapolis reporters were boiling at their inability to get straight answers from the Alexanders, porno czars of Middle America. Finally, Eric Pianin and Patrick Marx of *The Minneapolis Star* laced together a detailed series of articles, completing the national picture that north, south, east, or west, porno was the Mafia's easiest money-maker.

OFFICIALS FEAR PORN NEAR-MONOPOLY
by
Erick Pianin and Patrick Marx
(*Minneapolis Star* Staff Writers)

Ferris and Edward Alexander now virtually control

Minnesota's multimillion-dollar pornography industry, and federal authorities fear their near-monopoly provides the Mafia with an entree to this state.

The Alexander brothers, who made their start 40 years ago peddling newspapers in northeast Minneapolis, dealt directly with New York Mafia figures in the late 1960s. A government crackdown sent Ferris Alexander to a federal prison in 1972.

Most alarming, according to U.S. Atty. Robert Renner, was Ferris Alexander's acquisition last month of the four Wabasha bookstores in St. Paul and two others in Rochester and Duluth previously owned by Robert O. Carlson.

Before being squeezed out, Carlson reportedly owed the Alexanders between $60,000 and $75,000, was selling materials supplied by the Alexanders and was operating in buildings owned by the Alexanders.

"He [Ferris Alexander] has control of pornography in this state, for all practical purposes, and he's one of the biggest dealers in the Midwest," Renner said. "That's bad news, given his past associations."

"What I fear," Renner said, "is the association with organized crime—the subculture whose members seek each other out for mutual protection—and organized crime's potential for corrupting public officials."

Renner said pornography is "one of the more important means" by which organized crime raises money.

... The Alexanders are obliged to deal with distributors controlled by the Mafia, according to police in New York and Los Angeles, where most of the explicit-sex films and magazines are produced.

Moreover, some of these film distributors are pressing for a part interest in theaters across the country that show their films, police sources say.

Ferris and Edward Alexander have turned down repeated requests by *The Star* to answer questions about their activities.

A two-month investigation by *The Star* of the Alexanders and the adult bookstore and theater industry in the Twin Cities area has turned up evidence that tends to substantiate Renner's concerns. The evidence also underscores the Alexanders' influence. For example:

Two of the men convicted with Ferris Alexander in

a 1970 federal court case in New York have ties to the Mafia, according to New York City police and the FBI. The court case involved the interstate transportation of pornographic materials.

The Alexanders maintain close ties with the Minnesota Civil Liberties Union (MCLU), which has intervened in freedom-of-speech cases directly involving the Alexanders during the past six years.

Ferris Alexander contributes to the MCLU and owns the building at 628 Central Ave. NE. in which the private, nonprofit organization operates. *The MCLU does not pay rent to Alexander, according to MCLU officials. Randall Tigue, counsel to the MCLU, also is one of the Alexanders' private lawyers.*

Several of their former associates said the Alexanders buy some of their material from Star Distributors, New York City. Law enforcement officials there say Star Distributors has close ties with the Mafia.

Star Distributors controls the national distribution of *Screw*, a weekly pornographic tabloid newspaper that has a circulation of 85,000. Al Goldstein, publisher and editor of *Screw*, openly admits that he deals with Mafia-controlled distributing companies.

The Cornerstone of the Alexander fortune is a shabby outdoor newsstand at 401 E. Hennepin Ave. It is still run by Nick Alexander, who sells newspapers, used paperbacks, comics and plastic-bagged pornography.

After World War II, the Alexanders began selling "dirty pictures and books" under the counters of their newsstands, according to one former business associate.

In 1959, a Hennepin County Grand Jury indicted John Alexander for selling allegedly obscene materials at 310 Hennepin Ave., then an Alexander-run store. He pleaded guilty to the charge during a 1960 Hennepin District Court trial and was fined $500 and sentenced to a year in the workhouse. He served 30 days.

After court rulings in the 1960s, pornography was more openly displayed and hard-core materials became more available. Consequently, an Alexander sideline became a mainstay—a mainstay that made Ferris and Edward Alexander millionaires.

Today a patron of pornography can pay up to $10 for magazines showing pre-teen boys and girls performing anal, oral and vaginal intercourse. And there are full-color films and magazines depicting men and women performing sex acts with each other, with dogs, with donkeys and with pigs.

Yet the Alexanders deny even the existence of pornography and they cloak themselves with the respectability of the First Amendment.

After a Hennepin District Court hearing Oct. 7, a reporter asked Edward Alexander to discuss the subject of pornography and consent to an interview.

Pointing an accusing finger at the reporter, Edward Alexander said loudly: "Where were you when I was out defending your First Amendment rights? What's pornography?" he barked defiantly. "There is no such thing."

Since then both Alexanders have repeatedly refused to be interviewed by *The Star.*

Reporters, having failed to secure an interview with the Alexanders on their own, decided to seek one through an intermediary.

Edward Alexander again declined and told the intermediary: "My mother taught me never to talk to two kinds of people—whores and reporters." [13]

CHAPTER 2
How To Get Rid of Pornography:
Introduction

The report by the *Times, Minneapolis Star,* and San Antonio Grand Jury didn't shock vice-squads, district attorneys, and journalists. They were the targets of Mafia bribes. They were the recipients of bomb threats. And they were the ones investigating sex-crimes goaded by porno.

They knew what it was about and John Quinlan spoke their sentiments: "In the early years of the Christian Era a Roman emperor, speaking to the Roman senate concerning unrest among the populace said, 'Give them bread and Circuses.' And with that the Roman orgy began. A few years later the empire fell and we descended into the Dark Ages.

"Today's ultra permissive philosophy states, 'What's wrong with a person having a little fun if he is not hurting anyone?' Strictly speaking, a man spending his money to place a bet, pay a prostitute or buy a ticket to hard-core porno theaters and perhaps buy the services of a male prostitute in that theater is not physically hurting his neighbor. But multiply that 100,000 times every day across this nation, and let me ask this question. What makes up the moral fiber of the nation? What makes up its inner strength? Some Phantom Spirit? Or is it the collective discipline of the individual that makes up that nation?

"The salvation of our republic is in self-discipline, not self-indulgence.

"I'm always a little put out with the fact that every time our office investigates smut peddlers, the same hue and cry goes up from certain members of our community, 'Don't you have anything better to do?'

"Today we face a great conspiracy by organized crime to make its money on 'victimless crimes': gambling, prostitution, and the sale and distribution of pornography.

"How is this possible? Because this country is inhabited by a number of 'Good Time Charlies,' who march into the bookie joints, bordellos and porno houses of 'The Mob' and beg them to take their money. The reason gangsters are some of the richest people in this country is that too many of the adults of our society let their lust substitute for their spirit.

"And those 'Good Time Charlies' who aren't in these places spending their money are standing around my office like so many hooded monks mumbling their litany, 'Don't you have anything better to do?' or, 'What's wrong with a little porno?'

"Organized crime would like you to believe that all their bookstores and porno movie houses are run by dirty old men who might use the money they get for selling smut to buy their next jug of wine.... That's not true. The money that is eagerly spent by our citizens at $2 to $10 a clip doesn't stay here in our community. It is sent to New York, Atlanta, Los Angeles and Memphis or whatever other rock the smut peddlers are hiding under. There it is used to make their gambling, prostitution, or porno rig bigger and better and stronger by using their money and power to corrupt, if possible, your politicians, prosecutors and policemen, and in some cases the media. The dollars spent by 'Good Time Charlie' to buy his bag of filth may be used by the smut peddler to buy 'Charlie's' policeman."

Cities begin to rout smut peddlers, said Quinlan, by

first informing the community about the realistic nature of pornography:

> In San Antonio the methods we used to change the communities' feelings about pornography was to simply tell them what was going on in their porno film houses and bookstores. On every one of our Adversary hearings, which took place in the bookstores and movie houses, we took the news media along, with their cameras for a firsthand look. After they saw the hard-core films on the screen showing every perverted act imaginable; after they saw the used condoms and tissues on the floor of the theaters, and the sperm soaked peep shows in many of the bookstores; after they saw evidence of violations of health and fire ordinances abounding in many of these places, they printed what was there.
>
> Most members of the news media are people of a somewhat liberal nature, but after a visit to one or two of these holes, their attitude changed from that of mild skepticism to one of disgust. Whenever, in the course of executing a search warrant, we found films of a particularly disgusting nature, we would notify the media of its existence.
>
> The day my boss went on the 6 o'clock news and announced that we had seized a film showing child molestation, the last of the snickering died. At last the public was upset and, in many cases angry. Another method we used to get the facts to the people was to request a special Grand Jury to investigate the ties between organized crime and pornography. We got one. We issued subpoenas statewide and called in smut peddlers, landowners, employees, and experts on organized crime. The Grand Jury discovered that there were ties between certain Mafia families and the sale and distribution of pornography. At the end of 90 days they issued one of the strongest Grand Jury reports I have ever read. Portions of it were printed in every local paper and in one it was printed verbatim.[1]

Quinlan hit the three main issues: Pornography is a *spiritual problem*: "The salvation of our republic is in self-discipline, not self-indulgence."

Pornography is a *civic problem*: "In San Antonio the methods we used to change the communities' feelings about pornography was to simply tell them what was going on in their porno film houses and bookstores. At last the public was upset and, in many cases, angry."

Pornography is a *legal problem*: "Another method we used to get the facts to the people was to request a special Grand Jury to investigate the ties between organized crime and pornography. We got one. We issued subpoenas statewide and called in smut peddlers, landowners, employees, and experts on organized crime."

CHAPTER 3
The Spiritual Strategy

Two days ago a blizzard threatened Rhode Island. The temperature was 5°, winds gale force, and snow dropped heavily. The weatherman said driving would be treacherous.

My wife called Melanie Santos, telling her the party at our house was called off. Melanie said my wife caught her just in time: she was on her way out the door to pick up her hair-stylist husband, Dennis. Melanie was seven months' pregnant. My wife pleaded with her not to brave the impending blizzard. Overhearing the conversation, I got on the phone and *told* Melanie to stay home. I'd pick up Dennis myself. Which I did.

That's how I happened to sit in a beauty salon and hear two women arguing:

Cyrese: The Ten Commandments don't say nothing about fornication. It says, "Thou shalt not commit adultery." See—*adultery*! That's two married people.

Joni: That has to be wrong. You're telling me that shacking up is okay. That the Bible says shacking up is okay.

Cyrese: Listen, I go to church just like you. I help people, you know. Not always like I could, but the priest has never, never, never said fornication is wrong. It says, "Thou shalt not commit adultery."

Joni: You're wrong, wrong, wro—

Cyrese: If two people love each other . . . all right? If

> they love each other and aren't hurting anybody,
> it's all right. It's awwlllll right!
>
> Joni: Okay, so what's gon—
>
> Cyrese: Show me in the Bible where it says it's wrong.
> You can't do it.

My friend Dennis, a Christian, stopped removing Cyrese's rollers and broke in: "Wait a minute, wait a minute. You want to know where it's wrong? Really? There's a guy waiting for me right on the other side of the booth who knows the Bible better than I do. You want me to ask him?"

Cyrese said okay and Dennis whizzed around the smoked-glass partition. Everybody in the salon had overheard the conversation. I had my pocket New Testament ready. I showed her the Bible's teaching on fornication, and Cyrese, bless her heart, said she had been wrong.

Cyrese claimed to be a devout Christian, but her values didn't bloom from the Bible. They had long been drowned in the swamp of society. She and millions and millions like her *do not know* what the Bible teaches about nakedness, fornication, adultery, prostitution, homosexuality, bestiality, etc. Ignorant of the Bible's teachings on sexual abuse, they tolerate pornography. Ignorant of God's hatred of sexual abuse, they refuse to inspect porno magazines in the drugstore and scream at the manager. And, laughing at Johnny Carson's kinky jokes and Mary Hartman's cavalier sex, they allow pornography to flood the country.

If you're going to do anything about pornography, understand clearly that God *hates* sexual abuse; and, admit that you've been brainwashed and seduced by our "sexually free" culture.

Here is what the Bible says about sexual abuse:

Specific Biblical Teachings

Nakedness[1]

I heard thy voice in the garden, and I was afraid, because I was naked and I hid myself. (Gen. 3:10)

And Ham, the father of Canaan, saw the nakedness

of his father, and told his two brethren without. And Shem and Japheth took a garment, and laid it upon both their shoulders, and went backward, and covered the nakedness of their father. (Gen. 9:22, 23)

I counsel thee to buy . . . white raiment, that thou mayest be clothed, and that the shame of thy nakedness do not appear. (Rev. 3:18)

Fornication
(sexual intercourse between two unmarrieds)

If a man seduces a girl who is not engaged to anyone, and sleeps with her, he must pay the usual dowry and accept her as his wife. (Ex. 22:16)

If a man seduces a slave girl who is engaged to be married, they shall be tried in a court but not put to death, because she is not free. (Lev. 19:20)

Refrain from eating meat sacrificed to idols [and] from all fornication. (Acts 15:20)

I wrote unto you in an epistle not to company with fornicators:

Yet not altogether with the fornicators of this world, or with the covetous, or extortioners, or with idolaters; for then must ye needs go out of this world.

But now I have written unto you not to keep company, if any man that is called a brother be a fornicator, or covetous, or an idolater, or a railer, or . . . such an one, no not to eat. (1 Cor. 5:9-11)

Now the body is not for fornication, but for the Lord; and the Lord for the body.

Flee fornication. Every sin that a man does is without the body; but he that committeth fornication sinneth against his own body. (1 Cor. 6:13, 18)

But fornication, and all uncleanness, or covetousness let it not be once named among you. (Eph. 5:3)

Know ye not that the unrighteous shall not inherit the kingdom of God? Be not deceived: neither fornicators, nor idolaters, nor adulterers, nor effeminate, nor abusers of themselves with mankind. (1 Cor. 6:9)

Looking diligently lest any man fail of the grace of God; lest any root of bitterness springing up trouble you, and thereby many be defiled;

Lest there by any fornicator, or profane person, as Esau, who for one morsel of meat sold his birthright. (Heb. 12:15, 16)

Adultery
(sexual intercourse with another's spouse)

There must be no sexual relationship with ... anyone else's wife. (Lev. 18:19, 20)

If a man commits adultery with another man's wife, both the man and woman shall be put to death. (Lev. 20:10)

Know ye not the unrighteous shall not inherit the kingdom of God? Be not deceived: neither fornicators, nor idolaters, nor adulterers, nor effeminate, nor abusers of themselves with mankind. (1 Cor. 6:9)

Incest
(sexual intercourse with one's relative)

None of you shall marry a near relative, for I am the Lord. A girl may not marry her father; nor a son his mother, nor any other of his father's wives, nor his sister or half-sister, whether the daughter of his father or his mother, whether born in the same house or elsewhere.

You shall not marry your granddaughter—the daughter of either your son or your daughter—for she is close relative.

You may not marry a half-sister—your father's wife's daughter; nor your aunt—your father's sister, because she is so closely related to your father; nor your aunt—your mother's sister, because she is a close relative of your mother; nor your aunt—the wife of your father's brother.

You may not marry your daughter-in-law—your son's wife; nor your brother's wife, for she is your brother's. You may not marry both a woman and her daughter or granddaughter, for they are near relatives and to do so is horrible wickedness. (Lev. 18:6-17)

If a man sleeps with his father's wife, he has defiled what is his father's; both the man and the woman must die, for it is their own fault.

And if a man has sexual intercourse with his daughter-in-law, both shall be executed: they have brought it upon themselves by defiling each other. (Lev. 20:11, 12)

Everyone is talking about the terrible thing that has happened there among you, something so evil that even the heathen don't do it: you have a man in your church who is living in sin with his father's wife. (1 Cor. 5:1)

Homosexuality
(sexual relations between members of the same sex)

Homosexuality is absolutely forbidden, for it is an enormous sin. (Lev. 18:22)

The penalty for homosexual acts is death to both parties. They have brought it upon themselves. (Lev. 20:13)

And the men, instead of having a normal sex relationship with women, burned with lust for each other, men doing shameful things with other men and, as a result, getting paid within their own souls with the penalty they so richly deserved.

So it was that when they gave God up and would not even acknowledge him, God gave them up to doing everything their evil minds could think of. (Rom. 1:27, 28)

Know ye not that the unrighteous shall not inherit the kingdom of God? Be not deceived: neither idolaters, nor adulterers, nor effeminate, nor abusers of themselves with mankind, nor thieves, nor covetous, nor drunkard, nor revilers, nor extortioners, shall inherit the kingdom of God. (1 Cor. 6:9, 10)

Bestiality
(sexual intercourse with animals)

Anyone having sexual relations with an animal shall certainly be executed. (Ex. 22:19)

A man shall have no sexual intercourse with any female animal, thus defiling himself; and a woman must never give herself to a male animal, to mate with it; this is a terrible perversion. (Lev. 18:23)

If a man has sexual intercourse with an animal, he shall be executed and the animal killed.

If a woman has sexual intercourse with an animal, kill the woman and the animal, for they deserve to their punishment. (Lev. 20:15, 16)

Prostitution

Do not violate your daughter's sanctity by making her a prostitute, lest the land become full of enormous wickedness. (Lev. 19:29)

For this ye know, that no whoremonger, nor unclean person, nor covetous man, who is an idolater, hath any inheritance in the kingdom of Christ and of God. (Eph. 5:5)

General Biblical Teachings

Keep away from every kind of evil. (1 Thess. 5:22)

Fix your thoughts on what is true and good and right. Think about things that are pure and lovely. (Phil. 4:8)

Obey the government, for God is the one who has put it there. (Rom. 13:1)

Remember, too, that knowing what is right to do and then not doing it is sin. (James 4:17)

Let the word of Christ dwell in you richly. (Col. 3:16)

For we are not fighting against people made of flesh and blood, but against persons without bodies—the evil rulers of the unseen world, those mighty satanic beings and great evil princes of darkness who rule this world; and against huge numbers of wicked spirits in the spirit world. (Eph. 6:12)

God said it. I believe it. That settles it.

But, using these marvelous brains God has given us, we ask *why*? I *believe* He condemns sexual abuse, but *why* does He?

Does God think sex is dirty? Does He want to deprive us of fun? Or does He know, better than we do, that sexual abuse brings hate, depression, murder and suicide?

God condemns sexual abuse because sexual abuse is immorality, *par excellence*. And *all* immorality ravages people.

Here is immorality:

In our universe, there is a wide, thick, eternal line. Above the line are people, below the line are things.

People

Things

People are to be loved. Things are to be used.

Immorality is the reversal. It's immoral to love

things. It's immoral to use people.

$$\text{Immorality} = \frac{\text{Use People}}{\text{Love Things}}$$

It's immoral to use people for *any* reason. It's immoral to use people for political, racial, financial, or sexual advantage. People who are used are people who hate. Prostitutes confess that they hate men. Less than 1% of prostitutes successfully marry. They've never learned love. They've been used.

God likes sex. He created it. He wants men and women to enjoy it, not abuse it. It's lovely, passionate, and irreplaceable ecstasy. The Bible commends husbands and wives who sexually enjoy each other (2 Cor. 7:3, 4). God made Adam and Eve pure and nude. Satan made them prurient and naked. Sex, manipulated by Satan, is abuse, leading to death and banishment from God.

God wants His people to love each other, not use each other. He knows they'll be happier that way.

People who produce, sell, and buy pornography are not happy. Their lust, greed, and appetite for shock will never be satisfied. They traffic in hate. And hate is emotional cannibalism. Pornography is an extravaganza of sexual abuse, a relentless, vile outpouring of hate. It is the enemy of love, the enemy of God.

In fighting pornography, then, the first strategy is spiritual: know what the Bible teaches about sexual abuse. And then confess the following:

Confess you've been brainwashed by our Johnny Carson culture. Confess you've tolerated sexual abuse. Confess you've been seduced to believe (a) "We can't do anything to get rid of it." (b) "Some pornography's not so bad." (c) "Aaaaa, let consenting adults do whatever they want." All three are false.

Consider (a), *"We can't do anything to get rid of it."* "I don't like my children to see grotesque breasts on magazines and books at drugstores, airports and food stores, but there's nothing we can do about it."

That's what the mother said to me.

"That's trash . . . trash," said the man standing next to me at the airport bookrack, "but the Supreme Court has said it's all right to sell. What're ya' going to do?"

They're wrong! The Supreme Court still upholds convictions of sexual abuse. In the past ten years hundreds of pornographers have been arrested. We have pornography laws. We have civic instruments to trumpet moral outrage to get good laws enforced and better laws passed to clean up racks and screens.

The hundreds of successes in routing pornography chafe the indifferent, anger the playboy, and embarrass theological elitists. Together they bury news of the successes. You rarely read them in the paper and you never hear them reported on TV.

But the successes pile up: Millions of Americans in the past ten years have caught on fire and cleaned shelves and screens of their cities and states. They combined spiritual, civic, and legal power to do so. Housewives, college students, governors, senior citizens, businessmen, college professors, attorneys, clergymen, electricians, engineers, physicians, nuns, writers, secretaries, farmers—all cleaned their cities and states of pornography.

Consider (b), "*Some pornography's not so bad.*"

Martin Luther King said that it is no more possible to be half-free than it is to be half-alive. Ditto with purity vs. pornography.

It is no more possible for a book or film to be half-pure than for a person to be half-alive. It is no more possible to have pornography that's "not so bad" than a corpse that's not so dead.

Get this straight in your head. *There is no "hard-core" pornography.* There is no distinction between hard-core and the "other" kind. There is no "other" kind. It is *all* pornography: The slick porno magazines *Playboy, Penthouse, Swinger, Sir!* and a hundred others; the films "Deep Throat," "Last Tango in Paris"; the paper-pulp magazines like *Screw*; the crude, vicious and pagan TV shows where cavalier talk-show hosts joke about their divorces, preach homosexuality, laugh with prostitutes and applaud strippers as people with "great hearts"; the "comedy shows" showering blessings on fornication-with-everyone (not unlike the behavior of stray dogs)—I repeat, it's *all* pornography.

If you wish to tell me that *Playboy, Penthouse,* etc. are harmless because they carry occasional articles by John Kenneth Galbraith, Saul Bellow, and other notables, I'm leaving—because you're hopeless. (If you think *Playboy,* etc., are harmless, drop to your knees and ask God to crack the shell of paganism, encrusting your heart.)

For *one* feature article, *Playboy* pays $3,500. Anyone is tempted to prostitute his talents for $3,500 a shot.

Let me tell you about *Playboy, Penthouse,* etc. I was administrative assistant, Student Life Office, at a prestigious university in Texas. One of my duties was to periodically enter the rooms of the men in the dormitories, examining heating vents and thermostats. In every second room *Playboy* centerfolds were stretched on the ceilings directly above the beds.

After lounging in bed, feasting eyes and arousing lusts, the men sailed out to date an unsuspecting girl.

Read again the list of sex crimes in which *Playboy* (and others) were involved (pp. 21-23).

Three years ago, I had to crack the shell of paganism around my heart. I never attacked *Playboy.* What would people have thought of me?! After all, 80% of American college men read it. Even cabinet members and presidential candidates grant it interviews. (P.S. In his third debate, Jimmy Carter repented. He said if he'd had to do it over, he wouldn't have granted the interview to *Playboy.*)

And I was terrified to call it "pornography." I'd be laughed at. I'd be sued. (So I thought.)

Playboy is "porno-graphy" (writings of prostituted sex). And I said so, live, on a TV talk-show, debating a porno attorney. I challenged him on the spot—and the millions watching—to take me to court if I was lying.

Playboy is, in the words of Charles Keating (Commissioner, U.S. Commission on Obscenity and Pornography), "the most salacious magazine in America." *Playboy* blasted open the flood of abusive sex on a nation of decent citizens totally unprepared for relentless appeals to their lust.

Pray for the producers, sellers, and readers of *Playboy* (and all porno magazines). They need love. They need peace. And, after praying, turn on civic and legal power to blast magazines from the shelves.

Consider (c), *"Aaaaa, let consenting adults do whatever they want."*

If Jones consents to Smith's request to poison him, Jones is still a murderer. The "consenting adults" theory is a lie, and I'll talk more about it in Questions and Answers, in chapter 9.

Pray for yourself in exposing all the lies of pornography. Claim the power of 2 Timothy 1:7 (RSV): "For God did not give us a spirit of timidity but a spirit of power and love and self-control." And then ask the Lord's discipline, compassion, and courage for the civic outrage you'll lead.

CHAPTER 4
The Civic Strategy

> It is the ground swell of public opinion, not legal
> arguments, which moves events and nations.
> —Charles W. Colson,
> *Born Again*

Personal Action

Every time you enter a quick-stop store, drugstore,
supermarket, motel lobby, airport, bus station, look
at the magazine rack. Look at the cover and contents.
If there's something up there you know isn't right, take
it off the stand, turn to the worst paragraph or worst
photo, and march to the manager, saying, "Sir, did
you know this was on your shelves?"

Fifty percent of the time he will say, "Where did
you get that? You didn't get that in my store."

He's not putting on. Wholesalers whiz into a store,
fill up racks with paperbacks and magazines, and hand
a receipt to a clerk who simply counts the magazines.
Store, airport, motel managers rarely check their own
racks.

After he says, "Where did you get that?" guide
him to his own racks, open up more magazines and
show him.

I escorted a manager of a department store to his
own racks. He was shocked. He rolled a shopping cart
to the rack and—rather than simply removing the
Playboy joke-and-cartoon, sex paperbacks and re-

turning them for a refund—he ripped them apart. One at a time. And nearly filled his shopping cart.

I have talked with retailers in every part of America. I know there are many good men and women who simply do not know the contents of the magazines they casually sell.

One evening, speaking in Chattanooga on the subject of "How to Get Rid of Pornography," I shared with the audience the strategy of taking pornography directly to the manager. I told them that many managers simply did not know the contents of their own stores. Later, a man approached me: "Mr. Gallagher, I know what you're talking about. I'm a Christian and I own a drugstore in north Chattanooga. Last week while I was working behind the pharmacy counter, a customer came up and said, 'Joe, I just wanted to tell you I'm glad to see that you're finally starting to carry these books.'

"He held before me a copy of *Forbidden Lover*, a big-bosomed, naked woman on the cover.

" 'Come on, you didn't pick that up in here,' I said.

" 'Huh? Well, I sure did. Right down that aisle.'

" 'Get off it, you didn't get that out of my store,' I repeated.

" 'I'll show you; come here.'

"I went with him and there were more copies of the same book and others like it on my paperback bookrack. I told him it was a mistake and I took them all off and returned them to the jobber—and got a full refund, by the way."

Some managers think that they have to sell porno in order to receive *any* magazines from the wholesaler. They think (with a little bit of coaxing from the wholesaler) that if they don't sell porno magazines (*Playboy, Penthouse,* etc.) and the paper-pulp porno (*Teen, True Confession,* etc.), they will be denied a dealership on *all* magazines. In other words, they think they will be forbidden to sell *Reader's Digest, Time, Popular Mechanics, Christianity Today,* etc. They are told it's an "all or nothing" business deal. But it's not.

Managers, angry upon witnessing the sex-exploitation pornography slipped on their shelves, have bundled them up and returned them to the wholesaler, announcing, "I'm not going to handle this stuff. If that means I can't sell any of your magazines, that's tough."

Guess what? The wholesaler, anxious to keep profits rolling in from *any* magazines, *Reader's Digest, Christianity Today* or *Time,* lets the store continue to sell straight magazines.

Wholesalers had been bluffing. You know why they had been bluffing? Because they get rich on porno magazines—real rich. Estimates vary, but to produce a porno magazine costs 30¢ to 50¢. And they sell (are you seated?) for $2 to $15 each. That's a 600% to 3,000% mark-up.

It takes only a few years to get rich sucking in profits with a 600% mark up. And it takes only a few months to get rich from 3,000% profits.

Wholesalers and retailers know that lust is big, big money (that's why they'll fight like trapped rattlesnakes when you challenge them). In an eastern state, one wholesaler offers retailers a $400 bonus *just for displaying porno.* If they don't sell a single magazine, they still get $400. Wholesalers know that a glistening photo of a bare-breasted, pink-panty-ed, wet-lipped prostitute throws a man's hand to his wallet, jerking out $5 to buy the chronicle of lust.

Wholesalers want to get richer and richer and richer. So they tell retailers, "Sell the porno magazines or you'll get *no magazines.*" But that's false.[1]

And presidents of multi-chain stores don't know what wholesalers are putting on shelves in their own stores. Let presidents *know* what's on their shelves. Ralph Nader says that if you want something done, shoot right to the top.

Jack Exum did:

This week a very strange thing happened—I got angry!

While shopping in one of the more popular national chain stores, I noticed a most controversial book on display, "The Joy of Sex." It was placed on shelves that could easily be reached by a youngster, and I could just picture my 9-year-old daughter opening the book and paging through it. The book is replete with line drawings of every conceivable position of sexual behavior.

By long distance, I called the chief executive officer; his office was 3,000 miles away. He was appreciative of my interest and promised to look into the matter at once. Then I called the local store manager and explained that I had just been in contact with the executive officer of the chain. I gave him my name and address and read the letter that expressed my concern. He responded by removing the books from the shelves of his store immediately.

The following day I received a return call from the head office. Each store had been informed to remove the books immediately, and return them to the supplier, and refuse any further orders. He thanked me for my concern and interest. The answer to my anger was "action."

To this day, no one at the head office knows anything about me but my name and address, but they know more about us than we know about them. They know it is our money that builds their buildings, pays their salaries, clothes their children. They know that, when a reasonable complaint comes in, it represents one who in turn may reach hundreds in influence.

They know the POWER OF THE BUYER— we DON'T!

If one individual, unknown except by name and address, can exercise power in a giant corporation, that influences hundreds of stores, think what all of us could do in "turning the tide" on any important moral issue if we could just get "angry."

"I can't believe I'm that powerful." [2]

I want you to hear what I am going to say: *If EVERY Christian EVERY time he enters EVERY store complains about porno on the shelves, porno, nationally, will disappear in a month.*

There are fifty million active Christians in the United States (according to the wire services, reporting on Jimmy Carter's campaign).

A *conservative* estimate is that once a day each of us passes a newsstand, enters a drugstore, quick-stop store, or supermarket, or enters a motel, bus, train, or airport lobby. *Look at the racks every* time you enter!

Cut out the next paragraph. Xerox it, then tape it to your bathroom mirror or sun visor in your car, forcing you to look at it often: *If EVERY Christian EVERY time he enters EVERY store complains, porno will disappear.*

What about the *other* 50%, i.e., the managers who don't want pornography to disappear, who won't wipe it off immediately? They'll say:

> Yuh, I know it's there. Fact of the matter is, I sell fifty of those a week.
>
> If you don't want it, mister, don't buy it.
>
> I never read 'em myself.
>
> I put 'em up high where the kids can't get 'em. (The kids he's talking about must be those in diapers.)
>
> Nobody knows what's obscene. What's obscene to you ain't necessarily obscene to the next feller.
>
> What's wrong with a beautiful broad?
>
> I just sell them.
>
> Who the h— are you!
>
> I just sell whatever central office tells me to sell.
>
> No one's ever complained before.
>
> What are you talking about? Why aren't you out screaming about (pick one): All the hungry children in the world; getting capital punishment again so we can keep some of these cut-throat nuts off the street; drugs that are blowing everyone's mind; getting our taxes where we can live with it.
>
> C'mon, no kid's gonna' be ruined by looking at a few breasts.
>
> Get outa' here before I call the police.
>
> You think this stuff is illegal and obscene? Here's a dime. Go over there now and call the police.[3]

No matter what you say in response, you won't win. It's not a comparison of opinions to arrive at truth. The truth is already established. You're right and he's wrong. Better, the *Bible*'s right, and he's wrong.

And he knows he's wrong. That's why he's screaming and insulting. He knows *he*'s wrong, he knows *you're* right. Rather than admit it, he runs. Get this: The volume of his voice and the filthiness of his insults are in direct ratio to his anger-at-himself for being wrong. People who are right and know they are right do not scream and insult.

Sometimes I speed, zipping along the New York-Providence-Boston corridor of Interstate 95. Sometimes I don't speed.

One day my soft-spoken and infinitely patient wife said, "Sweetie, I think you've got a lead foot today. We're gonnnnnaaa—get a ticket." I looked at the speedometer and it was 50 mph. Casually and politely I said, "Honey, I don't think so. I just checked. But thanks anyway."

Another day I had a thousand things popping in my head and tried to get them all done before we left on a trip. I made us late, but I was determined that I was going to make us on time when we finished. I was hitting 70 mph and building.

After passing a commuter-Amtrak running parallel to us, my wife said, "Sweetie, I . . . ah . . . think you're speeding."

I said, "Would you please watch the kids. We coulda' got out in time if I hadn't had to watch them and pack too. When, huh, when in all the time we've been married have I told you how to drive? I'm telling ya'—that's one way where you're just like your mother —you think ya' need two people to drive. But, no, not when *you're* driving. I trust you. I know that you know what you're doing."

When we're wrong and know we're wrong, we attack the person whose presence and words expose our error.

When people are wrong and know they are wrong, they do one of two things: They admit it. That cleanses their guilt and allows them to start all over. Or they deny it—and keep running. Their guilt intensifies, like a shoe rubbing on a heel blister. And running makes it worse. You've got to admit you've got a blister, take off your shoe, and clean the infection. Then you can start all over.

Weekly, the newspapers carry a story something like this:

HONESTY CATCHES UP
or
A CONSCIENCE PAYS DIVIDENDS
or
TWENTY-THREE-YEAR THEFT ALL OVER

The manager of Best Buy supermarkets received on Wednesday $153 in cash in an envelope with no return address. The envelope contained a brief note:

Dear Sir:

When I was a boy, me and my buddies used to go in your store. I hate to tell you but I used to steal things. Candy, some cigarettes, packages of cold meat and cheese, chips and some other things. I knew it was wrong then, but I just gave in. All these years I've known it's wrong. Well, I've been waiting until I could get a big pay from an income tax return or a raise or something like that to pay you back. But it never came. Finally, I just went to a loan company to borrow the money which I figure is what I owe you plus interest for all the years in between.

The note was unsigned.

Criminals either give themselves up and praise the great relief they feel, or they commit more vicious, more frequent crimes, running from guilty consciences.

The more a store manager knows he's wrong for selling pornography, the more vicious and more frequent will be his insults. The more he screams at you, the more he's showing that he knows that you're right. He wouldn't scream and insult if he didn't feel threatened by your message.

If he immediately takes the magazines off, you've obviously gotten through. If he insults you, you've also gotten through. When you speak the right and good, you can't lose. People recognize the right and good when they hear it. Some admit it, some don't.

Those who don't want to hear it will let you know. You'll be called a trouble-maker, a publicity pig, a dangerous citizen,[4] a sex maniac, a prude (see ... you can't win), a Bible nut, a hypocrite, a censor, a no-good $¢@*&, a screw ball, and many, many, others. Some of the things will be said to your face, some not.

They know they're wrong for selling porno. If they won't admit it, they'll attack you. Bank on it—and praise the Lord.

> Blessed are you when men revile you and persecute you. ... Rejoice and be glad, for they persecuted the prophets before you.

"But won't I feel nervous and scared, even if the manager doesn't get angry with me? Won't I feel nervous and scared, just having to pick up that filth, open it up, and take it to the manager?"

I hope not. Because then you can call me—collect and immediate—and tell me how you did it *without* being nervous and scared. I want to know how to do it without feeling nervous.

In three years, I have been in hundreds and hundreds and hundreds of drugstores, supermarkets, quick-stop stores, airport/motel lobbies.[5] I've talked to hundreds of managers and I always feel nervous and scared.

It's called fear. And Satan is the author of it. I learned long ago to claim the power of 2 Timothy 1:7, "For God did not give us the spirit of timidity but a spirit of power and love and self-control."

Sure, sure, sure.

No, I mean it.

My pumping-iron frame of 5' 7 1/2", 145 lbs, goes bananas when I have to talk to a manager. My tongue turns to sandpaper, my stomach feels like a popcorn machine, and my knees turn to warm butter.

It makes me sick to look at that garbage. It makes me sick to handle it. But who is going to show a manager his magazines—which promote child-molesting, laughing about adultery, and abusing the female body —if you and I don't show him?

I take out my pocket New Testament and read to myself, "For God did not give us the spirit of timidity but a spirit of power and love and self-control." And I say, "Lord, you know I'm scared. I absolutely cannot do this on my own. If it's going to get done, it's going to have to be your power and love and self-control."

You ask for Christ's power and love and self-control and you'll get it. Then you speak to the manager with that power and love and self-control and—watch out! They'll respond to you just like people responded to Christ in the New Testament: They accepted Him gratefully, or rejected Him hatefully. There's no middle ground.

Managers have thanked me. I told you about the manager who immediately ripped up the porno books. I told you about the Chattanooga druggist.

Managers have cursed me. One man got so angry his eyes narrowed to slits like a cat, his chin turned white with hate, and his cheeks shook like a jackhammer. He dared me to use the phone to call the police. When I reached for the phone, he hurled it off the table. He screamed like a man having a leg amputated without anesthesia—curses, threats, four-letter hate words.

I didn't call the police. I drove directly to the police station. (More on that later.)

One woman told me to go-back-where-I-came-from and never-come-back-here while she slammed her two palms against my shoulder blades and pushed me out the door. (My ego was fractured.)

All I did was show these people what was in their magazines. And I asked them if they knew they were selling material like that.

Of those managers who refuse to remove porno, most won't react that violently. They recognize that their anger is a confession of guilt. They don't want you and other customers to witness their guilt.

Here are typical responses from managers and suggested answers:

"*Aw, those magazines don't bother anyone.*" Would you let your daughter or granddaughter date a boy who had just filled his eyes with one?

"*She's got a mind of her own—she can do what she wants.*" If she were pointing a gun to her head, would you say, "She's got a mind of her own—she can do what she wants"?

"*It's just the adults who get them. I don't let the kids read them.*" Of course, they can read them. They're right next to *Time* and *Reader's Digest*. Besides, you and I know that kids steal them.[6]

"*I just sell them. I don't think I can tell people what they can read or can't read.*" Correct. You can't tell the public what to read and what not to read. You *can* regulate what you sell. Once you circulate a product within a society, you are subject to the laws of society governing the circulation of the product. You're free to eat poisoned soup, but you're not free to sell it.

"*People will get sick of it after a while—it'll blow away.*" Are you going to wait until your wife is attacked before it "just blows away"? Or until your daughter is molested? Or until your son is picked up by a porno-goaded sex torturer? And it is not blowing away. Porno on open shelves and public theaters began about twenty years ago with "just" naked women. That didn't satisfy. Pictures of child-molesting and sex torture followed. That didn't satisfy. Pictures of bestiality followed. Porno is not fading away. It is engorging itself, growing —claiming victims every day like

"*I got to make a living.*" And that's exactly what a prostitute, hit man, drug-pusher, car-thief says.

"*Hey, I just sell whatever the office sends.*" A manager of a quick-stop store said he was helpless—it was up to the company. I bought his worst magazine and called the president and told him that there was something of questionable legality in his stores I thought he'd like to know about. Could I come see him?

I would not tell him over the phone. People have to *see* what it is to be shocked enough to move.

I saw him and laid out before him the worst pictures. The magazine left the store.

The answers are only suggested. Every situation will be different, but these are a guide. Whatever answer you give, respond with uncompromising firmness and uncompromising love. You hate porno and love the manager and you can tell him so.

Don't try to win an argument! You won't. He won't let you. Remember, he's on the run, escaping from a guilty conscience. He'll say anything to keep running from the truth.

You've given him the benefit of the doubt. He disappointed you. He used his free will badly and refused to admit his sin and change.

Then it's time for the next clout. You say, "Sir, if you continue to sell these magazines, I am not going to trade here, and I'm going to encourage my neighbors not to trade here."

And you'd better mean it. Be prepared to drive several blocks out of your way to do your shopping.

And then hold up the magazine to any adult or group of adults around you in the store and say, "Do you see this garbage the store is selling? Look at it. They don't care if children can pick it up or whoever. Are you going to let them continue to sell this garbage?"

Christians in New York, launching an effort to clean up Times Square, used the same strategy: Give the benefit of the doubt first; then hit hard:

> To combat obscenity and prostitution, Christians use what they call "operation olive branch." Their first step is to scout out a suspect establishment. For example, Paul Moore and Dick Lam of the Mayor's office recently decided to check out a massage parlor down the street. The place was advertised by a man walking around in front on the sidewalk, with a sandwich board that depicted a half-nude girl. Mr. Moore and Mr. Lam went upstairs and found "a middle-aged proprietor sitting in a sleazy lobby," Mr. Moore said. Through doors that

opened into the lobby, they could see several small rooms which contained beds.

"In the background, we saw six or seven nearly nude girls staring out of blank, expressionless faces," Mr. Moore recalled. "They might as well have been pieces of meat on a rack."

"How much does it cost?" Mr. Moore asked the proprietor.

"Ten dollars a throw," the man replied.

"Does that include everything?"

"Everything."

When it becomes clear that such a place offers illegal sexual services, Phase 2 of the operation begins. A representative of the church meets with the proprietor and the women and says, "We understand you want to make a living, and we'd like to explore how you can re-route your business into a more legitimate enterprise."

If they refuse the offer—or "olive branch"—then the church members and their secular supporters may resort to picketing and put pressure on city police authorities to enforce obscenity and prostitution laws.

Sometimes, though, the olive branch does the job. After hearing that pornographic movies were planned for a nearby theater, Christians voiced objections and suggested alternatives to both the theater manager and the corporate owner of the building. The theater is now showing general interest films.[7]

That works.

Everyone knows, I repeat, everyone knows, deep down in the silences of his soul, that sexual abuse is wrong. Many won't admit it. And many who do, can't or won't do anything about it. They're sheep. They need a leader. They need someone to speak their convictions, to give them courage, to remind them of purity, nobility, virtue and beauty.

Please don't give me this stuff about, "Oh, they won't listen to me. I'm just a preacher, an old lady, one businessman, a housewife, a college student, a tourist, a priest, an old man, an uneducated farmer, a nun, one customer. . . . "

Stop it! Right now . . . stop those damnable dodges:

If you're rich or poor, young or old, ragged or poised, farmer or stockbroker, Ph.D. or illiterate, male or female, Satan will always find an excuse for you *not* to speak up if you let him.

Claim 2 Timothy 1:7. "For God did not give us a spirit of timidity but a spirit of power and love and self-control."

After you finish your conversation with the store manager, go home and write a letter to the editor. Tell him what you saw and the manager's reaction. Write the same letter to your mayor, city councilmen, state representatives, governor, congressional representatives, and the President. You'll get a response full of cliche's or a response of real concerns and action —or no response at all. But you did what was right.

Oh yes, you'll be up past midnight, writing all those letters and buying all that postage. But I told you at the beginning that if you weren't willing to die to uphold God's standards, don't even start. Because if you start and quit, that discourages others. Unless you *will* pay the price in time, money, and reputation, don't even start. Please.

Next day, return to the store with a witness. Check the shelves. You may find that, despite his insults, the manager obeyed his conscience. He cleaned the shelves. Go thank him immediately. (Many managers clean shelves just because they're weary of the complaints.)

If the porno is still there, buy two samples of the worst. And buy a few grocery items or drug items to go with it. (Buying *just* the magazines arouses suspicion.) After you've purchased the magazines and have the evidence and receipt firmly in hand, look the clerk in the eye and say, "I bought these magazines to call for your arrest. I'm going to show them to my neighbors. I'm going to show them to the police." Return to the manager and tell him the same thing.

That works. One drive-in store had just put in a rack of fifty-six porno paperbacks—the kind that used to be hidden in adult bookstores. I bought one and told him I was taking it to the attorney general if he didn't remove them. I returned four hours later and they were gone.

Furthermore, telling the manager that you're going to take it to the police lets *everyone* know that you did not buy them to feed your own lust.

Then, take the magazines to the police, sheriff, or district attorney. If he's not in, return the next day. Show him the magazines and say you want to swear in a complaint. That's all there is to it. When legal authorities accept a complaint, you don't have to do another thing. They investigate, they bring the store to court.

If it's that simple, why haven't citizens been swearing in complaints for years?

Laziness, ignorance, and fear—that's why.

They're too lazy to bring in a complaint, or they don't know they can swear in a complaint, or they're afraid of being laughed at or sued. Even if some junior police-clerk laughs for bringing in a sex magazine ("in this enlightened and sexually free age"), you've still made your point: *This citizen wants the law enforced!*

And when your personal complaint is backed up by dozens of others, they'll enforce the law. Even if they're lazy.

I think most police, basically, want to do the right thing. But they're brainwashed too! Thinking that "porno's not too bad," they stall. In one city, I called for the arrest of a newsstand dealer. Police stalled. I wrote a letter to the mayor and newspaper. The police moved.

And you won't be sued. Once the complaint is accepted, the police department or district attorney becomes the plaintiff, not you.

The people who produce and sell pornography don't want to go to court. Because that means their magazines will be in court. They don't want an average jury to actually see what's in a porno magazine. That's why, on a talk-show, I called *Playboy* pornography and challenged a porno attorney to take me to court if I was wrong. It would be great to get it in court, so that more and more people would know the abusive sex in that magazine and its one hundred imitators. But the porno people want to stay out of court.

So far, I've talked about stores that *do* sell pornography. What about stores that do not? Good question.

(Remember. *Every time you enter EVERY store, look at the magazine rack.*)

If a store has a clean rack, seek out the manager and (with as many people around as possible) say: "Sir, I really appreciate you. I notice you weren't carrying those trashy magazines. Boy, a lot of those guys don't care what they sell. I tell you, I feel a lot better coming in here with my kids. I'm going to do all my shopping in here and encourage my friends to do the same."

That does two things for the manager: First, just in case the manager had been thinking about selling pornography, he won't now. Second, he probably knows he's been losing profit by not selling porno. You've let him know that someone recognized his sacrifice and praised him for it.

It teaches two things to the customers who overheard: Pornography is wrong; let's speak up against it.

Write a letter to the president of the store chain and tell him how much you appreciate his *not* carrying pornography. And send a copy of your letter to the manager, reinforcing your earlier compliment. If the president had been thinking of introducing pornography into his stores, he won't now.[8]

I need to say a word about films before talking about civic strategy that enlists *public* action.

Newspaper ads for films, these days, are sexually grotesque. Take your pick of the film you think is the worst and write to the manager. Give him the benefit of the doubt. "Sir, do you know what's in that film? Would you let your daughter or wife participate in such a film?"

If he writes back saying he never watches the films himself, call him for an appointment. Show him the worst porno magazine you can find and tell him *that's* what's up there on his screen.

If he refuses to stop showing the films, tell him you are going to swear in a complaint. Before you go to swear in your complaint, take ads from the last several weeks and make a small scrapbook, showing the insane escalation in sex-abuse movies.[9] Slap on the desk of the police chief, sheriff or district attorney your scrapbook, showing him the grotesque chronicle and telling him you want to swear in a complaint on the latest movie before the trend gets worse. I swore in a complaint against "Last Tango in Paris," the district attorney moved, and the film left town. That's not as good as getting the film in court and getting a conviction, but it was better than nothing.

Fighting porno magazines or films will create enemies. "A man's enemies will be those of his own household," Jesus said. You're going to be hurt when, opposing you, will be some neighbors and church members. You're going to find out that people with whom you'd been attending church all your life are church-goers and not Christians. They will do nothing, absolutely nothing, to halt sexual abuse. They will not write a letter, make a phone call, or sign a petition. They will not picket, boycott, or talk to a manager.

And they will criticize you for doing so. They will say: "Just preach the gospel," "The Church ought not to be involved in censoring," "We can't tell people what to read," or "I teach my children about what's right in sex at home. At home—that's where it's got to begin."

There's an answer to their responses, and I take them up in chapter 9 on Questions and Answers.

But there's no protection for the hurt you'll feel. Ever spill steaming-hot water on your hand? That's the pain you'll feel when friends desert you.

I want to relate two incidents, illustrating the intensity of this battle. One day a pastor of a large church of a major denomination called me.

"Mr. Gallagher?"

"Speaking."

"This is _____ at _____. Please take my name off the mailing list and phone committee."

"Sure, but, aah, would you mind if I asked why?"

"Because all I see is *hate* in this campaign. Hate, hate, hate. People are upset and hateful in what they're saying."

"Mr. _____, you called right while I was in the middle of a letter to the editor explaining my motives and trying to sort out a lot of things people are saying."

"No, I'd just rather you didn't call me anymore. I hear people talking at church. I read the editorials and letters.[10] It's hate, pure hate. That's the way I feel about it. We'll . . . see you."

"Yuh, thank you for calling."

I don't know why I didn't cry or throw up. I felt like doing both. I stumbled into a deep depression. His call came a day after a close friend at church said to take her off the phone committee. I groaned, pouted, and ached like Elijah thinking he was the last one left. Each step I took felt as if I was trudging through thigh-deep mud. The phone handle felt like a bag of lead.

Days later I saw it. The deserting pastor was absolutely right. Fighting pornography, fighting racism, and fighting pollution generates hate.

Profit-obsessed czars hate you when you demand pollution and safety control in cars and factories. They tried to impugn Ralph Nader.

Powerful bigots (North or South) hate you when you register blacks for voting and demand equal education opportunities. Martin Luther King was shot.

And the people who produce, sell and buy pornography *hate* you when you demand that sexual abuse stop. Harold Doran was beaten up.

Also hating you will be many parents (including church-goers) who tolerate pornography. Some allow their children to read porno. (One city councilman allowed his children to read pornography. He tried to run me out of town.) When you remind people that pornography is sexual abuse (which, deep down, they already know), they are ashamed. They hate themselves. But, rather than confess, they turn their hate toward you. And it hurts.

You'll be accused of "dividing families" and "dividing communities." The accusation is partly true. One day a woman called my wife:

"Mrs. Gallagher, you don't know me, but do you mind if I tell you something?"

"No, that's all right."

"Please tell your husband to keep on going in what he's doing. My husband used to get *Playboy* and other things all the time. And he used to show me them. We've had four kids and I keep a home—you know what I mean—you do too—and he says to me, 'Why can't you look like that?' I knew he was wrong in reading that swill, but I always felt cuckoo in saying anything. Since it's been on the news—you know what I mean—and in the papers, my husband don't feel so cocky anymore talking to me. And he's gotten kind of ashamed of himself I guess 'cuz he don't bring them home anymore. But he—well, I guess I'd have to say—he hates your husband. 'Cuz he don't have no excuses anymore."

I said the accusation was partly true. The division in families is *already* there. One family member tolerates sexual abuse, another doesn't. The division in the community (or church) is *already there.* Some members tolerate pornography, some don't. Your blistering, loud, and uncompromising condemnation of pornography is like fire salutes exploding in the sky Fourth of July night. Everyone sees, everyone hears.

People are forced to ask: Do I like what I see? They are forced to make public their feelings toward pornography. Are they *for* it or *against* it? No middle ground. Many who are for it would rather not let it be known. And they hate you because your stand in fighting pornography forces them to take a stand. It smashes their hard hearts to pieces. Jeremiah said: "Does not my word burn like fire? asks the Lord. Is it not like a mighty hammer that smashed the rock to pieces?" (Jer. 23:29).

When people express hate toward you, don't answer. Or simply say, "I love you, pray for you, and I am trying to do the right thing."

The most famous evangelist since the first century is probably Billy Graham. In an interview in *People* magazine, he said he early heeded the advice of a professor who told him, "Billy, don't answer your critics."

That's right. Don't answer your critics. Replying to criticism crowns their criticism with dignity. Replying to criticism acknowledges that their criticism is worthy of serious consideration and worthy of your time to respond. Replying says, in effect, "Your criticism is significant."

Replying is frustration. You get angry that they haven't heard a word you've said. You get angry hearing them vomit cliche after cliche, promoting sexual abuse. You go over and over and over in your mind, "What am I doing wrong that people misunderstand and impugn my motives?" It's not you—it's them.

Replying diverts your time. The best defense *IS* a good offense. Instead of answering a hundred hateful letters and phone calls, use that time to keep putting out your positive message: Pornography is sexual abuse. Most American's don't want it. The Supreme Court said that obscenity is illegal. Pornography kills kids, etc.

But be glad for the criticism. You learn from it. And it shows you're getting through. If you weren't getting through, you wouldn't be a threat to anyone and they wouldn't criticize you.

You'll make a lot of mistakes—no question. But the Lord will groom, discipline, and empower you through mistakes.

One day a church member called a friend of mine, Tommy: "Tommy, I'd like you to tell Neil that what he's doing in this pornography is—well—going about it the wrong way. Let him know that . . . (and he gave a long list).

Tommy said, "He may be making mistakes, but I prefer the way he's fighting pornography to the way you are not."

One person—black, white, red, yellow, brown; male or female; rich or poor; rural or urban; mistakes and all—can smash pornography.

What One Person Can Do

William Barclay said:

> Often in a church or a society a bad situation is allowed to develop because no one has the courage to deal with it; and often, when the situation has fully developed, it is too late to deal with it. It is easy enough to extinguish a spark if steps to do so are taken at once, but it is almost impossible to extinguish a forest fire.[11]

It takes only one to hurl water on a spark preventing a forest fire. And it starts today. At once. It's harder starting tomorrow.

We owe a great debt to thousands of people who extinguished sparks of pornography in their communities. Here are ten:

1

I stood in a long line, holding a jug of cranberry juice. I was fifth in line. I saw that No. 2 lady had a shopping cart full with magazines. I mean full. Two stacks of magazines grew like double skyscrapers from the bottom of the wire-netting to the top rim of the basket.

I groaned. Loud.

I hoped someone up ahead of me would see I had only one item, take pity on me, and usher me forward. No luck.

No. 2 lady, waves of palomino hair streaked with silver, circling under her jawbone and meeting below her firm chin, stood firm. She had brilliant green eyes glistening underneath contacts, a nose as small as a strawberry and just as red (she clutched a kleenex and kept sniffing), and hair-pin thin lips frosted with orchid purple and pressed together so tight the purple cracked in several places. She stepped up to take her turn at the checking stand. She took the magazines, four thick at a time. There were sixty, at least. By the time she slammed them on the counter and the checker began click-click-CHICK-CHICK-BANG, click-click-CHICK-CHICK-BANG, four people had lined up in back of me. We were backed up into an aisle.

No. 2 lady slapped the magazines face down. I saw only one or two. They were *Oui* and *Playgirl.* I didn't know what the other fifty-eight were. I found out.

The checker mashed the total button, shooting up a $104.36 total, and the four in front and four in back of me weren't bored. We were staring at magazine lady.

Right then, she hoisted two magazines, wheeled to the nine of us in line, and shouted, "D'you see the stuff they're selling in this store *out in the open* where even our kids can pick it up?"

In her right hand was a copy of *Playboy*. Against its slick, black background and in a variety of sitting, standing and supine positions were a collage of six wet-lipped, barebreasted prostitutes. In her left hand was *Man's Deluxe.* On its cover was a red-haired prostitute lying flat on a lemon-gold water bed. Her legs were spread wide, revealing the outline of her vagina and threads of vaginal hair spreading underneath pale-pink panties. Her left hand pointed to her vagina; her right finger, an engorged nipple. Slashed diagonally across the upper right-hand corner of the magazine was *Some Like It Red.*

The magazine lady continued: "Look at this!" She slammed back the covers of *Playboy* to a full-page cartoon showing an (apparently) just-graduated college man, raping a spread-eagled secretary atop a desk, and saying to the just-arrived boss, "Hire me, sir! I never take *no* for an answer."

She had handed it to the man next in line, nervously hugging a sweating, red-cardboard half-gallon of milk, a jar of Skippy, and a stalk of celery, yellow-green leaves brushing his chin. She said: "Here. Look for yourself," and threw it on the counter next to him. He hugged the food tighter, a shield against the magazine. Her hand dove into the cart and pulled up a

Penthouse. She slammed open a series of photos showing naked women spread over a white-sand beach, like
a cafeteria of whores.

"Isn't that sweet to sell next to the coloring books?!"
magazine lady screamed.

She threw it down the line of people waiting. It land-
ed in the basket of the woman in front of me. She
reached down and flipped through it. Magazine lady
again reached down, pulling up a magazine named
Hustler.

I can't tell you what picture she showed. I felt vomit
bubbling to my throat. You would too. Let me just
say it was a photo dealing with a man and a woman
during her menstrual period.

"*Are you glad to come into a store like this and
have your children around here*?! They've got the same
thing in that drugstore across the street, too." My knees
felt weak. I looked at the lady in front of me. Her
face was white, her eyes big as half-dollars, like she'd
just seen a baby eaten alive.

By now a man, apparently the manager, had responded to the checker's overhead calls, "Mr. Aylsworth, to the front please. Mr. Aylsworth. Mr. Aylsworth to the FRONT please. Mr. Aylsworth."

Magazine lady said, "Look at this! Look at this!
Just look at it!" and she thrust the magazine into the
hand of the sweaty manager.

She started to show him the nauseating photo in
Hustler. He stopped her, saying, "We need to let these
people check out." He guided magazine lady through
the chute.

After I checked out, I saw her and the manager
standing by the 5¢ bubble-gum, toy-and-trinket globes.
I walked over and nudged her hand (it was cold,
wet and trembling), saying, " 'Scuse me, lady. I just
wanted to tell you I appreciate you."

She shot, "Sir, I'm no pro. This isn't easy for me.
You do the same thing. If you're a fath-, if you're a
human being, you will. Don't thank me. You do it."

Next day the magazines were gone.

To this day, I don't know her name but she keeps me going.

2

It was five minutes to midnight, Monday, March 19, and Harold Doran didn't recognize the two men leaning against the corner of his garage. A late winter darkness swallowed up Chaplin Street in Pawtucket, Rhode Island. Doran couldn't see their faces.

No matter. Cold and sleepy, he wanted only to park, drag up two flights of stairs to his tenement, and fall into bed, clothes on.

His car heater hadn't worked. He shivered, driving home from his International Brotherhood of Electrical Workers' meeting where members—for the nineteenth straight year—elected Doran president of their angry local.

Monday night's meeting, like union meetings for two months, ran late. Members speeded up plans to picket, boycott, and run TV/radio spots to rout smut from Rhode Island. Under Doran's leadership, they had already saturated the state with phone calls and petitions, persuading other unions, Knights of Columbus councils, Protestant and Catholic churches, and a galley-full of legislators to support their Public Display Law now in Senate committee. Passage appeared more certain every day, and Doran was paying in time, money, and sleep. He forgot meals, forgot to fix the car heater, and forgot to watch himself. Doran didn't know how he had written the most enforceable anti-smut law in America. But the men leaning on the garage did.

Doran's headlights careened into the driveway, and the two men slid to the side. Doran saw the nickel-round end of two cigars punching holes in the blackness. Off-on, off-on, off-on like two caution lights. "Guys next door . . . smelly stogies . . . wives chased 'em out again," Doran mumbled in his head.

He parked the car and got out. The two figures, like huge oaks, floated out of the blackness.

"Mr. Doran?" the figure in front asked. He was wearing a hat.

"Yuh, whooh, I can smell those things from here."

Hat stepped in front of Doran. The other figure, shorter than Hat, stepped to Doran's right.

"Talk to you for a minute?" Short said.

Doran turned to Short on his right side. Hat's fist exploded on Doran's left lower teeth. He crashed into the car. He raised to his knees. Before he could straighten, Hat's brick fist shot in his throat. He choked and melted to the ground. He felt his stomach press against cold, hard cinders.

"We'd like you to lay off the books," Hat said.

"We don't want to come back to visit Denise and Melissa Jean," Short said.

Short's steel-tipped boot crashed into his ribs. He yelped like a dog hit by a car and jerked up his head. It dropped back on the frozen ground.

Hat and Short faded into the black, slid around the corner of the garage and disappeared.

Doran was lucky. His visitors were local. Small-time goons, they were protecting only a few thousand dollars' worth of smut. Had they been representing "The Family" and its two billion dollars' smut investment, they would have given Doran cement feet and dropped him in Narragansett Bay.

Doran had been threatened by small-timers before. They had called two months earlier when the Display Law was introduced at the State House. They "suggested" he remove the bill. They recited eleven-year-old Melissa Jean's walking route to St. Theresa's school. They recited three-year-old Denise's schedule at the neighborhood day-care center. Doran didn't comply. He called the FBI. They said that when a goon is really going to put the screws to you, he's not going to warn you first. He'll kidnap your kid—then talk. Besides, they said, they leave the decent citizens alone. The only ones they really lean heavy on are competitors. If "The Family" wipes out or kidnaps a decent citizen, it's blazed on the front page the next day. And they don't want that, the FBI said. They want to keep a respectable businessman image. These local goons may put a brick through your window or rough you up, but that's all.

Doran stuck with the Display Law, saw it pass by a 252 to 1 vote, and saw it become a model to clean shelves and screens in more places than Rhode Island. He received no more phone calls or visits. His children were never approached.

And what a law the Display Law has been! (See Legal Strategy, p. 109.)

3

On a Thursday morning early in February, 31-year-old Manhattan stockbroker Stephen E. Shapiro and his wife were having breakfast in their spacious, terraced apartment. The apartment is located in the area media people refer to as the "posh" Upper East Side. It also happens to be the area where Steve Shapiro was born and has lived all of his 31 years.

Steve and his wife were quietly going through the morning paper, when Steve threw down the paper in angry amazement. He had just seen an ad heralding the opening, the next day, of the sex-ploitation film "Deep Throat" at a theater right around the corner from his home.

Determination replaced anger. Something had to be done. "You let this go," he later told reporters, "and what comes next? The hookers, the massage parlors, porno shops, peep shows. The line has to be drawn somewhere. It has to be drawn here."

But, how was the line to be drawn? Who would help? Steve began to think and then telephone. Calls to the Trans-Lux Theaters Corp. and Aquarius Releasing got him nowhere. Political figures? One could see nothing wrong with the film being shown in the area; another told him, "We're not interested in this sort of thing."

He noted that there were three Roman Catholic schools and one public grammar school in close proximity to the theater. On the way to his office he stopped at the office of the New York Roman Catholic Archdiocese in mid-town Manhattan. Officials there suggested he contact Morality in Media.

MM had one suggestion for Steve Shapiro: call a community meeting of a dozen or so representative people and determine how and to whom the community can express itself to have the film removed from the theater.

Steve took off from that small launching pad, and at this writing had not yet splashed down. He spent several hours Thursday afternoon telephoning pastors and rabbis, in addition to school principals and PTA officers. Almost without exception they agreed to meet at his home Friday afternoon or send representatives. The film was to open Friday at noon. Realizing that many at his meeting would be clergymen and women, Steve dashed down to Times Square Thursday night to view the film, so that he would be able to describe it. "I personally think the film is worse than any stag film."

All at his Friday afternoon meeting agreed, however, that whether or not the film was declared legally obscene was not the issue. It was still in litigation in New York County. The trial had ended, and the judge's decision was yet to be handed down.

"The arrogance of the people," said one clergyman, "to move it into a neighborhood theater before the judge even hands down a decision." The point at issue, the ad hoc committee decided, was a basic one: The neighborhood did not want the film playing there because of the danger it presented to the community. Steve Shapiro repeated, "What comes next?"

The committee, after considering several plans of action, settled on a concentrated petition campaign. Petitions gathered would be delivered to Trans-Lux officers. They would be in churches and synagogues in the area for congregations to sign that weekend, and signatures would be gathered wherever possible. Petitions said simply that signees believed the showing of the film to be "detrimental and dangerous to our community."

Steve Shapiro didn't wait. "I've never been an activist," he said and swung into action. Early Saturday morning he called the local police precinct for permission to set up a table outside the theater. Before the theater opened, he had a sign tacked to a pole exhorting passersby to "Keep 'Deep Throat' Out of Our Neighborhood." People willingly signed. A little past noon, a local politician passed by and asked what he could do to help. Steve left him manning the table while he ran to telephone committee members to come help gather signatures on street corners in the area. As reinforcements arrived, he set up a second table outside the theater and then took off to make a few more signs.

By mid-afternoon, the campaign was in high gear. One thousand signatures had already been obtained. The cast of characters that had gathered was interesting indeed. Looking out from the lobby was a vice-president of Trans-Lux Corporation. Standing on the sidewalk observing were the president of Aquarius and an attorney.

Early Sunday morning, the first sign of victory appeared. The foot-high words "Deep Throat" had disappeared from the sides of the marquee. Theater employees said the marquee was being "repainted."

Residents obtained 2,000 signatures on the street Saturday and Sunday. By Sunday night when petitions began to come in from churches the number rose to over 7,000. Petitions were still coming in to Steve Shapiro on Monday when he had a tip Trans-Lux was having a meeting. At the meeting's end, he telephoned and was informed the film would be pulled on Wednesday.

Trans-Lux officials denied the decision came about as a result of community action. They said they had pulled the film because they had another booking. A TV newscaster told Steve Shapiro off camera, "I don't buy that." Neither did Steve, who had conducted the campaign with a great deal of skill and reason.

In the usual confrontations which were inevitably to occur, i.e., "Who are you to determine what people can see or not see in this theater?" Steve Shapiro kept his cool: "A community has a right to say what it wants and what it doesn't want. This neighborhood does not want this film playing here." [12]

<h4 style="text-align:center">4</h4>

A little town in Texas decided it would cash in on some of the big-city vice. It started selling porno magazines.

Sixty-four-year-old Rae Simmons knew it.

"What can an old woman do?" she sighed.

She continued to pick up her milk and bread at the store, avoiding the magazine rack. One day she was belted between the eyes.

A nine-year-old boy stood at the newsstand. His hands were in his pockets, sliding back and forth between his legs, while his eyes grabbed naked photos on the porno covers.

She choked for air.

She marched down the soda pop aisle, around the corner and up the chip 'n dip aisle, her brain a battleground of impulses and embarrassment. "What should I do?"

She marched to the newsstand. Pretending to scan the home-and-garden magazines, she said, "Oh, no! Look at what they've started to sell. That's awful—that's ugly, trashy. Big fella', when you go home, you better tell your mother not to let any of your brothers and sisters in here. Doesn't that make you sick?"

Then her tiny sweaty hands picked up two magazines. She held her rage as she walked to the checkout stand, but the veins in her forehead bulged out hard and tight like blue pencils. She fumbled in her purse for $5.50. She didn't look at the clerk.

Magazines in her hand, she screeched: "*You know what I just saw? You want to know? A boy—no more than nine years old—over there looking at this long and hard. That's gonna stop! This is swill. I don't care what you say. This is wrong. You're gonna stop it.*"

Mrs. Simmons took the magazines, got on the phone, and called several ladies to her home for coffee. At coffee, she opened up the magazines, reporting on what she had personally witnessed with the nine-year-old boy.

She gave them a petition to sign. She said she would not shop there as long as they sold porno magazines. She urged them not to shop there either.

The store stopped the magazines.

5

The bold, three-line headline of the *Rochester Democrat and Chronicle* said:

COLLEGE BOARD
CANCELS SHOWING
OF X-RATED FILM

Rochester Institute of Technology's College Union Board of Directors voted unanimously yesterday not to show the X-rated film "Wet Rainbow" next week.

A statement released by Steve Mahler, a spokesman for the board, said, "The College Board feels confident that if the film 'Wet Rainbow' is shown, all members of the College Union Board will face legal prosecution that would result in conviction."

The board made its decision after extensive discussions Thursday with a representative of the Monroe County District Attorney's office, an institute lawyer and a lawyer formerly with the American Civil Liberties Union.

"I feel it was unfortunate that we had to bow to pressure from outside groups, namely Mike Macaluso," Mahler said.[13]

The *Times-Union,* in an editorial credited Mike Macaluso with axing the X-film on the famed campus:

The students scheduled a film. Michael J. Macaluso Jr., chairman of Citizens for a Decent Community, said the film violated laws against obscenity and if it were shown, he would complain. An assistant district attorney said any such complaint would be investigated. If justified, those who showed the film would be arrested and charged. Then a jury would decide if the film was in fact obscene, and if so the promoters would face imprisonment or fine.[14]

"Mike the Porno Fighter," *Rochester Magazine* called him:

"Pornography is the basic evil," he explains. "It destroys anything good—all our virtues of love, compassion, and respect for other people. Eliminate pornography and you've taken a big step in setting society back on a straight and narrow path."

To do exactly that, five years ago Macaluso helped form Citizens for a Decent Community. He has been reelected chairman of the 3,500-member organization ever since.

Its purpose, Macaluso explains, is to "fight pornography and drive it out of the semi-respectability of movie houses and bookstores and back into the gutter." That, Macaluso insists, will go a long way toward damping the ripple effects of pornography—immorality, divorce, lying, cheating, illicit sex, stealing, abortion and the innumerable dishonesties that permeate life, from the kitchen cabinet to the President's cabinet.

"CDC began informally," Macaluso recalls. "The Coronet Theater on Thurston Road began showing X-rated movies on a regular basis. There'd been X-rated films in the city before, but they were mainly limited to the Lyric Theater. Their 'clientele' was mostly older men and the general feeling was, 'Aw, let the dirty old men have their kicks.'

"Well, then neighborhood theaters, like the Coronet, started showing the films. And we noticed that when the films began spreading out to the neighborhoods, the people going to them were much younger. Average age dropped, I'd guess, from 50's to late 20's or 30's. And we saw under-age kids getting in.

"So finally, in January, 1969, a group of us got together to picket the Coronet. That was the beginning of CDC, just a few people joining together to call attention to this trash infiltrating our neighborhood."

Macaluso's neighborhood is the 19th and 20th ward areas around his home at 222 Chili Ave. His house, some 70 years old, is of sturdy brick and frame construction. The furnishings are old, well worn, comfortable—and shoehorned in wherever space once allowed. It's fascinating, like an antique dealer's house-shop which is crammed full and which has no visible distinction between furnishings and wares.

To support this family, Macaluso works as an industrial designer and small businessman. In addition to the dozen or so optical equipment patents he produced in the early 1950's at Bausch & Lomb, he has six or seven personal patents. Since 1955, he's worked for himself and is founder and president of Maca Mfg., a three-employee shop that produces his two most successful inventions—an auto body-bending tool and an infrared auto paint drying system. It's a small but efficient operation and it keeps food on that large dining room table.

Macaluso averages about 90 speeches a year before groups as diverse as School Without Walls here in

Rochester and fledgling anti-obscenity groups in Massena and Watertown. Typical speeches are "Obscenity and First Amendment Guarantees," "Democracy and Pornography Don't Mix," and "Pornography and the Law."

Macaluso is also building an "effects" file, which, he explains, documents the effects of pornography. Presently, he's concentrating on the violent, criminal effects.

"There's an obvious correlation between pornography and sex crimes, but many people still don't admit this. The purpose of pornography is to inflame or incite. If it doesn't do this, it's not doing its job. Sex is a volatile instinct and the step from pornography to violence is a small one. We're gathering evidence largely from police testimony to demonstrate this. Police are always finding pornography in the possession of persons arrested for sex crimes.

"Recently, a young man came to see me and tried to convince me that we should focus some of our attention on violence as well as sex. We talked a long time, but I finally got him to see that pornography is the heart of all violence. If we solve the problem of pornography, we'll automatically solve the problem of violence."

CDC was also instrumental in banning topless dancing in the town of Gates. "There was a group of concerned people out there and they asked us for help," says Macaluso. "We advised them on how to get started and we gave them some legal advice. Later, I appeared before the Town Board and explained how harmful and corrosive these topless places are in a family community.

"You know, our Judeo-Christian values were the basic standards used when our forefathers established this country and wrote its laws. All the laws they set down were originally drawn from Judeo-Christian values and the intent was to protect and guard the sacredness of the family as the prime unit of our society.

"We've finally obtained some convictions and the battle has swung our way. I think I can say that we've turned the clock back six years in Rochester when it comes to X-rated movies. That may not sound like progress, but without CDC, Rochester would be where New York City is now. There are fewer X-rated films in town now and the really hard-core films aren't coming in anymore.

"I think we can also take some credit for closing down the Riviera and Monroe theaters. I want to make it clear that our intent is not to close down any theaters, but merely to keep them from showing pornographic films. We would prefer that they switch their bill of fare rather than close down, but that wasn't the decision of the owner.

"I know all about the argument that they have to show X-rated films because the G and GP films don't draw, and that claim doesn't hold water. Look at Jo-Mor. They're a very successful operation and they rarely have X-rated films. The only ones I can recall are 'Midnight Cowboy' and 'Last Tango in Paris.' Besides, if a druggist says he can't make a profit selling aspirin, do you allow him to start selling heroin?"

Macaluso is also familiar with the claim that CDC is trying to assume the role of community censor. He contends that claim doesn't hold water, either.

"We've got the American Civil Liberties Union and a lot of misguided people crying about freedom of expression and freedom of access and all sorts of other freedoms. Well, no freedom has ever been allotted to pornography. We're not taking anything away, because it never existed in the first place.

"For 200 years in this country, pornography has been kept in the gutter—legally. But all of a sudden the ACLU and the movie industry are trying to give the idea that there's some infringement of rights. Well, pornography is still illegal. All we're doing is saying that the law is being broken and that it should be enforced.

"We're not saying 'this shouldn't exist because we don't like it.' We're saying 'this shouldn't exist because it's illegal.' There's no censorship involved at all.

"The same thing goes for the 'consenting adult' and 'victimless crimes' arguments the ACLU makes. Just because you have fornication or homosexual relations between 'consenting adults' doesn't make it any more legal. 'Consenting adults' can't change illegality into legality.

"These aren't 'victimless crimes,' anyway. They're crimes against all society. The effects spread and touch everyone. The ramifications of a pornographic relationship don't end with just an illicit act.

"When you put a pornographic movie in a public theater, you're in effect legitimizing it. Pornography belongs

82

in the gutter, because when it's in the gutter, you have to go down in the gutter to get it. But if it's on display, and it's allowed, and it's publicly accepted, then it has respectability.

"Just one small example of the effect of public pornography was a phone call I got recently. Channel 21 broadcast a blasphemous show called 'Steambath,' a sick meandering of a degenerate mind. The lady who called me said it was terrible and something should be done. I agreed and suggested she write the station. But when she hung up, I thought, 'Lady, where have you been? If you'd helped us do something about public pornography years ago, it wouldn't be coming into your living room today.' " [15]

6

The *Miller* decision (U.S. Supreme Court, June, 1975) cripples pornographers nationwide. Represented among constitutional attorneys presenting briefs for decency in that decision were attorneys from Citizens for Decency Through Law.

CDL and its 350,000 members in dozens of chapters throughout America have routed pornography on the local, state, and national level. It began with one man, Charles H. Keating, Jr.

"Why don't the churches do something?" I asked.

Father Nick turned to me and said, "*You* are the church, Charlie. Why don't *you* do something?"

But back at work, I had forgotten it until now. "Oh, uh, yes," I stammered, "we'll have to figure something out."

A week later I happened to be chatting with the prosecutor at the police court. He handed me some magazines. I idly leafed through one, then recoiled at page after page of filth. "Where did you get these?"

"From a candy store near two grade schools. The seller's up for trial today."

"What do you think he'll get?" I knew there were laws against selling this kind of thing.

"Nothing, probably," sighed the prosecutor.

I nodded, remembering a previous local case in which a news dealer was acquitted when the judge said in effect,

"There is no law to define obscenity."

"Bob," I said, "can you get this case put over to another date?"

"Sure."

That was all I needed. I arranged the voluntary help of two respected psychologists and a psychiatrist as witnesses for the prosecution. Their testimony was clear and blunt: "This magazine . . . would encourage perverted forms of sex behavior which can lead to rape and other crimes." The verdict—guilty!

One small case—one neighborhood store. But the news flashed across the nation. The prevalent opinion that it was impossible to get a conviction under the laws covering obscenity had been disproved.

A community group in Cleveland asked me to address them. "Laws to combat pornography are on the books in practically every state," I told them. "It's up to the citizen to see that they are enforced."

The religious press picked up my speech, and my phone started ringing. Groups everywhere wanted advice. I couldn't handle it alone. So one evening about 12 friends and I gathered in my living room. Some of us were lawyers, another a druggist, a salesman, a banker. That night we formed Citizens for Decency Through Law.[16]

7

Robin Tellor is a former University of Minnesota football star who takes the ball and runs with it, and nothing stops him until he reaches that goal line.

Now he's a 36-year-old business executive in Duluth, Minnesota, and he's running fast to reach a goal: "To get it [pornography] out of town and accept nothing less, and to prevent it from spreading into other towns."

Robin had always been "strongly opposed to obscenities." In 1973 he happened to see the agenda of a City Council meeting where two anti-obscenity ordinances were being discussed. He brought up the subject at a Knights of Columbus meeting, and then represented the Knights when the City Council convened. The ordinances were passed, but later the Minnesota State Supreme Court ruled that they had to be approved by a majority vote in public referendum.

At the City Council meeting, Robin Tellor met "many

other interested people: John McAllister, Rose Johnson, Bob Wallin, Sister Petra Lenta; but we were all acting as individuals, and you've got to organize. You can't accomplish anything unless you organize."

So, with the ordinances coming up for vote in referendum in 1975, Citizens for Decency was organized with Robin Tellor as chairman. The appearance of the ordinances (based on the U.S. Supreme Court *Miller* decision) on the ballot generated a heated scare campaign in the media which strongly opposed them. Civil liberties cliches were quoted *ad infinitum.* Both newspapers editorialized, "You can't legislate morality..." "...an infringement on the rights of freedom and speech and expression," etc.

But Robin and his organization were determined. They traveled back and forth across the city speaking to community and church groups, filling eight or nine speaking engagements every week. Shortly before elections they called a press conference at which Robin took issue with the editorial stands of the newspapers, pointing to the endorsements of the ordinances of more than 2,500 people and countless organizations. The day before election day they took a full page ad in the papers, listing more than 1,500 endorsees. The ordinances passed by a 70% margin.

"And now," says the energetic Robin, "we're doing follow-up. We are encouraging police and prosecuting attorneys to enforce the ordinances."

In October of this year, Robin and the organization invited MM president Rev. Moron A. Hill, S.J., to Duluth. Robin whirled Father Hill and Rev. Paul Murphy, S.J. (founder of MM of Massachusetts) through a round of meetings, seminars, media appearances and press interviews. "That gave us a real spark."

Now the organization meets once a month and Robin has a 30-minute radio show once a month. There are three new committees, one to ask TV stations for uplifting fare; one to work with theater managers to gain cooperation; and one to work with the community to get community standards expressed. Robin Tellor is an organizer.

What makes handsome Robin run? Minnesota born and bred, he says: "The only thing I'm asking is to be able to raise my children (ages 9 and 10) in the same healthy environment in which I was raised. The pornography problem represents a real threat to our society. People have been passive and let indecencies be imposed upon them. If they want a community to be clean, they must stand up and make their opinions known." [17]

8

Sometimes the successes against pornography aren't dramatic like Mike Macaluso's, Rae Simmons', Charles Keating's, and Robin Tellor's, but they're still successes. They kick porno out.

A large drugstore has "Burton's Rules" taped to the cash register, visible only to the employees. "Burton's Rules" tells all employees—full-time, part-time, day or night—to check magazines carefully.

"Burton" is not the mayor, police chief, district attorney, or president of the drug chain. Burton is a customer. The father of two children, he checks the racks everytime he enters. And he screams to the manager or clerk if something is wrong. Weary of Burton's complaints, the manager taped "Burton's Rules" to the register.

9

The *Palo Alto Times* carried this item:

OUI ON 'OUI'—
IT'S OFF STANDS

Editor of the Times:

As the owner of Niven's International Foods, formerly Purity market, located in the Stanford Shopping Center, I agree with Mrs. Anita Dippery's letter to the editor (Forum, Nov. 26). I feel that the situation regarding magazines such as *Oui* has gotten far out of hand.

We have therefore instructed our supplier to discontinue shipping us that periodical and have removed all copies from the sales floor. We appreciate the concerns of Mrs. Dippery and her associates.

John Niven, Jr.,
Niven's International Foods,
Standord Shopping Center,
Palo Alto[18]

10

In Massachusettes, *Hustler* magazine was ousted from a *chain* of quick-stop stores because W. K. Currier looked at the magazine racks. He opened *Hustler* and recoiled. He called the president of the company, made an appointment, went in and showed him the contents of *Hustler*. That was enough.

It takes only one. One—who acts at once.

President Carter said:

> The course of human events—even the greatest historical events—is determined ultimately not by the leaders, but by the common, ordinary people. Their hopes and dreams, their courage and tenacity, their quiet commitments determine the destiny of the world.[19]

". . . ordinary people"—like you.

Public Action

Without men and women, *one at a time*, hating pornography, there is no public clout. There are, thank God, millions of committed men and women who hate pornography.

Even in "swinging" California, where in Los Angeles *alone* 114 porno shops flourish, this happened:

> A clear majority of California residents do not want newsracks in their communities that display sexually explicit materials for sale.
>
> A statewide survey revealed that of 1200 persons interviewed, 68.1 percent *disagreed* with the statement: "Newsracks placed on sidewalks and similar areas in my community that are available to the general public should be allowed to sell papers emphasizing sexual activity."
>
> The survey was sponsored by the Los Angeles County Sheriff's Department. Dr. Harvey Adelman, professor of public administration at Pepperdine University, and Bonnie J. Campbell, professor of mathematics and computer sciences at California State University, provide technical assistance.
>
> The survey also demonstrated that most Californians are opposed to porno theaters, bars and bookstores show-

ing or selling sexually explicit material to their communities.[20]

But how do you get them organized in Los Angeles, California; Hillsboro, Pennsylvania; Waco, Texas; or Tarrytown, New York? How do you get them organized to slam the porno people with public clout? You work hard; you endure insults; you pay—in time, money and sleep.

Organizing citizens into a porno-fighting army requires boycotts, pickets, public meetings, direct mail ads and letters, and newspaper ads. Personal calls to neighbors, friends, priests, preachers. Personal visits to neighbors, friends, priests, preachers. Personal calls and visits to police chief, district attorney, sheriff, city councilmen, city attorney and state representatives.

All it takes is one person to begin. You need no super organization, no rich treasury, and no influential backers. All you need is you.

Initial Action

1. Send a letter to your local newspaper, headlined "News Item."

On _____ at _____ a meeting will be held of all citi-
　　　　date　　　place
zens who are interested in stopping the flow of X-rated films, adult bookstores, and pornographic magazines in our drugstores and food stores.

Obviously, you alter this news item to fit the intensity of the problem in your city. Perhaps pornographic magazines are the only problem you have. Perhaps you've got massage parlors slipping in. Before you send in this news item, you will have already arranged for a meeting place. Avoid churches. If held in a Baptist church, people think, "It's a Baptist project." If held in a Catholic church, people think, "It's a Catholic project." You don't want to leave the impression that it's a pet project of any one group. Rent a meeting place from a school, bank, lodge, etc. (in most cases there is no rent or it's very low).

If there is nothing else available, use a church auditorium.

2. Run an ad. This will cost you money. Many won't thank you for spending your own scarce money to purchase an ad. You do it because it's right.

Once your army is off the ground, however, you will collect dues, letting all share in the expenses of routing pornography.

Run the ad in Sunday's newspaper (largest circulation).

3. One week before the meeting, ask people to go with you to buy samples of pornography. These people verify your purchase of the magazines and help in discretely displaying samples of pornography.

Prior to the day of the meeting, make contact with several key people to show them the pornography actually available. Visit ministers, priests, rabbis, nuns, friends, neighbors—as many as possible.[21] Show them the worst samples of pornography.

Review the facts on pornography published in the ad. And ask them if they will come to the meeting. If they say yes, ask if they will help you set up the meeting. Someone needs to make an urn of coffee, set up chairs, pass out registration of forms, usher in crowds.

Select the people who will help you from a diversity of racial, economic and religious backgrounds, establishing the fact that ousting pornography is a community concern. Many will volunteer to help.

But, even if no one agrees to help, *still hold the meeting.* You see this thing through not because it's popular but because it's right.

I will tell you, however, that in seventy-eight places where I've held workshops, there always has been a huge wave of people gratefully eager to help. They've waited for years to get rid of smut but never had a leader or encouragement.

Prepare Registration Forms and Pledge Cards which will be passed out at the meeting.

REGISTRATION

Name _____ Address _____

Home phone _____ Business phone _____ Occupation _____

Spouse's name _____ Address _____

Business phone _____ Occupation _____

Religious affiliation _____ Children (names & ages): _____

_____

1. For future meetings like this one, on what nights could you positively *not* meet? _____

2. Would you be willing to serve on a planning committee for future meetings of this group? Yes   No

3. Would you be willing to serve on a telephone committee for future meetings of this group? Yes   No

4. Would you be willing to serve as a hostess at future meetings? Yes   No

5. Would you be willing to help in the preparation of a newsletter designed to improve the quality of literature and films in our city? Yes   No

6. Would you be willing to help in the distribution of a newsletter designed to improve the quality of literature and films in our city? Yes   No

7. Concerning pornographic films or literature in _____, would you be willing, when necessary, to write a letter to:
                  —the district attorney?   Yes   No
                  —the county sherriff?   Yes   No
                  —the Editor?   Yes   No

8. (a) Funds for a newsletter, future meeting place, and legal assistance will have to come from strictly voluntary contributions. Would you be willing to make a contribution? Yes   No

Could you estimate the amount by encircling one: $100 $50
$25 $10 $5 $1. Itemized disbursement of funds will be reported to all contributors.

(b) In addition to an initial contribution for setting up a
continuing organization to examine films and literature in
_____, would you be willing to pay dues of $5 a
month? Yes   No

9. Would you be willing to participate in a legal demonstration
   against pornography in _____? Yes   No

(Registration forms will be collected later in the meeting.)

MEMBERSHIP PLEDGE CARD

Name _____

Address _____

Phone _____ _____ Individual _____ Civic Organization,
                                              Business or Church

In addition to my initial contribution of $_____, I pledge
$_____ ($5.00 for individuals or $10.00 for civic organi-
zations, businesses or churches) per month to fight pornography.

"YOU ARE WHAT YOU READ"

4. The night of the meeting, before people enter, take porno samples and lay out on long rows of tables. Cover with sheets, and position a man or woman usher before each table to be sure no one tampers with the tables.

Position ushers beside entrance handing out registration forms and directing people to the coffee urn. People are a little nervous coming to this initial meeting. A cup of coffee and filling out a registration form puts them at ease and gives them something to do immediately. And it shows them that your meeting has been well planned. Do not distribute the pledge cards as people enter.

5. Open the meeting by saying:

My name is _____ _____. I want to thank the many men and women who have helped make this meeting possible (acknowledge them publicly).

I think I can safely say that although the motivation for being here may differ slightly for each of us, generally we are here because we think sex is beautiful. We hate to see it abused or thrown in the gutter. We are angry to see our children assaulted by it everytime they go in a store and—increasingly—on some television shows.

We believe sex is a gift from God, and we want our children to grow up in a society where that healthy understanding is preserved.

To that end, I think we should ask God's help as we start on this community effort that we'll see it through to the end. Let's pray: (call on someone whom you've already requested to pray).

We are angry because we know God's gift of sex has been abused. And we know that—in America—there is something we can do about it.

We know that (according to the Harris and Gallup polls) most of the American people oppose pornography.

We know that, according to the June, 1973, *Miller* decision, the Supreme Court has declared that pornography is illegal. And we know that they've left it up to local communities, to us, to enact and enforce good strong laws against pornography.

We are angry at ourselves for letting this problem go so long. We know that we can get rid of pornography whenever we want to.

Tonight we want to.

If you say as you leave here, "Thank you, I enjoyed the meeting," you have missed it. There is nothing here to enjoy. There is admission of laziness, past failure, and compromising with low morals.

There is admission of neglect to our own children who see the grotesque ads in newspapers and see the magazines next to the coloring books.

There is nothing to enjoy here tonight. There is work. It'll cost you time, money, and sleep. You will not like this meeting. It will hurt.

Let us put our heads down in silent prayer and contemplation to see if we really want to see this thing through to the end. If there's anyone who's not sure, you may leave while we have our eyes closed.

(This is not histrionic. This is true. Pause for a few moments and let anyone leave who would like to.)

Welcome aboard fellow physicians. I address you as fellow physicians, because you are now going to inspect cancer. Not because you enjoy it, but *hate* it. It will make you angry. Please channel your anger toward expelling pornography, like Jesus Christ channeled His anger to expel money-sharks from a temple.

You have a choice. You may inspect this now, or wait until your children do. They can't help it. It's everywhere. Stores openly display it. Junior high through college students buy it or steal it to circulate at school. Eighty percent of movies project it, and television increasingly forces it before their eyes. Kids can't escape it. Legislation and civic indignation to stop the assault on children depends on us, not them.

Some people don't want you to inspect it. The pornographers. The pornographers want to continue to exploit our ignorance, and steal the money and minds of men.

The Supreme Court has consistently said that obscenity *is* illegal. Since June, 1973, it now also said that each community can determine what it allows *in its community*. Yet the pornographers have continued to violate both our existing law and community standards. What you will see tonight does not reflect the will of the people, but the will of pornographers. That will stop tonight.

But only if you hate pornography as God hates it. And upon viewing the samples you will hate it with a fury you didn't know existed in you. You will hate it as a physician hates cancer.

We are going to inspect that cancer.

It may make you sick.

It will make you angry.

Compress your anger and aim it toward the people who produce and sell pornography—in violation of purity, in violation of love, in violation of law.

6. Tell the audience that there are ushers at each table, preventing minors from viewing it. You then direct the men to one room, women to another.

Inspection is necessary. There are the people who will be the leaders in routing pornography. They will be talking to managers, city councilmen, and neighbors about pornography. They must know what they're talking about. They must see for themselves.

Jeremiah said, "You can't heal a wound by saying it isn't there" (Jer. 6:14).

You can't fight pornography by hoping it's not as bad as it really is. They must see that magazines on open shelves show: intercourse, bestiality, sex torture, child molesting. All the words in the world won't convince them.

They must see that many of the porno magazines actively promote and advertise *names* and *addresses* of people throughout the United States who advertise sexual services for adults or children, and artificial sexual devices, such as grotesque artificial penises, artificial vaginas, and 5'4" rubber dolls "anatomically complete."

They must understand that these magazines can be purchased by children.

If the immediate problem in your community is adult bookstores (perhaps one is erupting in your residential neighborhood), then go to the adult store and buy an assortment of the ugly sexual paraphernalia, including the artificial penises, vaginas and "sex dolls," and display them at the meeting. Make it very clear: this is what is sold in adult bookstores. Do we want this circulating in this community? Do we want our children playing at the playground, walking back and forth to school within blocks of this menace?

It is preferable to have men and women view the samples separately. They will take more time to really inspect what's there. But if separate facilities are impossible, there are a number of ways to display the samples discretely.

(1) In one-room buildings (including small church buildings), we opened up and laid out on the front pews the porno samples and covered them with sheets, shielding them from view before the meeting. After the opening speech preparing the audience to view the samples, we asked men and women to file down the center aisle, men to the left and women to the right. Men viewed the porno samples on the left aisle, women on the right.

(2) If there are no tables, benches, pews or rooms to openly display the pornography samples, place in folders or envelopes, and pass up and down the rows (after screening the audience for minors).

(3) If you can't segregate the men and women, you can still display the samples.

Half my workshops were in facilities where it was not possible to separate the men from the women. That's all right. If you prepare the audience, they'll understand, co-operate, and be appreciative of your efforts to help them.

Christians are not ashamed of sex. We have a robust, healthy, and grateful attitude toward sex. That's why we hate pornography. We are mature adults who can put aside feelings of embarrassment to fight a common disease. We are physicians who hate cancer.

The only reason that segregated facilities are preferable is that they allow longer time for more thorough inspection of the material. If segregated facilities are not available, you must find a way to display samples. If you will not discretely show samples, stop reading right here and concede the battle to the pornographers.

My audiences have been composed of a cross-section: nuns, priests, ministers, farmers, lawyers, businessmen, housewives, doctors, young marrieds, grandmothers and grandfathers. In my opening speech, I prepared them for the necessity of shock in viewing porno samples. In city after city after city, they viewed and exploded. They left the meeting boiling with righteous anger. And they cleaned their cities.

7. After viewing the samples, they are burning with one question: *What can I do?*

Review the registration form with them. Nearly all filled out their name, address, etc., but many—at the beginning of the meeting—didn't volunteer their services because they didn't see the need for it. They do now.

Remind them that they should fill out the form only

if they are willing to see the problem through to the end. No compromises, no retreats.

That's why organization is urgent. You need people who will volunteer their homes, invite neighbors in to show them samples and give them petitions to sign. (Better to write personal letters than to sign petitions.)

You need people who will help with the dull, monotonous chores of making phone calls, folding letters, typing letters, running a mimeo machine (or running back and forth to a printer's), licking stamps and sealing envelopes.

You need people to write powerful, personal letters to store managers, city councilmen, and state representatives. (Form letters are almost useless.)

Circulate a petition to sign. Make it clear and direct.

ACTION PETITION

No! We the undersigned do not want filth flowing in the streets of our cities.

We will protect ourselves. We will protect our children.

The filthy movies at _____
(or the filthy magazines at) _____
will go! Or Citizens for Decency in (name of city) _____
_____ will go!

Citizens for Decency are not leaving.

Those movies are wrong, those magazines are wrong, and everyone knows it.

We commit our lives, our fortunes, and our sacred honor to stopping them.

Signed, 1. _____
2. _____
3. _____
Etc.

Send this petition to the theaters and the press. Distribute names of stores, magazines, and city councilmen. Announce the time when all will go to the city council, collectively asking for passage of the Public Display Law (or Film Law or whatever law you need). Urge audience to personally call or write city council members.

96

Send the above petition to the mayor and city council with the added note:

> We expect the legislators of _____ to express their concern for our children by passing the "Public Display Law" (or "Film Law").

Circulate another petition:

> Sooner or later pornography kills kids. We have a right and duty to protect our children from moral pollution as well as air pollution. We demand that the city council pass the "Public Display Law" to halt the circulation of abusive sex in _____.

A cardinal principle of war against pornography is this: Every personal action, every public action must be directed toward the ultimate passage of a firm, clear pornography law or the enforcement of an existing one. If the pressing problem is massage parlors, adult bookstores, etc., then word the petition accordingly, pressing for passage of a law to halt them. (See Legal Section Chapter 5, p. 109, for a list of laws and how to implement them.)

Tell people to take petitions and circulate them. Tell them they'll be harassed. Some people will refuse to sign because of indifference. Some enjoy pornography and will refuse to sign. Some will say, "Oh, petitions don't do any good."

You'll be discouraged and depressed. But people who are discouraged and depressed are *not* losers. It's people who yield to discouragement and depression who lose.

In one city, signatures on a petition (1,000 of them) knocked a lazy D.A. out of his seat (he previously said nothing could be done) and compelled him to take action against a theater showing an X-rated movie.

Distribute *Pledge Cards* and take up a collection. Point out the cost of ads, postage, stationery. Point out that the pornographers have a two billion dollar war chest to draw upon.

Tell the audience that you will incorporate your group.

Remind the audience that you are a deadly serious group formed to pass and enforce laws to get rid of pornography.

If your city is so large (or if you are co-ordinating a statewide effort) that you don't have the names of the stores carrying pornography, you're not at a loss. Urge the audience to check every store they enter. Urge them to pick up the worst porno they find, open it and show it to the manager. Many stores, tell them, will remove porno voluntarily. Those who don't will be boycotted and picketed. Urge people to keep a file on stores selling porno.

Tell the audience a Board of Directors will be formed to guide the organization in its activities. Welcome suggestions. Announce the time and place of the next meeting, emphasizing that regular meetings will be held to be sure that tough pornography laws are enacted and enforced.

8. After the meeting and from the list of names, draw up a list of names of men and women to serve on the Board of Directors.

Organize the names into committees and put into action a day or two after the meeting. (See Chart in Civic Action, Appendix 2, p. 209.)

Place another ad in the newspaper making it clear that war has been declared on pornography by a large community of people.

Call together a group of volunteers to send direct-mail ads to homes throughout your city. (See sample: Direct Mail Ad in Civic Action, Appendix 2, pp. 209-213.)

Have telephone volunteers call all members, asking which stores complied with request and which stores refused. Draw up separate lists.

Run ad in the paper announcing time of next meeting.

Second Meeting

Introduce Board of Directors. For people who were not at earlier meeting, show samples. At each meeting show samples of pornography to any in audience who had not previously inspected them.

SECOND PETITION

No!!

We still don't want filth flowing through _____.

We refuse to patronize your stores until you stop selling pornography—*Playboy, Penthouse, Oui, Hustler,* etc.

Signed,

1. _____
2. _____
3. _____ Etc.

It is important that you name the magazines because this makes your goal clear to the supporters of decency, clear to the city council, clear to the managers; and it makes clear that you are *not* gunning for magazines which necessarily and tastefully use the nude form, i.e., medical textbooks, bona-fide art books.

Write a similar petition if the particular problem is with films.

Circulate a "We Appreciate You" petition, praising stores and theaters which do not traffic in filth (or formerly trafficked in it but stopped because of citizen concern).

WE APPRECIATE YOU

We appreciate your concern for the citizens of _____ by not selling pornographic magazines. We pledge ourselves to actively patronize your store.

Signed, 1. _____
2. _____
3. _____
Etc.

An appreciation petition is important because the store is obviously not receiving the large commissions which come with the sale of pornography magazines. You want him to know that not only do you appreciate his sacrifice but that his sacrifice will, in fact, generate more business for him.

It is also important because in the future—should

he be tempted to entertain the idea of selling porno magazines—your petition of appreciation will serve as a great deterrent.

Circulate a second action petition stating,

> "We refuse to patronize your store unless you stop selling *Playboy, Penthouse, Oui, Hustler* and other magazines which abuse sex,"

This means that you have made a commitment to boycott those stores.

A boycott is simply a public and outspoken refusal to patronize a place of business. It dramatizes a clear commitment to refuse to patronize the store.

Boycotts require commitment. You've got to be willing to put your name behind your commitment:

"Hello, is this the manager of WHIZ IN 'N OUT store? This is Mrs. Blackstock. I've been in your store. I usually come in about once every two days for milk and bread. Anyway, I don't feel I can continue to give you my business because of the pornographic magazines you sell. I will shop there again when you get rid of the magazines."

Ditto with a theater.

Boycotts require sacrifice. You've got to be willing to drive out of your way to shop, or pay extra for milk somewhere else, or deny yourself a chance to see a good "G" movie at a theater because that theater chain also regularly shows "X" movies.

Boycotts work. In one city I received this phone call at noon:

"Hello."

"Hello. Is this the Neil Gallagher that's been going around telling people what they can read and can't read???!!!"

"This is Neil Gallagher, but I haven't told anyone what they can read and can't read."

"This is Jack Lebrun at Sunnydale Drive-In. What the hell's going on? Six people called me this morning and told me they aren't going to shop here anymore. When's 'zis gonna' stop??"

"Well, first I think you'd like to know that it's a

question of selling, not reading. Anyone may read whatever he likes to read, and I don't want anyone telling me what I can read and what I can't read. Second, I didn't tell anyone not to shop at your store, in particular. We circulated a list of all stores selling pornography. You were not singled out. Those who called your store did it on their own. And I guess they've called other stores too."

"It's my damn store!! Don't tell me what I can sell. I'll sell what I d—"

"You mean even if it's illegal? If some—"

"It ain't illegal. And those magazines are my business."

"But that's not the way the law works. If the community says they don't want those magazines and since laws reflect the will of the community, then we have to go by it, whether we like it or not. That's one of the joys—and burdens—of living in a democracy."

"Look, this is my store. Leave it alone!! And we ain't got a law that says it's illegal."

"We do, but it's not very strong. That's why we've submitted to the city council a much clearer and more enforceable law. The legal thing is really not the most important. You're a father probably and I don't think you want that stuff circulating. Just because something is legal doesn't mean that it's moral. We've got a lot of laws which aren't exactly up to the best moral standards. Fortunately, prostitution is illegal. But, ah, let's say it weren't. If prostitution were legal, would you offer it in your store, or on your premises?"

" 'S not the same thing."

"But the point is there's a difference between something being legal and moral. If heroin were legal, would you sell it on your premises? If prostitution were legal, would you, really, sell it on your premises?"

"It's my store and I would!"

This store manager was not exactly co-operative. Furthermore, his college buddy was on the city council, the councilman who subscribed to *Playboy,* and let his children view it as well.

But this store manager cleaned his shelves. Even before we got the Display Law passed.

Boycotts work.

Please remember, give the manager the benefit of the doubt.

We've got our heads on straight in fighting pornography. We're not witch-hunting or store lynching. We appreciate sex. We affirm the goodness of people.

Show the man the worst porno he's got. Give him the benefit of the doubt. "Sir, I don't think you realize what's on your own shelves."

Give him a chance to voluntarily remove it. You'll know in a day or two if he will comply. If he doesn't, then you swiftly return to the store, make a scene in the store, get samples of porno, take them to the police, boycott and picket. Hit the store swift and hard.

It was Friday afternoon and during a routine physical, a doctor detected a growth on two vertebrae of the bare-chested, muscular man on the office stool. Monday morning the man was under a surgeon's knife in the Medical Center.

Cancer—moral or physical—won't wait.

Picketing

Why do you suppose homosexuals (a small minority) and extremist wranglers of ERA (a smaller minority) are able to swing legal clout and get things done? Because they scream. They picket, boycott, sit-in, and march. They grab the media. They're willing to "make fools" of themselves. And they get what they want. I know . . . you say:

"I could never picket. I'm just a woman, a preacher, an old man, a kid. I'm too old, too young, too ugly," and on and on.

Do you want to rout pornography? That's the only issue. Do you want to stop the aggressive circulation of child-molesting, rape, sex torture, intercourse-with-animals, and the brutalization of the female body?

Picket. Day and night, 95° or 15°, man or woman, black and white.

Picket. Walk up and down past that theater or bookstore or grocery store selling *Playboy, Penthouse,* etc. Picket massage parlors. Picket police stations where police won't enforce the good laws you've got in effect. Picket City Council chambers demanding they pass the Display Law.

Pickets work.

The report in the *National Decency Reporter* said:

PICKETERS CELEBRATE ANNIVERSARY

October 1 marked the one-year anniversary of the picketing of the only "adult" bookstore in the Alhambra community. Pickets have been protesting the store every hour it has been open since September 30, 1975. The citizen group called "People Against Obscenity" has broad-based support from churches and other community organizations who have volunteered to man the picket lines at specific times each week. Mrs. Barbara Messina, one of the organizers of PAO says, "If it takes forever, we'll drive smut out of Alhambra.[22]

And, so far, in Alhambra there are five lawsuits pending against the porno shop; three civil actions by the city, a misdemeanor criminal charge by the district attorney, and an eviction suit by the landlord.

Warner Jenkins, editor-publisher of *The Post Advocate* (Alhambra, California) said:

If and when anyone ever gets around to passing out hero medals, I'm going to place in nomination the names of all those unsung Alhambrans who have volunteered for picket duty in front of the adult bookstore at 25 W. Main St.

They have been terrific.

They have been more than that.

They have been sensational.

David Guthrie, whose wife, Jan, co-chairs CAP (Citizens Against Pornography) along with Barbara Messina, describes Alhambra's response to this pornographic invasion as a "great moral revolution."

He's right.

It takes courage, guts and raw determination to work

that picket line. Make no bones about that.

I am positive that some of our good citizens have been exposed to more foul language and harassment from roving goons than in all of the rest of their life combined.

A filthy expletive, a rotten egg, a thrown beer can can be a shocker.

But the pickets, the majority of which are women, have persevered.

They have defied a growing tradition that it doesn't pay to get involved.

These people are involved.

They have the courage of their convictions and they have had the determination and the motivation to carry them out.

The uprooting of the adult bookstore has become Alhambra's No. 1 community issue.

I have been a resident here since 1948 and I have never seen such unflinching resolution. Not even flouridation or the most sizzling of municipal elections could begin to compare in community interest.

Conservative, staid and sometimes stuffy Alhambra has awakened.

Smut and all of its offensive ramifications has rallied our community as has no other single issue.

Those sign-carrying pickets deserve a pat on the back.

The bookstore is open seven days a week—many days from 9 a.m. to 2 a.m. the next day.

The pickets are always there—no matter how foul the weather; no matter what day of the week.

It's an unbelievable and most welcome display of community unity.

A tip of my tattered editor's visor to the people, the churches and all other individuals and organizations who are willing to stand up and be counted. There was even a nun in the picket line Monday afternoon. Bravo.

They are proving in the most visible fashion possible that there is still plenty of kick in the old hometown.

Mrs. Messina has advised me that another mass rally of citizens is planned by CAP in the next week or two.

Watch for the date and place.

It should prove to be another demonstration of "people power."

Citizens in Fremont, California, picketed.

The people of Fremont, California, a community of

120,000 on San Francisco Bay, used more imaginative tactics in their war on porn. Pickets suddenly began appearing in front of the city's massage parlors, often late at night. They usually marked the license numbers of parlor customers on their signs. After recognizing the family car's license number on the sign, some angry women joined the picket lines; others burst into the parlors searching for their husbands. Through a combination of harassment and regulations enacted under California's red-light-abatement law, Fremont eventually closed five of its nine parlors. A new city ordinance restricted hours for the others from 10 a.m. to 10 p.m., and not all are operating full time (perhaps because the ordinance also forbade nude massages). One parlor operator who said she did half her business between 10 p.m. and 2 a.m., tried to have the ordinance overturned, but so far the courts have refused.

Other citizens' groups have concentrated their attack on one of the most objectionable forms of smut: child pornography. Encouraged by permissive social attitudes and—more significantly—boredom with "conventional" adult entertainment, some pornographers have begun to exploit children. Magazines like "Young Stud" or "Chicken Supreme" show pre-teen boys, sometimes masturbating or engaging in homosexual acts. Boys and girls in movies like "Children Love" have sex with each other; they are so inexperienced that they can sometimes be seen looking off-camera for instructions on what to do next.

Filmmakers have no trouble finding the stars for their movies. Some simply use their own children; others rely on runaways. In Los Angeles, where much of the child pornography is produced, police estimate that adults sexually exploited 30,000 children under 17 last year, and photographed many of them during the act.[23]

Rhode Islanders picketed stores and State House, demanding the expulsion of pornography and the passage of the Display Law.

The law was passed.

Most police departments quickly took action under the law. One did not. And they were picketed:

POLICE STATION PICKETED:
SMUT ACTION VOWED

Woonsocket police said last night that they will notify certain store owners in the city about a state anti-smut law after the police station was picketed.

Capt. Horida Ledoux made the announcement after being confronted with allegedly obscene newspapers purchased at three stores in Woonsocket. . . .

Harold Doran, president of Local 1208 of the International Brotherhood of Electrical Workers, . . . two other union officers, a photographer and his girlfriend picketed the police headquarters before entering the station at about 6:50 p.m. They carried signs which said, "Stamp Out Smut."

The police notified the three stores. Arrests were made.

How do you get people to picket?

You show them samples of pornography. They're enraged by what they see. You ask, "Will you join some other citizens in carrying a sign in front of the store (or theater) that sells this?"

You call the people who—on their registration forms —agreed to picket.

You carry signs, peacefully, up and down, up and down, up and down in front of the store or theater. You don't yell, shout, curse, or insult. Your presence and your sign tells all they need to know.

Make the signs clear to read and clear to communicate. In bold, bright letters, march with:

SAVE OUR CHILDREN
STAMP OUT SMUT
PORNO KILLS KIDS
WOMEN HATE PORNO
YOU ARE WHAT YOU READ
ROLL BACK FILTH
SWEEP FILTH IN THE GUTTER
FILTH IS FOR GUTTERS
STOP MIND POLLUTION

What Reactions to Expect

When you picket, you may get people who will counter-picket, chanting the tiresome slogans of "Freedom to Read." (Again, it has nothing to do with freedom to read. The issue is freedom to sell. And the community determines what may be legally sold.) Say nothing. March quietly. Answer no catcalls.

You'll get threats of lawsuits. The manager will say he's going to call police. You hope he does because that will bring more publicity to your cause.

You won't be arrested. You won't be sued.

A public street is a public street is a public street.

A lazy police chief threatened to lock me up. A rich lawyer protecting a rich store threatened to sue me. They couldn't. All of that, however, is secondary. If you were arrested, if you were sued, so what? You echoed the commitment: "Our lives, our fortunes, our sacred honor."

Most people who see the picket line, however, will join it or openly praise it saying, "Right On!" "It's About Time!" "I'm With You!"

If you're a Christian businessman and you sign a boycott petition, expect to be counter-boycotted. The stores you refuse to patronize because of their smut will remove the smut—or vent their anger by refusing to give you any business.

Count the cost before you join the porno fight.

I must tell you this story. A Christian mechanic signed a boycott petition against a theater. He serviced vehicles of the theater chain.

They called and cancelled their heavy business with him.

Eight days later people, *appreciating* his public stand against pornography, began taking their cars to him.

You'll be insulted, criticized, and misunderstood. And *praised*.

The more vocal the opposition, the more you cheer. It shows your message is getting through. They wouldn't attack if they weren't threatened.

One campaign against pornography generated, within a month, mountains of letters to the editor, the year's hottest news item. "Letters to the Editor" fall in three categories: (1) praise, (2) insult and character attack, (3) irrelevant (a vehicle for people to simply release steam).

(See sample letters—Appendix 5.)

Some "Letters to Editors" are easy on the eyes and nourishing for the brain. Others are muddy and weak.

When you write, write clear and direct. Rewrite and re-rewrite, packing a bomb to blast behind men's defenses. Slam on the issues. Leave people alone.

Don't worry about "on the fence" letters. Their writers won't actively support decency—and they won't actively oppose decency. Their toleration of pornography is covert. They won't bring it out in the open.

You'll get several "on the fence" responses—by mail, or phone, or personal meetings, or in "Letters to the Editor." They fall in five categories: (1) "Let's compromise." (2) "Why don't you fight something more important than pornography?" (Abortion, poverty, etc.) (3) "Let's just preach the gospel and leave politics alone." (4) "Let's just teach our children the beauty of sex at home." (5) "Let's be *for* something instead of *against* something."

I deal with these issues at length in the Question and Answer section but a brief note is needed here. Some of these people are hiding, but some are confused. Clarity and patience will swing them to fight pornography. You can tell them: (1) You don't compromise with racism, pornography, or drug addiction.

(2) We fight pornography *and* abortion *and* hunger, etc. It hasn't failed yet. Across the country, people who fight pornography also fight abortion and hunger, etc.

(3) Jesus said, "You are the light of the world." The very presence of Christians exposes the darkness of pornography. Or they're not Christians.

(4) We teach our children not to ride with strangers. When we see strangers soliciting kids (ours or others),

we report them to the police. We teach our children the beauty of sex. When we see retailers selling abusive sex, we report them to the police. If police say they don't have the laws to arrest, we give them a law.

(5) People who are *for* the beauty and privacy of sex are *against* pornography.

But after all the words are said, action is needed. You read a lot of steaming lava-hot, insulting letters from people who "oppose censorship" and support "freedom to read" and uphold man's "enjoyment of his own body." Those letters are mild. I couldn't print the hate letters I received in the mail.

Yet, in that city, the supporters of decency won. The racks were cleaned. The screens were cleaned. Here's why:

A few opponents of decency went to the city council to complain. One or two tried to sic a lawyer on me, and others. They went back home and wrote a lot more angry letters to the editor.

The supporters of decency, however, had pledged "their lives, their fortunes, their sacred honor." They wrote and called and boycotted. They wrote and called and boycotted. They wrote and called and boycotted. They kept it up long past the point of exhaustion.

CHAPTER 5
The Legal Strategy

"Good laws supported by good men and good women make good government."

Civic actions must be aimed at the passage of clear, enforceable laws. Martin Luther King said: "Direct action is not a substitute for work in the courts and halls of government. Indeed, direct action and legal action complement one another; when skillfully employed, each becomes more effective." [1]

I have grieved after holding workshops in cities where citizens were satisfied to clean racks and screens *without* demanding clear, tough laws.

Porno lawyers are rich. They are rich because they glue strategy to greed. They tell their theater, bookstore, topless bar, and massage-parlor clients, "Look, take the stuff off. Close up for a while. Let 'em 'win'!"

No more dirty books and magazines. No more dirty drive-ins, massage parlors, or topless joints—and no tough law.

Porno lawyers know that you can't call, write, boycott, and picket forever. Some day you'll die. Some day you'll move. Some day you'll get sick and lay in the hospital. Some day people will forget the insanity of *Hustler*, the brutality of *Penthouse,* the exploitation of *Playboy*—some day.

On that day, they move in again.

This time, it's near impossible to get citizens

alarmed and active again. "Look, all that work for nothing! Ahhhhhh, it doesn't do any good. I'm just going to keep my kid away from there."

Bang. You're dead.

That's just what the porno people wanted.

But "some day" never comes with a clear, tough law on the books. It doesn't matter who dies, moves or gets sick. The law is on the books—permanently.

If, thirty years hence, your grandchildren see a porno magazine crawling its way back on a shelf, they simply report the crime. Just like that.

But the example with "grandchildren thirty years hence" is weak. Because thirty years hence, your grandchildren won't see pornography on public display in theaters or stores—*if the enclosed laws are enacted by American states and cities.*

With clear, tough laws you report the crime of the sale of pornography, and the criminal is arrested—just like you had reported the crime of robbery.

When the enclosed laws are enacted nationally, porno will be shucked of its legitimate skin. It'll still circulate (lust will end only in heaven), but it'll be back in the gutter. People, again, will have to shovel in sewer holes to get it.

Laws work.

In February, 1977, in Cincinnati, Larry Flynt, publisher of *Hustler* magazine was convicted. He received a 7 to 25 year jail sentence and a $1,000 fine. The reason prosecutors secured a conviction was, in part, because of a provision in the June, 1973, *Miller* decision (U.S. Supreme Court).

Miller was a crucial obscenity decision. You should know what it said and did not say.

Marvin Miller, a book dealer, had been convicted by a local court on the grounds of mailing "sexually explicit" materials, violating a California law, which had reflected the court's earlier test for obscenity in *Memoirs* v. *Massachusetts*. Miller appealed, and the Supreme Court upheld his conviction.

In *Miller*, the Court said (1) *on First Amendment rights*: "This much has been categorically settled by the Court, that obscene material is unprotected by the First Amendment."

"The protection given speech and press was fashioned to assure unfettered interchange of *ideas* for the bringing about of political and social changes desired by the people. . . . But the public portrayal of hardcore sexual conduct for its own sake, and for the ensuing commercial gain is a different matter."

"One can concede that the 'sexual revolution' of recent years may have had useful by-products in striking layers of prudery from a subject long irrationally kept from needed ventilation. But it does not follow that no regulation of potently offensive 'hard-core' materials is needed or permissible; civilized people do not allow unregulated access to heroin because it is a derivative of a medicinal morphine."

(2) On *Roth:* " . . . There are certain will-defined and narrowly limited classes of speech, the prevention and punishment of which have never been thought to raise any Constitutional problem. *These include the lewd and obscene. . . . It has been well observed that such utterances are no essential part of any exposition of ideas, and are of such slight social value as a step to truth that any benefit that may be derived from*

them is clearly outweighed by the social interest in order and morality....'" Emphasis supplied by Court in *Roth* opinion.

"In sum we (...) reaffirm the Roth holding that obscene material is not protected by the First Amendment...."

(3) On a working definition of obscenity: "The basic guidelines... must be (a) whether 'the average person, applying contemporary community[2] standards' would find that the work, taken as a whole, appeals to the prurient interest.... (b) whether the work depicts or describes, in a patently offensive way, sexual conduct specifically defined by the applicable state law, and (c) whether the work, taken as a whole lacks serious literary, artistic, political or scientific value."

(4) On sex and nudity: "Sex and nudity may not be exploited without limit by films or pictures exhibited or sold in places of public accommodation any more than live sex and nudity can be exhibited or sold without limit in such public places."

(5) On the primacy of the jury system in determinations of obscenity: "In resolving the inevitably sensitive questions of fact and law, we must continue to rely on the jury system, accompanied by the safeguards that judges, rules of evidence, presumption of innocence and other protective features provide, as we do with rape, murder, and a host of other offenses against society and its individual members."

In two ways, the *Miller* decision empowered Cincinnati to secure a conviction against *Hustler*:

(1) The definition of "obscene" includes three parts: whether "the average person, applying contemporary community standards" would find that the work, taken as a whole, appeals to the prurient interest; whether the work depicts or describes, in a patently offensive way, sexual conduct specifically defined by the applicable state law; and whether the work, taken as a whole, lacks serious literary, artistic, political or scientific value.

(2) "Community standards" was important in the

Hustler decision. Here's why: In America there are pockets of people who do not find *Hustler* obscene. Neither do they find *Playboy*'s recreational sex, child-molesting, sex-whippings, nor women mating with horses obscene.

But—since *Miller*—these pitiful sex-addicts, choking Boston's "Combat Zone," New York's Times Square, and Los Angeles' Hollywood strip, no longer can slap their barbaric sexual standards upon a nation of decent citizens.

It's up to each community to decide their own sexual standards. That's what *Miller* said.

In *Miller*, however, the Supreme Court did *not* say that certain magazines were obscene and others were not. The Supreme Court, according to the Constitution, is not empowered to do things like that. The Supreme Court does not "make laws for the nation." The Supreme Court *analyzes* laws, including laws containing strategic legal terms like "obscenity," and then says: "This law or this legal definition is constitutional," or "This law or legal definition is unconstitutional." In *Miller*, the court said that whether "the average person, applying contemporary community standards" would find that the work, taken as a whole, appeals to the prurient interest; whether the work depicts or describes, in a patently offensive way, sexual conduct specifically defined by the applicable state law; and whether the work, taken as a whole, lacks serious literary, artistic, political or scientific value—all add up to a constitutional definition of obscenity. The Supreme Court, in effect, said to states, cities, and towns: It is constitutional to use this definition of obscenity in arresting and prosecuting pornographers in your community.

Cincinnati said they wanted *Huslter* arrested and convicted. The *Miller* decision empowered them, and empowers citizens in *any* community to do the same. It's up to a local people.

Pornography remains in a city only as long as citizens want it.

The enclosed laws have cleaned up several communities. But it takes people to slap these laws into the hands of city councilmen and state legislators and fight for their passage.

This is not an exhaustive treatment of the legal battle against pornography. Here I am giving the laws you need to rout porno and the actions you need to get the laws on the books.

1

THE PROBLEM: Weak, vague, outdated, and/or unconstitutional state and local obscenity codes

THE SOLUTION: Model Ordinance—Obscenity, based on Miller definitions

MODEL ORDINANCE—OBSCENITY

SECTION 1. Definitions

For purposes of this Ordinance:

(A) "Matter" means any book, magazine, newspaper, or printed or written material or any picture, drawing, photograph, motion picture, or other pictorial representation or any statue or other figure, or any recording, transcription, or mechanical, chemical or electrical reproduction or any other articles, equipment, machines or materials.

(B) "Performance" means any play, motion picture, dance or other exhibition or presentation, whether pictured, animated or *live*, performed before an audience of one (1) or more person(s).

(C) Any matter or performance is obscene if:

(1) the average person, applying contemporary community standards, finds that the matter or performance, taken as a whole, appeals to the prurient interest, and

(2) the matter or performance depicts or describes in a patently offensive way, sexual conduct, normal or preverted, actual or simulated, and

(3) the matter or performance, taken as a whole, lacks serious literary, artistic, political or scientific value.

(D) "Sexual conduct" means acts of masturbation, excretory functions, lewd exhibition of the genitals, sado-masochistic abuse, homosexuality, lesbianism, bestiality, sexual intercourse or physical contact with a person's clothed or unclothed genitals, pubic area, buttocks, or the breast or breasts of a female for the purpose of sexual stimulation, gratification, or perversion.

(E) "Sado-masochistic abuse" means flagellation or torture by or upon a person as an act of sexual stimulation or gratification.

(F) "Person" means any individual, partnership, firm, association, corporation or other legal entity.

(G) "Distribute" means to transfer possession of, whether with or without consideration.

(H) "Knowingly" means knowing or having good reason to know the character of the matter or performance.

(I) "Owner" means any person who owns or has legal right to possession of any matter.

SECTION 2. Prohibited Acts—Matter

Every person who knowingly sends or causes to be sent, or brings or causes to be brought, into this (Political Subdivision) for sale or distribution, or in this (Political Subdivision) possesses, prepares, publishes, or prints, with intent to distribute or to exhibit to another, or who offers to distribute, distributes, or exhibits to another any obscene matter is guilty of a misdemeanor.

SECTION 3. Prohibited Acts—Performances

Every person who knowingly engages or participates in, manages, produces, sponsors, presents or exhibits any obscene performance is guilty of a misdemeanor.

SECTION 4. Defenses

It shall be an affirmative defense to a prosecution under this ordinance for the defendant to show:

(A) That the distribution was made to the recipient by a bona-fide school, museum, or public library or by an employee of such organization or of a retail outlet affiliated with and serving the educational purpose of such organization acting in the course of his employment; or,

(B) That the act was done for legitimate scientific or education purposes.

SECTION 5. Arrest and Seizure

Where the subject matter is offered for distribution

to the public as stock in trade of a lawful business or activity, or, as in the case of films, is exhibited at a commercial theater showing regularly scheduled performances to the general public, no person shall be arrested for a violation of any of the provisions of this chapter unless the arresting officer shall have first obtained an arrest warrant, and no property shall be seized as evidence unless a search warrant shall have first been obtained pursuant to the provisions of this ordinance; Provided, however, that the quantity of matter seized shall encompass no more than is reasonable and necessary for the purpose of obtaining evidence.

SECTION 6. Hearing

At any time after arrest and seizure, and prior to trial, the state, defendant, owner, or other party in interest of any matter seized, may apply for and obtain a prompt adversary hearing for the purpose of obtaining a preliminary determination of obscenity, the defendant or owner of any matter seized may apply for and, upon a showing that other copies of the film or motion picture are not available to be exhibited, the court shall order that the applicant be permitted to copy the film or motion pictures, at his own expense, so that showing can be continued pending a judicial determination of obscenity in an adversary hearing.

SECTION 7. Penalty

Any person who violates any of the provisions of this ordinance shall be guilty of a misdemeanor, and shall upon conviction, be fined in any amount not to exceed one thousand dollars ($1,000) and, may be imprisoned for any period not to exceed six (6) months.

SECTION 8. Severability

If any provision or clause of this ordinance, or its application to any person or circumstance is held invalid, the invalidity does not affect other provisions or applications of this ordinance which can be given effect without the invalid provision or application, and to this end the provisions of each section are declared to be severable.

Optional: SECTION 9. Effective Date

Whereas an emergency exists for the immediate taking effect of this ordinance, the same shall be in full force and effect from and after its passage.

Notes on Obscenity Ordinance:

1. Ask your state representative (or Attorney General) if your state's obscenity code incorporates the *Miller* definition of obscenity. If your code does not, it's probably unconstitutional or hopelessly weak. Ask your state representative to introduce this obscenity ordinance.

2. The rigorous enforcement of the obscenity ordinance will virtually wipe out all pornography (except the *Playboy*-genre pornography; the public display law wipes that out).

3. In addition to the obscenity ordinance, you should enact and enforce the following laws. The more bullets in your gun, the more pornography you kill.

2

PROBLEM: Pornography on open shelves in public places (food stores, drugstores, quick-stop stores, airports, motels, newsstands)

SOLUTION: Public Display Law

Mrs. Dedra Wharton grabbed her eight-year-old's hand, wheeled, and shot down the quick-stop store's aisle. Whizzing by the check-out counter, she slammed on it the sweating milk jug she had intended to buy. Outside, little Bret continued, "Mommy, what was that lady on the magazine doing? Huh? What was she doing?"

The "lady" was a wet-lipped, football-sized breast prostitute, lying naked on the cover, her right hand stroking her vagina—thinly veiled behind pink-bikini panties—her left hand squeezing her engorged nipple. Licking her lips, she, and the dozen other cover prostitutes, say, "C'mon and take me."

Mrs. Wharton was used to it. She had seen the nightmarish wallpaper before: *Oui, Penthouse, Hustler, Playboy, Cavalier*, and twenty other slick, popular porno magazines. And, she now realized, Bret and his buddies must have seen them too, buying comic books on the same rack. But today was the first time she had been in the store *with* Bret. It didn't dawn on her until today.

Mrs. Wharton did not live in Rhode Island. If she did, that wouldn't have happened. The slick, popular porno still sold in Rhode Island is behind-and-under-the-counter, out of arm's reach and eye-view of children and adults.

The *Public Display Law* did it (hereafter, Display Law). And did it so effectively that other state legislatures are studying it and several cities have already adopted it as a local ordinance.

Taking porno out of public view, the Display Law restores to parents their right to protect their children from abusive sex in public places, and restores to adults their right *not* to see abusive sex. The law restores these rights without exercising censorship and without infringing on an adult's right to read. That is one reason why the law was upheld in Superior Court; second, the law is rooted in a Supreme Court Decision (*Ginsberg* v. *New York*, 1968); third, its language is simple, clear, and enforceable.

The law spells it out:

PUBLIC DISPLAY-MINORS LAW

Sale or Exhibition to Minors of Indecent Publications, Pictures, or Articles.

Every person who shall willfully or knowingly engage in the business of selling, lending, giving away, showing advertising for sale or distributing to any person under the age of eighteen (18) years or has in his possession with intent to engage in the said business or to otherwise offer for sale or commercial distribution to any individual under the age of eighteen (18) years or who shall display at newsstands or any other business establishment frequented by minors under the age of eighteen (18) years or where said minors are or may be invited as a part of the general public any motion picture or live show, or any still picture or photograph or any book, pocket book, pamphlet or magazine the cover or content of which exploits, is devoted to, or is principally made up of descriptions or depictions of illicit sex or sexual immorality or which is lewd, lascivious, or indecent, or which consists of pictures of nude or partially denuded figures posed or presented in a manner to provoke or arouse lust or passion or to exploit sex, lust or perversion for commercial gain or any article or instrument of indecent or immoral use shall, upon conviction, be punished by a fine of not less than one hundred dollars ($100) nor more than one thousand dollars ($1,000) or by imprisonment for not more than two (2) years, or by both such fine and imprisonment.

For the purposes of this section, "description or depictions of illicit sex or sexual immorality" shall mean (1) human genitals in a state of sexual stimulation or arousal; (2) acts of human masturbation, sexual intercourse or sodomy; (3) fondling or other erotic touching of human genitals, pubic region, buttock or female breast; "nude or partially denuded figures" shall mean (1) less than completely and opaquely covered (a) human genitals, (b) pubic regions, (c) buttocks, and (d) female breast below a point immediately above the top of the areola,[3] and (2) human male genitals in a discernibly turgid state, even if completely and opaquely covered; "knowingly" shall mean having knowledge of the character and content of the publication or failure on notice to exercise reasonable inspection which would disclose the content and character of the same.

The law does not use evaluative words like "abusive" or "pornographic." It uses the word "objectionable" (empowered by *Ginsberg* v. *New York*, 1968) providing *ad hoc* definitions for "objectionable." The simple, clear definitions make the law eminently enforceable because no jury or judge has to guess at what "obscenity" is (The Display Law eschews that oft-misunderstood word.); no prior (and usually lengthy) pre-judiciary hearings are needed; and no "expert witnesses" are needed.

Anyone—district attorney, sheriff, policeman, or average citizen—can tell if the cover or content of the magazine fits the definitions. Instead of asking, "Is this magazine 'obscene'?" you ask, "Does the cover or content show 'human genitals in a state of sexual stimulation or arousal'?" or "Does it show the 'female breast below a point immediately above the top of the areola'?" or "Does it show 'less than completely and opaquely covered buttocks'?" If so, you call for an immediate arrest.

The law is eminently enforceable. I asked the city attorney and police chief in Everett, Massachusetts (suburb of Boston), how enforceable it was as a city ordinance. They replied:

> In regard to your letter [city attorney's letter— WNG] of November 20th, referring to a communication from a Mr. Gallagher, chairman, "Citizens for Decency through Law" the following is a brief comment of how the police department handled the enforcement of same.
>
> When our ordinance became law, we contacted every person handling publications that were or could be the subject matter of the law, and gave them a copy of the law. We told them that they would be given a week to cull out the books and magazines that were in violation of the law.
>
> Original and follow-up contact was made by the Liquor & Vice squad. Store owners and managers were encouraged to ask questions on the law. Any questions officers could not answer were referred to the police prosecutor and his answer brought back to the store owner.
>
> Store owners were notified that there would be strict enforcement of the law.
>
> Uniformed officers were given copies of the law and informed by their superiors that there was to be strict enforcement.
>
> Any complaints made by a citizen would immediately be processed and investigated by the Liquor & Vice squad. If there was a violation, it would be prosecuted in District Court. The Officer would sign the complaint.
>
> As a result of the above actions, (1) we have had no arrests, (2) no convictions, (3) no violations, (4) and best of all, no display of magazines or books of the type mentioned in the law. Our youth are protected completely from such displays in our city.

In court a jury does not have to maneuver around a definition of "obscenity." It simply has to determine: (1) Does the cover or content contain material fitting the definitions? (2) Was the material on public display in a business establishment accessible to minors?

Experience in Rhode Island (and other communities) shows the law works. Here's why:

(1) Retailers welcome it. For years, wholesalers have demanded that reluctant retailers sell *all* magazines on aggressive, open display—porno magazines, especially. (One wholesaler offers a $400 bonus *just for displaying* porno magazines.) If you don't, they say they'll stop delivery of *all* magazines (*Time, Reader's Digest, Good Housekeeping*, etc.). Display and sell *all*, wholesalers say, or none. The Display Law gives retailers the "out" they were looking for.

(2) It removes from popular porno its aura of public acceptability. The open sale of any product *means* that society approves of the sale of this product (else, it wouldn't be sold openly).

However, taking the magazines from the open shelves and forcing them behind the counter *now* says this: Society thinks there's something amiss with these magazines; look, their visibility must be restricted. And that's a plus, especially for children. The more children witness the aggressive marketing of abusive sex, the more they accumulate an impression that, well, abusive sex must be okay. Here it is, in the open.

(3) Display Law arrests lead to convictions, and convictions—when challenged—are upheld. Law officers are thereby encouraged to enforce the law, knowing their work will not be in vain.

The Display Law does not deal with adult porno shops which, presumably, are not accessible to minors. The Display Law deals only with "business establishments frequented by minors."

Adult porno shops are *not the main porno* problem in the United States. Adult porno shops erupted like pimples on a face already clogged with acne. Adult porno shops erupted because, for twenty years prior, Americans had gradually allowed the display of abusive sex in public stores. Americans became jaded. Nothing shocked them anymore.

The Display Law helps restore sex to its place of

privacy and beauty. And returns to parents (like Mrs. Wharton) their sense of outrage when witnessing the privacy and beauty of sex abused—before their children are smacked at eye-level with that abuse.

The Display Law was upheld in Superior Court. In that decision, the court acknowledged that Supreme Court decisions upheld and undergirded the Display Law.[4] Of the Display Law, the *Boston Herald-American* said:

RENEWED DRIVE AGAINST SMUT

Within a few days an initiative petition will be circulated throughout the state to prohibit the display of hard-core pornography in places frequented by minors.

The petition is the handiwork of two Boston legislators, Rep. Raymond P. Flynn and James F. Hart, who introduced similar legislation in the form of late-filed bills at the recently concluded session, only to have time run out in the rush of prorogation.

They deserve the encouragement and support of the general public and have already been assured the backing of organized labor and other civic and religious organizations.

Experience in other states, notably nearby Rhode Island, has demonstrated that despite prior court rulings, smut peddling can be controlled and substantially reduced through carefully drawn legislation designed to stand the test of constitutional challenge and give police something to work with.

A year ago, Rhode Island passed legislation which avoided the pitfalls which had proved fatal to prior efforts and concentrated its direction toward safeguarding its youth.

As a result, sales of obscene publications have dropped 95 percent. Encouraged by that record, other states are taking up the battle against the smut traffic.

While it is difficult to define obscenity in relation to adults, the U.S. Supreme Court in the Ginsberg case four years ago carefully distinguished the right of the states to prevent the distribution to children of objectionable material.

The constitutional shield for adults does not apply to those corrupting children for financial gain, and the state can protect the morals of the community by barring the distribution to children of books and other materials which the courts recognize as suitable for adults.

Without the teenage trade, the proft from pornography is doomed. Smut peddlers feed on the youth market. The new legislation, by isolating those under 18 from exposure, can drive the entire operation out of business or under the counter where it was ten years ago.

Concerned citizens of Massachusetts should remember that when they are handed an initiative petition to sign. At least 56,000 signatures, three percent of the vote cast for governor in the last statewide election, are needed. There ought to be ten times that number eager to respond to the call.[5]

And Knights of Columbus said in an editorial entitled "The Cancer of Pornography":

There are times in everyone's life when he or she is shocked beyond belief. It might be a senseless and brutal murder of a young child, an old masterpiece of art vandalized beyond repair, or a loved one wasting away from the ravages of cancer before our eyes and all available resources unable to stem the tide of the destroyer since the cancer has progressed too far.

Medical science, human techonology and common sense urge us all to check the danger signs of cancer. This makes good sense since it could and many times does save the individual. But many do not heed the danger signals—due to fear or "it can't happen to me" attitude.

A cancer has been introduced into our society; a cancer that affects those whom all right-thinking men and women would fight to protect our children.

Our country was designed upon the strong foundation of the Constitution and Bill of Rights, States Rights and a system of Checks and Balance between and among the Presidency, Legislature and/or Judiciary. No one branch of government was to be more powerful than the other.

Recently the cancer of hard-core pornography has been seeping into our society from all the media. This hard-core pornography is out-and-out filth. It must be recognized as such and accepted by citizens as a challenge—as much of a challenge in fact as is communism, heart disease, cancer.

The state council of Knights of Columbus has for the

past ten years attempted to alert the public to this growing evil. But to little avail, due to a combination of apathy and a feeling that this is a purely Catholic issue. The Knights of Columbus effort was thought by many to be a Catholic effort only. It was and is an effort of men who are concerned about children, their future and the nation's future.

Another group of men has stepped into the breach, *The International Brotherhood of Electrical Workers* AFL-CIO and CLC. This group of men under the leadership of their President Harold E. Doran, Business Manager Cloris Gauthier and Recording Secretary Anthony Almeida have made specific in-roads on the purveyors of filth.

History and society have always condemned those who exploit, harm, or in any way affect youth in a negative way. Socrates, one of the greatest minds of all time, was condemned to death by his Grecian peers because of his activity toward the young.

The men of the IBEL are no different from any other group of men. They see an obvious wrong and are doing all in their power to eliminate this wrong from the hands of the young.

These men are not attempting to drive anyone out of business, or judge one's willingness to sell this filth to young children; they wish rather to protect the young mind in the formative years from being exposed to a distorted and gutter perspective of life.

Mr. Doran and his union must be commended for their actions, and must be given tangible support from the citizenry. The Knights of Columbus strongly urge all Catholics, Protestants, Jews to support the stand taken by the Electrical Workers.

These men need support from all of us. Men, no matter how dedicated, get discouraged when they feel their positive actions are falling on deaf ears.

The cancer of the body will some day, through the concentrated effort of medicine, be controlled. The cancer of hard-core pornography can be effectively controlled only by the concentrated effort of the citizenry and all the resources they possess.

Hard-core pornography will strangle in its own filth. Strangle only when the supply exceeds the demand. When a profit isn't realized by these "men" who live off the innocence of children and youth: Then and only then will these "men" taste the bitter hemlock or channel their energies elsewhere.

A state law in Rhode Island, the Display Law has been enacted in a city ordinance in Nashville, Tennesee;[6] Everett, Massachusetts; Lawrence, Massachusetts; Poplar Bluffs, Missouri; and New Fairfield, Connecticut. At this writing, it is under consideration in several other cities and states.

The law is clear, tough, and enforceable. You will want your city councilmen, state legislators, attorney general, city attorney, and local judges to read the enclosed "open letter" which Harold Doran (author of the law) sent to thousands of inquirers:

Dear Sir/Madam:

Congratulations. You now have in your hands one of the most effective anti-smut laws in our nation.

This law can be introduced as a city ordinance or as a state law. Here in Rhode Island it is a state law and a felony offense. Several cities in other states now have it as a city ordinance. Everett, Massachusetts, had a serious smut problem. They introduced our law and within a week the city was cleaned up. This was two years ago, and as of this writing, they have no problem.

This may shock your local attorneys and perhaps even your state Attorney General. Here in Rhode Island we are, and have been for the past four years, making arrests *without* "obscenity" *warrants*,[7] and *without a probable cause hearing on obscenity.* I am enclosing a copy of one such court decision for your investigation, written by the Honorable J. MacKenzie of the Rhode Island Superior Court.[8] In another decision, the court *denied* a motion to suppress and dismiss. The defendant had argued that the arrest was illegal and void because no probable cause for the arrest of the defendant existed, as no judicial or other legal determination of obscenity was made prior to the arrest. *The court stated, however, that a judicial determination of obscenity, expert testimony, as well as an arrest warrant was not needed because the law has been so written to avoid this problem.* This statute has also withstood court challenges concerning *Scienter* and vagueness. This should be good news for your Attorney General's office. There are two important root factors that are responsible for this great success, and in the remainder of this letter I will attempt to clarify them. (1) We avoided the definition of obscenity (with all of its confusion), and we treated the material as *objectionable* rather than obscene material. (2) We did not prohibit adults from purchasing the material.

As of this writing, two hundred thousand sex publications have been removed from store displays in the State of Rhode Island. This even includes paperbacks (without photographs) as well as the previously untouchable *Playboy* magazine. I have also effectively applied this law to the motion picture classification system in our state and a city library that was making available sex paperbacks such as the *Joy of Sex* to our children. I also successfully applied our law to a talk-back radio station show that was entertaining sex conversations. And when a local CBS TV station advertised they were to air an "X" rated film at 11:30 p.m., I immediately challenged the station and made them aware of the Rhode Island law. The station manager told me, "We are not governed by state law but rather federal law!" I then called CBS in New York City and I was told the same story; however, there was a flaw in their story.

CBS did allow the local TV station the option to air the "X" film or substitute it for another. I then called our state Attorney General and made him aware of the TV station's option, and he stated that if the descriptions or depictions of sexual conduct in the film violated this section in our law, he would take action. Our newspapers and the A.C.L.U. joined with the TV station and screamed "Censorship." I then made a strong public statement that if the film were aired, I would call for their arrest. The TV station publicly countered me and said they would air the film. However, two days later when the film was scheduled for showing and without any public explanation, the TV station substituted another film.

We have effectively applied our law to written material, the spoken word, and photographs.

Now, if you are an attorney and after what you have just read, you are probably thinking, "This guy is nuts. This can't be. This violates every obscenity ruling of the United States Supreme Court." What you are overlooking, however is that almost all major obscenity rulings by the high court concerned *adults*. True, the United States Supreme Court said that in determining obscenity and before an arrest the state must first hold a judicial hearing on probable cause, and the trier of the fact must find that (a) the work taken as a whole appeals to the prurient interest in sex. (b) The work or material is patently offensive. (c) The work taken on the whole lacks serious value, etc. This test on determining obscenity is mostly from *Miller*, U.S. Supra.

It would be wise now to stop and think, did the United States Supreme Court in the *Miller* decision specifically mention "children"? The answer, of course, is "No." The states, then, do not have to incorporate the *Miller* decision in their minor statutes nor in their city ordinances. However, because of this confusion concerning the definition of obscenity, we are now witnessing a great tragedy unfolding in this country. Good state legislators and dedicated citizens in their eagerness to insulate their states from moral decay have and at this present time are incorporating the test of obscenity as stated in the *Miller* decision in their state minor statutes and city ordinances. How sad and foolish this is, unaware that what they are doing is to legally expose their children at any age to frontal nudity and open display of sex acts. Unless this is checked soon our children will fall before the onslaught of pornography in their schools, libraries, TV, and in all local stores.

The answer to this massive national disgrace is so simple. It is so close and yet so far. *Do exactly as I have done in Rhode Island.* Avoid at all cost the definition of obscenity. Do not even use the word "obscene" in your minor state or city laws. Do not use the test for obscenity as stated in the *Miller* decision, *taken on the whole, lacks serious value, and taken on the whole is patently offensive,* etc. Again I say, *Miller* was set down by the United States Supreme Court for adults, *not children.* We do not have to prove obscenity where children are concerned. The United States Supreme Court years before the *Miller* decision stated, *"States can suppress books for children even though they are not necessarily obscene for adults."* Rhode Island Superior Court Judge, J. MacKenzie, in his brilliantly written decision, makes strong reference to these decisions by the highest court in our land.

I stress the importance of avoiding the word "obscene" for good reason. Two years ago and with great personal expense, I had the Rhode Island law introduced in the State of Massachusetts. However, unknown to me, in committee they put it in with their obscenity laws. Because of this error, the law is practically worthless. Only the cities of Everett and Lawrence, Massachusetts, who introduced the Rhode Island law without change as a city ordinance, are enjoying the fact that their children are not exposed to smut.

If you do dearly love your children and want to protect them, then just introduce the enclosed law under the title of *"Objectionable Shows"* and *"Publications,"* but above all, avoid like you would a *rattlesnake* the word *obscene.*

I have witnessed the effectiveness of this law in our state, and I am firmly convinced that if it were nationally implemented, our country would once again enjoy the decency it once had. Maybe then our children would be free of V.D., illegitimacy, and suicide epidemics. Stores in the State of Rhode Island, who are no longer displaying sex publications, have told us *their sales have dropped by 95%! Out of sight, out of mind!* And most stores no longer even sell *Playboy* or other sexually oriented magazines and paperbacks. It is important to note that many, many paperbacks are responsible for the pollution of our children's minds from coast to coast.

And the total, constant expense of the abuse of sex has conditioned many lawyers, judges and *juries* to let anything slip by because "it's not as bad" as some novel sex abuse they saw yesterday. (Some juries pass favorably on photographs showing a spread-eagle view of a woman's genitals because "it's not as bad" as the photographs of intercourse they've seen, or some pass favorably on photographs of intercourse because "they're not as bad" as pictures of child-molesting currently circulating. Get the point?)

The Rhode Island Display Law insulates adults and children from the constant exposure to sexual abuse. If the Display Law is not enacted in all states soon, all adults will be conditioned to accept *all* sex perversions. They will find *nothing* obscene; and neither will any judge or jury.

The Display Law takes the sex-abuse magazines (*Playboy* and its thousand imitators) out of public exposure and isolates them, making them (again) vulnerable to personal and community attack.

All of this is important to know. There is a great financial loss to pornographers because of this law and there are tremendous evil forces fighting this new law throughout the country. I pray that God will give you the strength to overcome this evil force.

Harold Doran

How do you get the Display Law enacted?

1. Call a public meeting.[9] Discreetly show samples of pornography to mature citizens.

2. Invite people to your home. Discretely show them samples of pornography. They'll say, "What can I do?" Give them a petition to sign, pushing for passage of the Display Law. Tell them to call and write city councilmen, pushing for passage of the Display Law. And also tell them to invite people into *their* homes, spreading the word on the terror of porno and how to get rid of it.

3. You and a committee of concerned citizens visit city councilmen and the mayor and show them the worst samples.

Tell them you want the Display Law passed to stop the open peddling of that insanity.

You keep on packing the pressure through boycotting and picketing, as outlined on pages 87-105.

Enacting the law *statewide* is best. For two obvious reasons: (1) As a state law, the Display Law cleans the shelves of *every* city and town at one whack. (2) When ten states have the Display Law enacted, the glossy-porno market will be crippled out of business nationally.[10]

At their own admission, pornographers will not be able to withstand the losses.

As I write this, I am aware my words are being read by publishers and peddlers of *Playboy, Penthouse, Oui, Hustler,* etc. I'm not giving away secrets. I am articulating what they already know.

I am simply letting the public know what pornographers have been hiding—*there are laws to stop porno.*

(I am also aware that the Display Law puts some people out of work, like drug laws put pushers out of work. I help porno peddlers and drug pushers to find new work. That I can do. To allow the circulation of porno or drugs, in the name of jobs, that I cannot do.)

To enact statewide, do the following:

1. Call, unite, and visit people throughout the state. Start with church leaders, PTA leaders, Boy Scout or Girl Scout leaders, or, with just one friend in another city.

All it takes is one. Contact one and he or she helps you contact two and the two help you contact four, etc. You show them the samples. They'll gasp and ask what can be done. Give them the Display Law and names and addresses of all representatives and senators, emphasizing those from that person's district. (You get the names and addresses from the State House Library, which you call, write or visit.)

2. Tell people to hold meetings at their churches, clubs and homes, discretely showing the samples and telling others to write and call legislators and Governor, pushing for passage of the Display Law.

3. Arrange for a delegation of people to visit the Governor and key legislators. Show them the samples, explaining the urgency of having the Display Law passed.

I've opened the pages of savage pornography before Governors and legislators. It shocked them and hurt them. It shocks me and hurts me. But *then* they understand the problem and they *do* something.

The Display Law was passed in Rhode Island partly because Harold Doran showed then-Governor Frank Licht the insane photographs of women-mating-with-horses, sold next to coloring books. Governor Licht acted, eventually issuing a proclamation calling for Decency Week in Rhode Island to herald the passage of the Display Law.

Push for the Display Law first.

But wait a minute, I hear what you are saying, "This Display Law protects only children. But porno hurts everyone. Are you one of these squareheads who believe that strychnine stops being poisonous at age 18?"

No, I'm not. I know that pornography rapes the mind and blisters the consciences of everyone.

The reasons for stressing the Display Law are these:

(1) You can get it passed. Even the most jaded city councilman or state legislator will pass a law protecting children.

(2) The law attacks the porno problem at its two malignant roots: public acceptability and public visibility. Forcing the magazines from public view dramatizes the community conviction that the community emphatically does not want these magazines.

(3) You immediately protect adults and children from viewing ugly, abusive sex on porno covers when they enter an airport, drugstore, or food store.

(4) You *do* (ultimately) cripple the sales of all porno magazines. That's why *Playboy* fought so hard in Rhode Island. They know that most men buy porno on impulse—the impulse of lust. The wet-lipped, bare prostitute on the cover goads men to snatch and buy.

The consciences of some men have been so brutalized that they'll fish in a gutter in public to get a porno magazine. They don't care. But most men in America still have sensitive consciences. They cannot look a clerk (usually a female clerk) in the eye and say, "Give me the latest *Playboy*."

It's like looking at the woman clerk and saying, "Give me the magazine that treats you like a 'nigger.' "

The Display Law forces the magazines behind and under the counter. If there is no public display, there is no goading, no impulse to buy. Out of sight, out of mind.

The Pentagon adopted a Display-type law with the following results:

GROTON, Conn. (UPI)—Men and women too embarrassed to ask for adult magazines kept behind the counter at the U.S. Naval Submarine Base Exchange have caused a 75 percent drop in magazine sales during the past three weeks.

Capt. Robert D. Rawlins, commanding officer of the base, said yesterday the Navy Resale System Office in Washington about three weeks ago ordered "adult-type reading material" taken off the open display rack and placed behind the counter.

Lt. Cmdr. Urlich Kusker, in charge of the store where military personnel can buy discounted items, said magazine sales have dropped more than 75 percent because people are too embarrassed to ask for the magazines.

"A woman won't come in and ask for *Playgirl*, and a man won't ask for *Playboy*, but they will buy it if it is on display," Kusker said.

The order Rawlins received said, "The open display of adult-type reading material in magazine racks at Navy exchanges is considered detrimental to high moral standards, and easy access to these magazines by young people is of growing concern."

Rawlins said the order didn't specify which magazines were considered "adult-type reading material," so the choice was up to him. He selected 12 magazines, including *Playboy, Playgirl, Penthouse, Oui* and *Hustler*, to be placed behind the counter.[11]

The law also silences paranoid libertarians who boil about an "adult's right to read" (again, it's the *right to sell*). The Display Law says: Sure adults can still buy it. All they have to do is ask for it.

The Display Law undergirded by a Supreme Court decision, *Ginsberg* v. *New York*, states:

The state also has an independent interest in the well-being of its youth. . . . Chief Judge Fuld emphasized its significance in the earlier case of *People* v. *Kahan*, 15 N.Y. 2d 311, 206 N.E. 2d 333, which had struck down the first version of 484-h on grounds of vagueness. In his concurring opinion, id., at 312, 1 206 N.E. 2d at 334, he said: "While the supervision of children's reading may best be left to their parents, the knowledge that parental control or guidance cannot always be provided and society's transcendent interest in protecting the welfare of children justify reasonable regulation of the sale of material to them. It is, therefore, altogether fitting and proper for a state to include in a statute designed to regulate the sale of pornography to children special standards, broader than those embodied in legislation aimed at controlling dissemination of such material to adults." [12]

(5) The law avoids the firecracker word "obscene." Remember, the law deals with business establishments frequented by *minors* (incorporating about 99% of all business establishments). Because it is a *minor* statute, it *does not have to meet adult standards of "obscenity."*

It's a *minor*'s statute. It's not restricted by definition of obscenity in state adult statutes.

Because it is a minor's statute, it may be written more stringently than an adult statute. It may use the word "objectionable," providing *ad hoc* definitions of "objectionable."

Ginsberg said that laws for minors may be "adjusted in the interest of protecting youth":

That the state has power to make that adjustment seems clear, for we have recognized that even where there is an invasion of protected freedoms "the power of the state to control the conduct of children reaches beyond the scope of its authority over adults. . . .' " [13]

The beauty is that it is a minor's statute which *also* protects adults from being smacked with abusive sex every time they enter a food store, drugstore, or airport lobby.

Press for the Display Law first. And prepare for pornographers to fight. Prepare for them to lie, insult, and scream.

One thing they cannot say. They cannot say it's unconstitutional. That appears to be already settled.

No Supreme Court decision on obscenity touches this law. Because it is *not* a law on obscenity. It is a law designed to protect minors. It, therefore, doesn't fall within the restrictions of "obscenity." The High Court has ruled that stricter laws (stricter than "obscenity" laws) may be written where minors are concerned.

3

PROBLEM: Porno films: drive-in theaters showing movies whose sex scenes are visible from roads, houses, playgrounds, shopping centers and other adjacent areas

Don't trust movie ratings.

Unless it's a Walt Disney movie, don't let your kids go to a movie alone. Go with them to *every* movie.

Like TV shows, you never know for sure what's going to be shown. Don't go by the rating system.

Even if the film is decent, you don't know what the previews (or commercials) will be.

Jerry Lewis called the flood of sex films "trash." Art Linkletter went further:

> Entertainer Art Linkletter says he is disgusted with talented actors who are resorting to "shameful pornography" for movie roles. The radio-television host said that 10 years ago pornography was content to use unknown actors, but the public became bored with those films. "Now we have the spectacle of big-name stars making the cheap, sensational films. They're making a lot of money, but they'll wear out," he predicted. He singled out two actors by name for censure. "Warren Beatty in 'Shampoo' is an example of a young man who at the height of his star powers has debased the whole business by putting on a movie with major celebrities that caters to the lowest common denominator of taste." "Marlon Brando, in my opinion, is on par with him. A star of that caliber doing 'Last Tango in Paris' is, to me, disgusting." [14]

Art Linkletter was kind. He underestimated the situation.

Savage-sex films have crawled onto American screens so gradually, we may not be aware of what's hit us. Every night, in most large metropolitan newspapers, movie ads assault the eyes with such titles as: "Fourteen and Under (Too Young to Know Better, Too Old to Say No!)," "Teenage Sex Fantasies," "Teenage Sorority Girls," "The Intimate Teenagers (What Really Happens Between Her First Desires and the Age of Consent)," "Love Camp No. 7," "The Swappers Wives

(They Were Ready and Willing to Trade Anything)," "Teenage Sex Therapy," etc.

The "X" films of a few years ago are the "R" films today. The "R" films of a few years ago are the "GP" films today.

The Motion Picture Association of America (MPAA) writes the rating code and classifies the films. They obviously write it in their own best interest.

Legally, the code means nothing. There is no law to enforce it.

"X" films are savage sex, raping the minds of actors and spectators alike.

"R" films (restricted to adults) are largely abusive sex, gang violence, and raw language. Few are suitable for adults.

"GP" films (children admitted with parental guidance) are spilling over into "R" content. (One "GP" film showed a prostitute undressing.) Few are suitable for children.

This is an updated classification of the films:

G   Sexually pure, little beyond conventional.
PG   Moderately explicit indication of sex. Later, "long shots" or "brief flashes" of nudity.
R   Breast and buttock nudity. Touching and caressing breasts. Simulated intercourse.
X   Anything and everything that doesn't fit in "G," "PG," and "R." In other words: the sewer's the limit! Intercourse, full nudity, sodomy, fellatio, masturbation, the full barrage of 4-letter words and more.

SOLUTION: Publicly Visible Films Law

NUDE MOVIES VISIBLE FROM STREET PROHIBITED

It shall be unlawful for the owner, manager, assistant operator, ticket seller, ticket taker, usher and/or any other person connected with or employed by any motion picture theater or drive-in motion picture theater to show or exhibit at a motion picture theater or drive-in motion picture theater in the city (or state) of or to aid or assist in such showing or exhibition any motion picture, film, slide or other exhibit which is visible from any public street or highway in which there are depictions of illicit sex or sexual immorality or, depictions of nude or partially denuded figures.

"Description or depictions of illicit sex or sexual immorality" shall mean (1) clothed or unclothed human genitals in a state of sexual stimulation or arousal; (2) acts of human masturbation, sexual intercourse or sodomy; (3) fondling or other erotic touching of clothed or unclothed human genitals, pubic region, buttock or female breast.

"Nude or partially denuded figures" shall mean (1) less than completely and opaquely covered human genitals, pubic regions, buttock, and female breast below a point immediately above the top of the areola; and (2) human genitals in a discernibly turgid state, even if completely and opaquely covered.

4

PROBLEM: "Adult" films
SOLUTION: Obscenity Ordinance
(See pp. 114-116.)

5

PROBLEM: "Adult" bookstores
SOLUTION: Obscenity Ordinance
(See pp. 117-119.)

6

PROBLEM: Live sex shows

Item: Old Law Ruled "Vague"
TOPLESS DANCE LEGAL IN TULSA

Tulsa, Okla. (UPI)—Prosecutors couldn't find a half dozen persons in town who were offended by topless dancing, so it became legal Friday.

Municipal Judge Laurence A. Yeagley declared "vague and overly broad" a city law forbidding toplessness and said it was a violation of civil rights. "It is no longer an offense simply to expose the breasts," the judge said. "It would be up to a jury now to decide whether a person has outraged public decency based on the standards of a community."

Yeagley ruled on an appeal for dismissal of a complaint brought by police against Ella Lou Ridgeway, 20, who was arrested for appearing topless in a nightclub May 27. Her trial ended in a hung jury and some city officials felt Yeagley's ruling would make convictions almost impossible in the future.

"The [jury] cases cause me to think that we are in a downhill slide toward degradation," City Prosecutor Jack Morgan said.

"We just couldn't find six persons who were offended by nude dancing," said Assistant Prosecutor Mike Fairchild.

Officials said that would mean, with the exception of topless waitresses, it would now be legal in Tulsa to dance topless as long as the audience was aware that such acts were to take place and was not outraged. The only restraints would be state laws prohibiting outraging public decency.

This teaches two lessons:

1. SPEAK UP!! Write, phone, picket, petition! But scream your moral convictions! Obviously, more than "a half dozen persons" in Tulsa find topless dancing offensive.

Tulsa has oil wells and churches—hundreds of each. It has Christian colleges and seminaries. The hundreds of thousands of Christians didn't speak up.

2. Vague laws are useless. Get a clear, tough law enacted, like the Obscenity Ordinance (pp. 114-116), or the following:

SOLUTION: Indecent-Show Law

Section 1. Sale or exhibition to any person of indecent shows or performances or presentations. Every person who willfully or knowingly promotes or wholesale promotes within the community any show, performance, or other presentation or material which contain depictions of sexual conduct or live sexual conduct for the purposes of commercial gain or public entertainment shall upon conviction be punished by a fine of not less than _____ nor more than _____ or by imprisonment for not more than _____ or by both such fine and imprisonment.

For the purposes of this section, sexual conduct means
(1) showing or the depictions of acts of sexual intercourse, sodomy, or masturbation, including genital, anal-
genital, or oral-genital intercourse actual or simulated,
whether between human beings or between a human being and an animal; (2) depictions or the showing of
the excretory functions including the male semen, actual
or simulated; (3) depictions or the showing of the
female genitals in a state of sexual stimulation or
arousal, any explicit close-up representation of human
genitals, female with legs spread or openly displaying
her genital organs, male genitals in a discernibly turgid
state even if completely or opaquely covered; (4) depictions or the showing of fondling or other erotic
touching of the clothed or unclothed human genitals,
pubic region, buttock, or female breast, whether alone
or between members of the same or opposite sex or
between humans and animals, actual or simulated in
an act of apparent sexual stimulation or gratification.

Depictions means the showing or the representation
of physical acts or conduct.

Material means anything tangible which is capable
of being used to record, show, reproduce or vividly
represent physical acts or conduct.

Community means the geographical area of the
state, city of (   ).

Promote, means to manufacture, issue, sell, give, provide, lend, mail, deliver, transfer, transmit, publish, distribute, circulate, disseminate, present, exhibit, or advertise or to offer or agree to do the same for resale.

Wholesale promote means to manufacture, issue, sell,
provide, mail, deliver, transfer, transmit, publish, distribute, circulate, disseminate or to offer or agree to
do the same for purposes of resale.

Knowingly means having knowledge of the character
and content of the material or failure on notice to exercise reasonable inspection which would disclose the
content and character of the same.

If any of the depictions of sexual conduct described
in this section are declared by a court of competent jurisdiction to be unlawful because such are constitutionally
protected, such declaration shall not invalidate other
provisions of this section.

Section 2. This act shall take effect upon passage.

7

PROBLEM: Topless bars, nude beaches

SOLUTION: Indecent Exposure Law (or Obscenity Ordinance)

Section 1. Every person who willfully or knowingly displays his or her body in indecent exposure in a place of public accommodation in (name of city, state) shall upon conviction be punished by a fine of not less than _____ nor more than _____ or by imprisonment for not more than _____ or by both such fine and imprisonment.

For the purposes of this section, "indecent exposure" shall mean (1) the display of the unclothed human male genitals or buttocks, or the clothed or the unclothed human male genitals in a state of sexual stimulation or arousal; (2) the display of the unclothed human female genitals or buttocks or breasts below a point immediately above the top of the areola, or the clothed or unclothed human female genitals or breasts in a state of sexual stimulation or arousal.

Section 2: This law shall take effect upon passage.

Michigan and Florida made it clear that they didn't want topless bars or nude beaches:

TOPLESSNESS IS LAWLESS

Port Huron, Mich. (AP)—Voters in Port Huron, given a chance to set their own "community standard," have voiced their disapproval of topless entertainment.

With about 23 percent of the registered voters going to the polls in a special election, the City Council's enforcement of an obscenity code prohibiting topless bars was upheld 2,932 to 643.

The City Council had scheduled the vote to allow Port Huron residents to set their own standard of decency, City Clerk Guy Provost said.

"All the court decisions on obscenity talk about a community standard," Provost said. "This should tell us what our standard is."

The first and only topless bar in Port Huron opened late last year, but city officials closed the establishment after one day.

"The owners had a liquor license, but no entertainment license," the city clerk explained. "After they were closed, they applied for a license for such entertainment, and were turned down under the city's obscenity code." [15]

The Florida Supreme Court has decided that the Bible argues against topless sunbathing by females. The court upheld, 5-2, the disorderly conduct conviction of two women arrested last year at Ft. Pierce beach.

Writing for the majority, Justice Joseph Boyd said, "Public nudity has been considered improper" since the beginning of civilization. He quoted Genesis 3:7: "And the eyes of them both were opened and they knew that they were naked; and they sewed fig leaves together and made themselves aprons." [16]

8

PROBLEM: Massage parlors

Massage parlors frequently are fronts for masturbation parlors. Like all abusive sex, if not stopped immediately, they devour a community like ravenous cancer.

FORMER BOULEVARD MASSAGE PARLOR EMPLOYEE TELLS HOW BUSINESS OPERATES

(Because the woman interviewed wished to remain anonymous for the newspaper interview, we shall call her Barbara. All other events she relates to are based on factual happenings as she saw them.—Ed.)

Now employed in another line of work, Barbara is a licensed massuse. She received her training at a local school of massage for which she paid $325. Upon completion of instruction, she received a certificate noting she was a trained massuse. She says the certificate is not authorized; "it is just a piece of paper." Neither is it governed by laws of the State of California such as a beautician or realtor.

But in the trade this piece of paper is called a license and a girl can use it to work in a massage parlor much like a private, self-employed contractor.

During her course she practiced her learnings in the

school, also doing business as a massage parlor for which she received no pay. Her school instruction was for straight legitimate massage. However, upon graduation from the class, she was immediately taught the finer keyed methods for pleasing male customers. Special portions of the groin area were noted and results of such massages pointed out. Other areas were also discussed and their particular ramifications noted.

A pretty blond woman with dark brown eyes, Barbara told vividly about this portion of instruction and one particular incident that resulted from it. "The operator of the business showed us how to do a 'local' (masturbation). One of the girls, a little Korean, really innocent, was present also. That night she went home and showed her husband what she had learned at school that day. The next day he came down to beat up the owner."

Of course, all the girls were not that naïve, recalls Barbara. "In fact," she said, "most of them were out hustling the owners, especially the male owners. One of the girls was even selling marijuana to her customers. But I don't think the owner knew or she would have been fired for that.

"The girls where I worked received the minimum hourly wage plus 50 percent commission on their tips."

How much and what were the tips for? According to our source, "the average was $5 for a 'local' or 'complete' massage, a 'table job' [straight sex] was more, and an 'oral' was $25. Sometimes we received more, depending on how the customers liked us and if he had money.

"We used talcum powder for French finger tip massages and oil for the traditional Swedish massage."

Barbara was somewhat horrified to learn the oil was regular garage oil purchased in large quantities from a local gasoline station.

In the beginning, did Barbara and the other girls know what kind of business they were getting into? "Yes," she said. "I was told by another massage operator outside of town that all the massage parlors in Whittier were 'whore houses.' We all saw the massage parlors as a place to make a lot of money. I knew two girls who had made over a thousand dollars a month."

Barbara admitted to making as much as $200 a week before leaving the business.

Was there other vice, such as gambling, and did she believe that organized crime was present?

"At one of the places on Whittier Boulevard, down near the freeway, there was a regular poker game going on out behind one of the massage parlors. But I don't think everyone knew about this."

As to organized crime taking over in Whittier, "this was discussed amongst the girls and their boy friends. But I don't know for sure. Except that I had heard two years ago there was a Las Vegas connection with one of the places."

Barbara was equally unsure about payoffs. "Some of the girls were 'busted' but the businesses still remained open and some of those girls came back to work. But I don't think the police ever got paid off. Someone else maybe. Why else do they stay open?" [17]

SOLUTION: Model Ordinance for Massage Parlors[18]

It shall be unlawful for any establishment, regardless of whether it is a public or private facility, to operate as a massage salon, bath parlor, or any similar type business, where any physical contact with the recipient of such services is provided by a person of the opposite sex.

This section shall not apply to a physician, surgeon, chiropractor, osteopath or physical therapist duly licensed by the Commonwealth of Virginia, or to a licensed nurse acting under the direct prescription and direction of any such physician, surgeon, chiropractor or osteopath. Also, this section shall not apply to barbershops or beauty parlors in which massage is given to the scalp, the face, the neck or the shoulders.

Any person who shall violate the provisions of this section shall, upon conviction thereof, be fined not more than one hundred dollars, and each day's operation shall constitute a separate offense.

9

PROBLEM: Exploitation of children in pornography

SOLUTION: Child Pornography Law

Exploitation for Commercial Purposes.—(a)

"(b) Every person having the custody or control of any child under the age of seventeen (17) years of age who shall in any manner or under any pretense sell, distribute, let out or otherwise permit any such child to be used in any book, magazine, pamphlet or other publication, or in any motion picture film, photograph or pictorial representation, in the nude in a setting which taken as a whole suggests to the average person that such child has engaged in, or is about to engage in, any sexual act, which shall include but not be limited to sodomy, oral copulation, sexual intercourse, masturbation, or bestiality, shall, upon conviction thereof for the first offense be punished by imprisonment for not more than five (5) years or a fine of not more than five thousand dollars (5,000), or both; upon conviction of a second offense be punished by imprisonment for not more than ten (10) years, or a fine of not more than ten thousand dollars ($10,000), or both, and, upon conviction of a subsequent offense, be punished by imprisonment for not more than fifteen (15) years, or a fine of not more than fifteen thousand dollars ($15,000), or both.

"CHILD NUDITY PROHIBITED IN PUBLICATIONS.—Every person, firm, association or corporation which shall publish, sell, offer for sale, loan, give away, or otherwise distribute any book, magazine, pamphlet or other publication, or any photograph, picture or film which depicts any child, or children, under the age of seventeen (17) years in the nude in a setting which taken as a whole suggests to the average person that such child, or children, are about to engage in or have engaged in, any sexual act, or which depicts any such child under seventeen (17) years of age, performing sodomy, oral copulation, sexual intercourse, masturbation or bestiality, shall, for the first offense be punished by imprisonment for not more than five (5) years, or by a fine of not more than five thousand dollars ($5,000), or both; for the second offense, by imprisonment for not more than ten (10) years, or by a fine of not more than ten thousand dollars ($10,000), or both; and for any subsequent offense, by imprisonment for not more than fifteen (15) years, or a fine of not more than fifteen thousand dollars ($15,000), or both."

Section 3. This act shall take effect upon its passage.

CHAPTER 6

Pornography and Art

1. When is nudity pornography?

In his *The Nude: A Study in Ideal Form* (A. W. Mellon Lectures in the Fine Arts, Princeton University Press, 1971), Kenneth Clark says:

> The word "nude" . . . carries, in educated usage, no uncomfortable overtone. The vague image it projects into the mind is not of a huddled and defenseless body, but of a balanced, prosperous and confident body: the body re-formed (p. 3).

But:

> To be naked is to be deprived of our clothes, and the word implies some of the embarrassment most of us feel in that condition.

The difference between the nude and the naked is the difference between nudity and pornography.

Nudity uses the unclothed body for the expression of (1) order and energy, (2) aloneness and despair, and (3) detail and perfection.

Pornography uses the unclothed body for (1) lust, (2) shock, and (3) greed.

Order

"For soule is forme, and doth the bodie make," said Spenser in his *Hymne in Honour of Beautie*. A study of the nude body is a study in symmetrical form. Nothing is more beautifully balanced than the human body.

"Bearded God of Histiaia" [1] is majestic. A nude man stands erect. His left arm, like an arrow, shoots to his left from his shoulder and flows into a palm-up hand, stretched in a point. His right arm, shooting to the right, flows into a palm-up hand, cupping a smooth stone.

His proud head, angled over his left shoulder, glistens within a circle of hair. The bushy, trim beard and razor-sliced bangs of hair meet in a round frame, encircling a set of eyes frozen on an object to which the outstretched fingers of the palms-up, left hand points.

We see two sweet-potato shaped triceps—packed in the extended left arm and right arm—like two smooth weights balancing each other. The trunk-round legs are spread, the heels angled inward, each set of toes pointing in the same direction as the outstretched arms. The perfectly balanced legs, uninterrupted by clothing, rise to meet at the site of genitalia, above which is a tight, rippled stomach.

The balance of symmetrical form is so striking that we think, surely, a man like this could stand forever.

We look at Michelangelo's "Detail of David" [2] and see cigar-thick veins plunging from the neck into the upper breast. A rude, deep cleft splitting the platter-size breasts spreads above a tight, flat stomach. A navel hole, centered three feet below the cleft, looks like a bull's-eye on the stomach's hard surface. The stomach muscles roll into the bottom of a V, at the point of which erupt the genitalia. The lines of the body, unbroken by clothing, then flow into watermelon-round hips.

This body was no accident. It has a flow, form, and order.

Energy

Michelangelo's "Samson Defeating Philistines" [3] shows a nude Samson, his legs intertwined with Philistine warriors, raising a brick-sized fist whose hammer blow we feel. We feel the blow because this pure, nude frame reveals waves of muscles rolling from his ankles up his straight legs, over his unclothed torso, building speed and strength in his chest, and crashing into power through a raised fist.

Giambologna's *Mercury* floats.[4] The delicate and detailed god of mythology is on a rude stump, balancing on the ball of his left foot, arched and crowned with a winged heel. The single, tense foot supports a nude body whose muscles point and strain up, up, up, up, racing into an L-shaped right arm, shoulder to elbow the base of the L, elbow to wrist stretched into the column. The wrist races into an open hand—palm up— the index finger stabbing into the air, like an antenna thrusting a skyscraper deeper into the sky.

In his left arm and curled into a large pocket formed by a wrist and palm turned inward, he balances a caduceus. His sharply angled nose points to his outstretched right finger and his head melts into a winged helmet. We think that, instantly, he will rise and float.

Aloneness

The nude form dramatizes aloneness, accenting expressions of grief. The "Unknown Soldier"[5] of the Greco-Roman "Soldier's Gravestone" shows four mourners tugging and heaving a nude corpse. The corpse's right arm plunges down. His large, square head sinks over his right shoulder toward the dragging knuckles. The nude buttocks and hips plunge toward the knuckles, making us feel not only the dead weight of the corpse, but his comrades' heavy grief.

Despair

Michelangelo's charcoal-and-ink of the nude Christ hanging from the cross is brutal despair.[6] (Many historians feel that Christ was crucified nude, the ultimate in Jewish humiliation.) Because the body is unbroken by clothing, we feel the stretching and tearing of muscle. The trauma begins with the spiked left wrist and spiked right wrist, shooting down through the forearms and biceps and shoulders to the bottom of a V. At the

bottom is the spit-smeared head of Christ. The length-
ened tail of the V is a pole of tortured muscle, dotted
in the middle by a shadowy outline of genitalia, and
split at the bottom by the faint outline of two crossed
feet nailed fast.

Detail

DaVinci's *Muscular Legs*[7] show a nude male from
navel to feet. From navel to knee are thick, tight muscles, like football padding stuffed between skin and
femur, from knee to ankle are smooth, curved muscles, like long cucumbers packed under the skin.
The exposed genitalia, neither prominent nor offensive,
flow naturally with the detailed lower body.

Michelangelo's *Creation of Adam*[8] shows the reclin-
ing, flawless, and nude Adam supported on his right
elbow, the strain adding definition to his right bicep,
round as a softball. His right side facing the viewer,
we see an exquisite body arched forward in a C-shape,
the left arm straining forward, melting into his outstretched left finger pushing towards God's finger.
His right leg, the bottom of the C, lies full and flat
on a pristine forest bed. His left leg is bent, the heel
pressing against the right thigh, the knee cocked
straight up and supporting the outstretched left arm
straining toward God.

Lust

The nudity of art, inviting contemplation, differs
from the nakedness of pornography. Lust, shock, and
greed are motives of pornography.

W. H. Auden said, "Pornography is whatever causes
an erection." That hits the nerve of pornography.

It is, of course, possible that a classical nude stimulate an erection in a viewer. But that would be an
accidental consequence. With pornography, the aggressive attention is to stimulate erections.

In classical nudity, the genitalia are displayed casually and naturally. The genitalia of the naked prostitutes in pornography are displayed with gorilla-sized

proportions. In pornography there is no attempt to use the nude to express energy, despair, or detail. The naked body, rather, serves as a backdrop for oil-massaged, bulging genitalia.

It is for those reasons that one never finds centerfolds from *Playboy, Penthouse, Oui, Playgirl,* etc., in art museums. They do not use the nude for aesthetic enjoyment. They do not use the nude at all. They use a naked prostitute.[9] And they use him or her to excite lust.

Incidentally, one need not blush about identifying *Playboy, Penthouse,* as pornography. They have been convicted of violating obscenity laws. Appearing with a porno-lawyer on a TV talk-show, I identified them as pornography and the centerfold "bunnies" and "pets" as prostitutes. I invited the lawyer and the viewing audience to sue me if I misrepresented the magazines.

Some porno-publishers are embarrassed by their exploitation of lust, and attempting to cover it, have included elitist articles in their magazine. Mr. Hugh Hefner pays $3,500 to worthies like John Kenneth Galbraith and Saul Bellow to write economic and fiction pieces in between the bunnies. He then insists that the cerebral articles are the selling points of the magazine. (To test that thesis, Mr. Hefner was once challenged by Dr. William Banowsky, president, Pepperdine University, to remove the naked prostitutes to see what happened to sales. Hefner declined.)

Shock

The classical nude has been displayed for at least 5,000 years without insane escalation in showing his/her body or sexual activities. Since 1955, however, when mass-market pornography began, the breast-nakedness of prostitutes has steadily escalated to include pictures of women masturbating horses, children engaged in sex acts, and Jesus Christ involved in sex acts.

Once a person feeds lust, he's hooked. The "old" shock wanes into the familiar and dull, requiring a new, more insane shock. The "new" shock shortly becomes familiar and dull, requiring a "newer," more insane shock. And it grows and multiplies and ravages, not unlike a malignancy.

Greed

Starving artists are picturesque and plentiful. Starving pornographers there are not. The pornography industry in the United States alone peaks $2 billion annually.

A full-color porno magazine, showing a three-some sweating through a marathon of intercourse, fellatio, and cunninglingus, costs about $.50-$1.00 per publication. It sells for $15.00.

One prominent attorney, arguing pornography interests before the Supreme Court, earns $750,000 annually. Mr. Hugh Hefner collects mansions.

The stacks of money are so deep that pornographers have recently discovered an occupational hazard. The Mafia wants in. And, according to New York City and Bexar County Organized Crime Bureaus, they get in either by buying the porno markets at skyscraper prices or blatantly plagiarizing and peddling all the best-sellers. There have been no reports of anyone suing to stop the plagiarism.

The artistic expression of the nude—like all art—does not aim for stacks of money.

Money, for the artist, is incidental. His goals, in aesthetically displaying the nude, are love, truth, and taste.

2. *"Most people recognize that pornography is cheap writing and cheap photography. Let's just leave it alone and not even give it the dignity of talking about it. It's trivial trash. Let it die."*

No writing is trivial. Written words affect readers:

Lincoln, Illinois (A.P.) December 7, 1976—Michael Edward Drabing, who said he wanted to rid the world of rich people, has been convicted of murdering three of them. . . . Drabing testified that he was following the philosophy of the Charles Manson family as outlined in the best-selling book, *Helter Skelter*. He said the Manson family "killed all those rich people and I saw if you killed them, that erases the problem."

Odd, but the very people insisting that "pornography reaps no harm because no one's affected by it" belie that statement in their own professions.

The pornographer, remember, argues that what we see or read doesn't affect us. So you have to conclude that all literature is irrelevant and all art morally trivial, because what we read and what we see doesn't affect us. And the writers and the professors go along. Here's a person who booms behind a college lectern, sweat exploding from his armpits and running down his side in a stream. He stabs the air with gestures and scratches the board with chalk cartoons—rock-sure that his words and pictures will affect, influence, and persuade listeners. Here's a person hunching over a typewriter twelve hours, neck straining, fingers limp, his Roget's thesaurus like shredded gauze from hourly use building a novel. And rock-sure that his words will affect, influence and persuade. (They'd better or no one will buy.)

And these are the guys who say, "Aw, leave porno alone. Words and pictures don't affect anyone."

3. *"Obscenity is honest. It betrays what really happens in the world—just like Shakespeare and the Bible."*

The Bible and Shakespeare treat art realistically but not pornographically. Homosexuality, fornication, adultery and rape are included in their pages, but not exploited. In pornography, sex is so exploited that it is *stronger* than the narrative. It steals the narrative. It becomes the narrative itself. The pornographic use of sex overwhelms the intellect and emotions. In pornography no deeper meaning exists for contemplation and profit. Playboys, for example, lionize Marlon Brando for his raping and sodomy in *Last Tango in Paris*, but they do not acknowledge the report of the journalist who upon interviewing patrons of *Tango,* received these replies: "I never did get hold of the plot line." "I didn't see the story in it." "It was just sex, sex, sex." "I didn't understand where it was all going."

In the Bible and Shakespeare, sex is included because it is one part of a total narrative. The narrative is stronger than sex. Not so in pornography where sex *is* the narrative. The biblical narrative, note the difference, includes a story wherein Isaac takes his wife Rebekah into his tent on their "honeymoon" night. The story *then* moves on with the *more important* narrative of the life of Isaac and history of the Jews. That is not the way the pornographer would handle the narrative. He would rip open the tent curtain, blare every sigh and whisper of the biblical lovers, and verbally describe or pictorially photograph every genital part of Isaac and Rebekah before, during and after intercourse. In the pornographer's handling, sex would be indulged in for its own sake, not as a minor part of a more important narrative. The narrative of Jewish history would be slurred over in the pornographer's exploitation of the sexual lives of Isaac and Rebekah.

Art encompasses the whole of reality. Pornography does not. The pornographer dramatizes a man and woman blithely copulating night after night. There the pornographer stops. He doesn't show the effects of fornication on the later lives of the couple or their bastard children. The pornography of sex is as reprehensibly *unrealistic* as the pornography of violence projecting from television and theater screens. Writers and producers prolifically show smashed teeth, crushed jaws, and bullet-spattered bellies, but *never* show the dentist bills, widow's grief, or lonely lives of fatherless children victimized by violence. "Bang, you're dead" does *not* mean the whole narrative is dead. The whole story hasn't been told or shown. The lives of survivors continue, radically changed by the death or injury of the loved one. But the television producers eschew that, and so the realistic effects of violence are distorted. So with the pornography of sex. Pornography does not show the guilt and anger arising in people who come to realize they have used each other as sexual machines. The pornographer does not show the *true* yearning of every playboy for a loyal, compassionate and virgin life-mate. The pornographer does not dramatize *every human's* hatred of being used. He does not show the bitterness and resentment arising in people who come to realize they have been "machines of masturbation" for another "swinger." He does not show that every civilization favoring free sex has rotted from within and tumbled. The pornographer not only lacks art and realism, he lacks truth. He is a liar.

Veteran actors denounce the pornography in film. Loretta Young, gracious queen of television and theater screens and now a member of *Morality in Media* planning board, has long fought for decency and morality in public media. Ronald Reagan said he was "ashamed of the motion picture industry for production of X-rated movies." Katharine Hepburn, commenting on the current crop of films, said: "It's pornography. Nothing more or less than pornography. It appeals to the lowest possible level of human experience. I think it's atrocious." Of *Carnal Knowledge*, she said: "It's a picture about lust. That's all it is—lust. Two dull, self-centered men and their sex problem."

A statement from a district attorney tells why artists of all professions condemn pornography:

> It seems to me highly questionable that an approach of extreme permissiveness which lets the bars down on the circulation of all manner of pornography, really advances the cause of intellectual freedom or contributes to a more effective, artistic and intellectual life. The avalanche of shock for shock's sake ... has distracted public attention from authentic works of art (and) ... has had the ultimate effect of debauching and trivializing our artistic and intellectual life rather than enhancing its vitality and richness.[10]

4. *"Must anti-pornography laws necessarily conflict with legitimate art and literature? Or is all nudity immoral?"*

The laws cited do not conflict with legitimate art and literature.

The display of the nude is not immoral at all. The apostle Paul didn't think so. He distinguished between soma (the body) and sarx (the flesh). When we use our bodies for *fleshly* purposes, i.e., to arouse lust, make a quick buck, or engorge our appetites, that's immoral. And all three describe pornography.

Pornography prostitution is a Grand Canyon width from nudity and art.

5. *"Pornography is an idea and ideas ought to be expressed."*

Castrating Jews is an idea too. So is hanging blacks. Some people would like to aggressively circulate those ideas in words and pictures. Are they free to circulate them in America? Sure.

Are they free from society's penalties in circulating them? No.

The point is this. Everyone, at some time, says, "Those words, those pictures are wrong. They hurt people. We need laws to protect us from those abusive pictures and words and the harm they cause."

One person says, "We ought not to enforce laws against slick porno like *Playboy*, but we ought to enforce laws against adult bookstores."

Why? Why does he draw his line of values at adult bookstores?

Another person says, "We ought not to enforce laws against adult bookstores, but we ought to enforce laws against child pornography."

Why? Why does he draw his line of values with child pornography?

Everyone has a point where he says, "No! That's wrong. That's too much. That ought not to circulate. We need laws to halt that!"

Some people reach that point with child pornography; others with women-fornicating-with-horses; others with sex torture; others with any form of sexual abuse, beginning with the glossy-porno market (*Playboy*, etc.).

Why do people have different points of toleration?

Because some have *inconsistent* standards of value.

Ask him, "Why do you tolerate glossy-porno but not adult bookstores?"

"Because *I* think they're bad," he says.

Ask her, "Why do you tolerate adult bookstores, but not child porno?"

"Because *I* think child porno is bad," she says.

So who are *you*?

What's his authority for saying adult bookstores are wrong? What's her authority for saying child porno is wrong?

If sexual abuse is okay anywhere, it's okay everywhere. There is no authority, no standard of value, to discriminate between different kinds of sexual abuse.

The only consistent standard of value is the Bible.

Why do you not tolerate *Playboy* sex, an adult bookstore's books, or child porno, etc.?

Because the Bible condemns sexual abuse. That's the authority, that's the standard of value.

6. *"Obscenity laws crush free expression."*

During the first 200 years of America, while common sense obscenity laws prevailed, America enjoyed unprecedented and vigorous political and artistic expressions. Today, ideas of purity, discipline, and decency are blatantly censored.

CHAPTER 7
Pornography and Christian Activism

"The sin of respectable people is running from responsibility."

—Dietrich Bonhoeffer, *Life Together*

1. "What 'scriptural authority' is there for Christians to oppose pornography?"

No scriptures exonerate Christians from resisting and defeating the pornographic abuse of God's gift of sex.

2. "Can Christians use legal means to advance spiritual ends?"

Paul did. (1) In Acts 25:11, Paul, believing that his arrest was illegal according to Roman law, appealed to Caesar. He invoked his right as a Roman citizen to advance a spiritual end. (2) In Acts 23:13-23, Paul, hearing of the Jewish conspiracy to kill him, appealed to the Roman guard for protection. He invoked his rights as a Roman citizen. (3) In Acts 16:37-40, Paul, who had been illegally arrested, invoked his rights as a citizen to be publicly released and exonerated. He was. Therefore he was able to continue to preach and advance spiritual ends.

Dr. Ronald J. Snider says:

Social concern involves both relief for those suffering from social injustice and the restructuring of all of society, saved and unsaved, for the sake of greater social justice. Unfortunately, not all societies provide as much opportunity for political action as does the United States. Living in the totalitarian Roman Empire, Paul did not have the political opportunities available in his day. But he was not apolitical. He insisted on due process of Philippi (Acts 10:35-39). He took advantage of his right to appeal to Caesar as a Roman citizen (Acts 26:32).[1]

3. "How can I know God wants me spending all this time and money on pornography instead of saving souls?"

a. Can a Christian doubt that God wants his gift of sex exalted and cherished? God's gift of conjugal sex was meant to be the final, holy, and romantic union between a woman and a man who had bethrothed their lives to each other. Today, the conjugal gift is slandered in hundreds of magazines, thousands of movies, and 'on millions of television screens. In the Old Testament, adultery was punished by stoning to death. God hates sexual sins. Today adultery and fornication are glorified before millions of viewers and readers. Pornography not only teaches that adultery and fornication are permissible but that they are *desirable*! (How much more could anti-Christ doctrines be on the rampage!) Further, the same magazines actually say that there's something *wrong* with a virgin lady, or something wrong with a man saving his virility for his wife.

b. According to the Bible, we cannot "love souls" or want to "save souls" unless we love the whole person and minister to his whole life. "Soul" in the Greek means "life." People's lives are at stake: their spiritual, emotional, moral and physical lives. If we love them, we serve them in any way we can. The same motives which compel a Christian to "spend a lot of money" and "spend a lot of time" to build a climate of clean media and clean literature are the same motives which compel him to "spend a lot of money" and "spend a lot of time" building orphanages and hospitals.

Furthermore, decency campaigns dramatically bring before the community the Christian concepts of purity, holiness, beauty and the rightful place of God's gift of sex.

4. *"Why should I start or join any decency group?"*

Jesus said that His followers are "the salt of the earth" and "the light of the world" (Matt. 5:13-14). Salt is worthless without some degree of contact. If Christians are the salt of the earth or the preserving power to save a decaying earth, we must be "in touch." Marshall Keeble, famous Negro evangelist, said, "Salt is no good if it's left in the salt shaker!"

To be the "light of the world" is necessarily to expose darkness or sin and evil. The primary tool of Satan is deception. He works best in darkness or obscurity. Satan would like nothing better than for people to think that he is nothing more than the character on the chili-powder can. Deceit is a master tool for Satan. Sometimes he even appears as an "angel of light," or as porno promoters have described, "a work of art." Jesus did not say that Christians "ought to be" the light of the world. He did not say that they "should be the light of the world." Jesus said, "You *are* the light of the world. A city set on a hill *cannot* be hid!" It is not a matter of a Christian's influence "ought to be exuding" or "must" but it *cannot* be concealed. To be the light of the world is to not only show the way to go, to reveal the way to live, but lights of the world, to expose dangers and anything that keeps one from discovering the meaning of life. Pornography keeps people from seeing sex as God created it.

5. *"Why not just preach Jesus and quit minding other people's business?"*

I'll tell you why! In the last ten days, I have counseled with five adults, all of whom have had serious problems arise. I'm not surprised when a young man advertises his station wagon for sale with the added explanation: "Great for drive-in movies, equipped with curtains for you and your date." You see, these other people, whose business you accuse me of minding, are the same people who have called me in tears, requesting help for their daughter who is pregnant, but doesn't know who the father is. I am the Christian who gives money for the preaching of the gospel and benevolent good, and the same Christian man or woman drilled by calls to help children who are victims of a marriage involving sex without love.

"Minding somebody else's business?" I think not. I am the man who is burning my gasoline, giving my clothes from my back and food from my pantry to rehabilitate a man. It's not easy to mend men who have been in prison (for sex crimes) and are now trying to find a place once again in society. I am the man who gets long distance telephone expenses and counseling expenses to place an "unwanted child of passion" in the best possible home.

You bet it is *my* business. Would the porno promoters, or some of their colleagues, like me to refer to them—for counseling and answer to those problems —the angry, bitter and broken victims of "free sex"? Have the porno promoters *ever* been involved, during agonizing midnight hours, counseling and consoling twisted emotional lives ensnarled in the snare pit of sex divorced from love and sex divorced from life-commitment?

6. *"But the Bible says* nothing *about pornography."*

Jesus said, "One who looks on a woman lustfully has already committed adultery in his heart" (Matt. 5:28). A Christian who is against adultery is against pornography. We are living in a world of persons and things. *One* person is of more significance than *all* things. It is wrong to view a person as an object or thing instead of as a person; pornography is as much wrong as the philosophy of Marx which holds that persons are only of value as they provide things (labor). For porno promoters, a woman's thing (or use) is carnal satisfaction.

Matthew 5:44 says, "Love your enemies." This word for love comes from the Greek word meaning "to do" or "to make" and another word for "goodness." It is impossible to love *anybody* without being fully committed to bringing about goodness in his or her life!

7. *"But aren't I judging and condemning retailers and wholesalers of porno magazines?"*

In Matthew 6:1 Jesus said, "Beware of practicing your piety before men." For one who does so already has his reward. Likewise to *fail* to practice one's piety ("charity" or "good deeds") before men because of fear of contempt or ridicule is to be no different in character or spirit than the one who *does* practice his religion before men for the purpose of approval of men.

In Matthew 7:6 Jesus said, "Do not give dogs what is holy and do not throw your pearls before swine." The superficial statement that "Christians are out of the judging business" is not according to scripture. The same Jesus who said, "Judge not" in Matthew 7:1 gave the command concerning dogs and swine! The disciples would not have known among those to whom they preached which ones not to "cast pearls before" had they not exercised definite judgment as to who the "dogs" and "swine" were. After all, they were handling "the pearl of great price" and couldn't prostitute it on "dogs" and "swine." They had to judge.

Paul said the spiritual "judge all things." The spiritual, which in the New Testament means *all Christians*, have the mandate to mark those who promote evil (e.g., pornography) and rebuke those who tolerate evil (e.g., pornography), because promoting as well as tolerating evil are both Satan's work.

Revelation 2:2 says, "I know what you have done; I know how hard you have worked and how patient you have been. I know you cannot tolerate evil men."

8. *"We ought to just preach the gospel."*

Thank you very much. And please forgive me. I may be egregiously wrong, but the people who shout that do neither. Preaching the gospel from the Sunday pulpit is, I submit, not preaching the gospel at all. It's earning a salary. If Jesus does not irresistibly work through you in all social concerns, you don't have Him.

People who shout, "We oughta' just *preach the gos-*

pel" are justifying inaction. Please forgive me if I'm wrong, but I felt it must be said since some of them are priests, preachers and Bible professors who influence thousands. One Bible professor said, "Well, in Acts 19 when Paul went to Ephesus, he didn't appeal to law to get rid of the bad books. . . . He preached the gospel!" Terrific. The reason Paul did not appeal to Ephesian law to get rid of the bad books was that he could not. There was none.

In those places, however, where Paul could appeal to existing law, he did. Three times in Acts, Paul appealed to relevant Roman law for bodily protection. He appealed to *legal means* for the ultimate promotion of *spiritual ends.*

Preach the gospel *and* fight pornography! It's amazing how the Lord will use you when you make yourself totally accessible to Him. Through this ministry, He's allowed me to preach the gospel to more people in more places where, normally, I would never have access, i.e., public high schools, service clubs, talk shows, etc. When they ask me why I fight porno, I tell them: Man was made in the image of God; man was made for friendship with God available only through Jesus Christ; anything assaulting that image and threatening that friendship is dangerous and worthy to be crushed.

The same motives which compelled me to nurse lepers in Northern Thailand and to picket American supermarkets selling "blood-soaked" lettuce and grapes compel me to oppose pornography.

Christ in Christians compels them to hate and fight any abuse of human beings.

9. *"Many ethicists believe that Christian ethics are 'kingdom ethics'—that our standard of morality requires the infusion of the Spirit of God and is not really to be expected of 'the world.' "*

The greatest thing about a democracy, like America, is that obedience to (if not enjoyment of) "kingdom ethics" can be a legal reality. If most Americans want laws projecting respect for sex, we can have them. (Gallup and Harris polls say that 80% of America opposes pornography.)

True, if Christ's kingdom were *in* everyone, we would not need laws curbing abuse of sex (or abuse of property or abuse of reputation, etc.). People would *want* to obey God's laws. The ice-hard fact is, however, most people do not want to obey God's laws. Now the question is: Can Christians expect legal protection from those people? Yes, Paul says (Rom. 13).

I can, I must appeal for passage of laws reflecting Christian respect for sex. Such laws not only protect my wife, children and me from the pornographers but they provide a healthy social climate. Such laws, of course, do not—presto!—zap the playboy into a Christian. But they remove from him the pseudolegal cloak for his aggressive hedonism.

10. *"My wife (or my husband) doesn't want me to get involved in it. She (or he) thinks it's wrong for me to be near the stuff at all."*

This is a Christian with a shaky marriage. A wife feels threatened by her husband's inspection of porno magazines. She doesn't want him inviting church members in to show them what's on the racks. She's afraid she doesn't measure up to what he's inspecting.

This couple needs to take off for a couple of weekends by themselves to get to enjoy each other again— and trust each other. They need to practice the beauty and passion and excitement of sex in marriage that God promised them in 1 Corinthians 7:3, 4: "For the body of the husband belongs to the wife and the body of the wife to the husband."

11. *"Christian activism in politics is the first step toward the Social Gospel. I don't want to take even that first step."*

Let Dr. Stan Mooneyham, president of World Vision International, answer that one:

> In London, the editor of a weekly evangelical Christian newspaper ran a series of articles on such subjects as abortion, narcotics, homosexuality, and mental health. The series, timed to coincide with discussions in the British Parliament, provoked an avalanche of mail. Not

a few were vitriolic. A Christian's duty (the letters said) was to preach the gospel and keep himself unspotted from the world till the coming crowning day. There was to be no truck with the Social Gospel. The aborted, the stupefied, the perverts, and mentally disturbed were an intrusion in an orderly Christian perspective, not to be mentioned in pious company except in outright condemnation.

More baloney.

Gandhi said: "In my judgment the Christian faith does not lend itself to much preaching or talking. It is best propagated by living it and applying it. . . . When will you Christians really crown Jesus Christ as the Prince of Peace and proclaim him through your deeds. . . ?" [2]

12. "Christians are supposed to be unspotted from the world!"

But not out-of-touch with the world. Or unsympathetic to the world.

Protected by Christ, Christians plunge into a world of greed, pride, and lust to rescue the addicts of greed, pride and lust.

A Christian group, called the "Lambs" are changing the appearance of Times Square in New York. *National Courier* said:

> To combat obscenity and prostitution, the Lambs Christians use what they call "operation olive branch." Their first step is to scout out a suspect establishment. For example, Paul Moore (director of the "Lambs") and Dick Lam of the Mayor's office recently decided to check out a massage parlor down the street. The place was advertised by a man walking around in front on the sidewalk, with a sandwich board that depicted a half-nude girl. Mr. Moore and Mr. Lam went upstairs and found "a middle-aged proprietor sitting in a sleazy lobby," Mr. Moore said. Through doors that opened into the lobby, they could see several small rooms which contained beds.
>
> "In the background, we saw six or seven nearly nude girls staring out of blank, expressionless faces," Mr. Moore recalled. "They might as well have been pieces of meat on a rack."

"How much does it cost?" Mr. Moore asked the proprietor.

"Ten dollars a throw," the man replied.

"Does that include everything?"

"Everything."

When it becomes clear that such a place offers illegal sexual services, Phase 2 of the operation begins. A representative of the church meets with the proprietor and the women and says, "We understand you want to make a living, and we'd like to explore how you can re-route your business into a more legitimate enterprise."

If they refuse the offer—or "olive branch"—then the church members and their secular supporters may resort to picketing and put pressure on city police authorities to enforce obscenity and prostitution laws.

Sometimes, though, the olive branch does the job. After hearing that pornographic movies were planned for a nearby theater, the Lambs Christians voiced objections and suggested alternatives to both the theater manager and the corporate owner of the building. The theater is now showing general interest films.[3]

13. "Why is it necessary for people to inspect samples?"

Because most people don't know what pornography is. It breeds and grows in darkness—like green mold on bread. Exposed to light, it vanishes.

Many legislators and law-enforcement officials don't know the problem. One district attorney repeatedly told me that he had more to do than fight "phonography." (A police chief told me the same.)

Then I showed them samples. Then they knew the word and the problem.

Jeremiah 13:1-10 says:

The Lord said to me, Go and buy a linen loincloth and wear it, but don't wash it—don't put it in water at all. So I bought the loincloth and put it on. Then the Lord's message came to me again. This time he said, Take the loincloth out to the Euphrates River and hide it in a hole in the rocks.

So I did; I hid it as the Lord had told me to. Then, a long time afterwards, the Lord said: Go out to the river again and get the loincloth. And I did; I dug it out of the hole where I had hidden it. But now it was mildewed and falling apart. It was utterly useless!

Then the Lord said: This illustrates the way that I will rot the pride of Judah and Jerusalem. This evil nation refuses to listen to me, and follows its own evil desires and worships idols; therefore it shall become as this loincloth—good for nothing.

Did Jeremiah know what would happen to a loincloth buried in mud? Of course. Had he ever seen mildew before? Yes.

God gave him, a righteous man, an object lesson in the corruption of Judah. Then Jeremiah's "bones were filled with fire"—he had to speak out.

I know I'm vulnerable. I know adults who inspect are vulnerable. I pray: "God, cleanse my motives, cover me with your blanket of protection." And say, "Satan, in the name of Jesus, I command you to leave me alone in this work."

I screen others, telling them, "If you have any doubts about your motives, leave."

God led me into this ministry, kicking and screaming. I never sought it. But I was there in a place and time when no one would lead an effort to rout smut and save kids. I quit a $1,000 a month job and went to work for $0.00.

God guided me day by day—through dozens of cities —to show hundreds of thousands how to get rid of smut. We've routed a lot of smut.

And I have to believe the success of this ministry is (1) trusting God—willing to be beaten, bruised, and taught by Him to be used by Him, and (2) showing the samples, so people *know* what's at arm's-length, eye-grabbing view of children.

14. *"America is presumably a Christian nation. How did it happen that things like child-prostitution,* Playboy *recreational sex, and masturbation parlors became so open and permissive?"*

Watch a chameleon in spring grass. He's neon green. Pick him up and put him in a hole of rocks and sand.

His color changes from neon green to sand brown. But not smash-bang! He changes gradually. He changes from neon green, to lime green, to olive green, to burnt green, to burnt greenish-brown, to burnt brown, to walnut brown, to sand brown.

As *Playboy* breast-nakedness—twenty years ago —changed *gradually* to worse exploitations of sex, so did Christian tolerance. Or ignorance.

Twenty years ago Christians were embarrassed to demand the halt of breast nakedness. They tolerated it. Which conditioned them to tolerate the next abuse. Which conditioned them to tolerate the next abuse. Which conditioned them to tolerate the next abuse. . . .

We did the very thing God condemned in Romans 12:1, 2, "Don't be conformed to this world."

We forgot Proverbs 11:11, "The good influence of godly citizens causes a city to prosper, but the moral decay of the wicked drives it downhill."

15. "I don't read it or buy it. I don't go to dirty movies. I don't watch permissive TV programs. I do read the Bible with my children and teach them the beauty of sex. That's how I'm fighting pornography."

You're right. If every person didn't read porno or go to dirty movies or view permissive TV; or if every parent read the Bible with their children and taught them the beauty of sex, there'd be no need for this book. There'd be no pornography.

But you are different. Most Americans don't do what you do. We are a minority in a heathen nation. Either we retreat or invade. If we retreat, we are murdering them by neglect—especially the children.

Dr. T. W. Wilson, vice-president of the Billy Graham Evangelistic Association, said:

> Do you know what a witness for Jesus Christ is? Did you know that in England, for instance, they have what they call murder by neglect? Many people in Britain have been put behind prison bars simply because they *neglected.* . . .
> I wonder what a Christian witness says. Let's use

an illustration.... Let's suppose I go over here and see a house on fire. I see some little children there. They don't know what to do. I hear them scream. I realize that the mother and father are gone. I say, "It's no business of mine. I don't know these people. Why should I jeopardize my life and go in and try to help them? They don't mean anything to me."

No matter how I try to argue, if I let those little children burn and I neglect to rescue them, whether I call myself a Christian or not, I believe I'm a murderer. I believe I could have spared their lives, but I just neglected. I just let them go ahead and be burned to death.[4]

16. *"But we can't legislate morality."*

We can't legislate *spirituality*

We can't make people love what's right. But we can make them *obey* what's right. That's what laws are for.

You can't legislate the end of racism. You can't make bigoted whites love blacks. But you can make them obey laws—Civil Rights laws.

Law is the morality of millions expressed in public law. Law starts with the cold fact that some people's hearts aren't right. Some people give in to lust, greed, and hate. Law won't change their hearts. That's not what law is for. Law is to protect the innocent from those giving in to lust, greed, and hate.

Prohibition against murder is public morality expressed in law.

Prohibition against theft is public morality expressed in law.

Prohibition against abusive sex is public morality expressed in law.

You can't make people respect life, property, and sex. But you can legally restrain them from abusing life, property, and sex. That's what civilized cultures do.

17. *"I am a follower of Jesus Christ. And I am also proud of the freedom we fought for in America. I have to believe that the freedom to read is an absolute right."*

Right. But the freedom to sell is not.

You are free to eat poisoned soup. You are not free to sell it.

In America, the democratic rule is this: Once you circulate a product in society, you are answerable to the laws of society.

18. *"When boycotting, do we boycott the stores or the products?"*

Both. I earlier discussed the effectiveness of boycotting stores. Sam Taylor explains the boycotting of products:

HOW WE SUPPORT PORNOGRAPHERS

Each day many of us, unknowingly, support pornography. How? By buying products from companies which spend millions of advertising dollars every year in the *Playboy*-type magazines.

There are those who tell us that if we ignore pornography, it will go away. Films and printed material dealing with explicit and illicit sex will eventually bore us, they say.

Any right-thinking person knows this to be utter nonsense. *Playboy* magazine recently completed its twentieth year. In that period of time, the publication of just one such periodical of filth has multiplied 50-fold! In that 20 years, millions of children have reached young adulthood—and have reached for *Playboy* and *Penthouse* and *Viva* and *Hustler*. Readership figures are astronomical, particularly on college campuses.

Television glorifies the hedonistic, Playboy philosophy with coverage of the Bunny-of-the Year Awards, as well as hundreds of jokes and gratuitous plugs each season. To better their image, the perverted publishers utilize interviews with all manner of prominent people, including presidential candidates.

No, boredom has not set in, the blight has not gone away. This writer examined four issues of *Penthouse* magazine, for April, June, August and October of this year. Aside from the approximately 50 ads for sex-oriented materials, each edition had up to 14 cigarette sponsors and up to 18 advertisements for hard liquor products.

Not counting the liquor and cigarettes (which are too numerous to list), here are just a few of the national advertisers actively backing pornography in the pages of *Penthouse*: Acme Boot Company, Bell & Howell, the (Jacques) Cousteau Society, English Leather toiletries, Fiat, Honda motor cars, Kawasaki motorcycles, Longines-Wittnauer, Memorex, MG (British Leyland Motors), Minolta Camera Co., Old Spice, Panasonic, U.S. Pioneer (stereo equipment), Revlon, Subaru, Toyota and Volkswagen.

(We should emphasize, happily, that no American automobile manufacturers advertised in *Penthouse*, at least not in the issues checked.)

Boycotting of these products can be helpful, but local dealers and distributors should also know why you are boycotting. Major automobile dealers, for example, have been able to change the advertising policies of the manufacturers. Whether you're in the market for a car or not, tell such dealers how you feel.

Letters to the parent companies will have an effect. Public libraries usually have a book called the Standard Directory of Advertisers, with addresses of the firms and names of the presidents. It will list by brand names as well, i.e., Old Spice is a product of Shulton, Inc. Individual letters are fine, but protests and boycott threats on company letterheads will carry more weight, as will communications from lawyers, doctors and owners of businesses.

Finally, the letters might add, in each person's own words, something about corporate responsibility. This means more than accountability to stockholders, if the company is publicly held. Private industry, in concert with church, government, education, labor and other institutions, should share the responsibility for the common good. Few leaders in any of these fields would argue that the Playboy ethic—which has generated media vulgarities and obscenities of monstrous scope, and is associated by endeavor if not by financial ties with organized crime—serves the common good.[5]

19. *"Why the emphasis on* Christians *fighting pornography?"*

Because, in the long run, it is Christians who see

it through. I have worked with Christians and non-Christians:

1. Non-Christians give up. They don't have a deep source of power to draw from. (Some "Christians" give up too—but fewer.)

A Christian continues to fight because it's *right*.

That's the only motive that lasts.

2. Non-Christians eventually feud among each other.

3. Non-Christians get so zealously involved in fighting pornography that they neglect wife, husband, or children—not just for a day or two but for months.

Christians keep balance in their lives. Christians still make love to mates, get out and exercise, read the Bible, go to church, play with the kids, etc.

4. Non-Christians are not openly supportive of each other in open criticism, love, trust, and praise.

CHAPTER 8

Pornography and the Law

1. "Why hasn't legislation stopped pornography?"

Legislation has. Good legislation (like the Display Law) demanded by citizens has been passed and upheld.

Some legislation, however, has been ineffective. Because for many years,

> prosecutors had to prove that "obscene" works were "utterly without redeeming social value." Now the DEFENSE must prove that a challenged work has "serious literary, artistic, political or scientific value." [1]

Under the impossible test of "utterly without redeeming social value," it was nearly impossible to secure a conviction. And many states *still* (implicitly) require "utterly without redeeming social value" as a test—even though the Supreme Court has scrapped it in favor of "serious literary, artistic, political or scientific value."

Another reason legislation has been ineffective is because citizens have not demanded good legislation from city councilmen and state legislators. Citizens have not demanded enforcement of law by local police and state police.

In America, power belongs to the people. When people hurl their collective weight against legislators and police, things get done. All you have to do is show people the problem and *they'll* show their power.

A third reason is that the quality of our judges is

poor. (See Appendix 4, pages 237-239.)

2. *"What if someone wants to feed on pornography?"*

Many people want to feed on heroin, but (so far) Americans have recognized that engorging oneself on drugs ultimately affects everyone. It is the same with pornography.

Pornography ultimately affects everyone because individual discipline (or lack of it) breeds national character.

John L. Quinlan III, Chief of Special Crimes Division, Bexar County, said:

> Today's ultra permissive philosophy states, "What's wrong with a person having a little fun if he is not hurting anyone?" Strictly speaking, a man spending his money to place a bet, pay a prostitute or buy a ticket to hard-core porno theater and perhaps buy the services of a male prostitute in that theater is not physically hurting his neighbor. But multiply that 100,000 times across this nation and let me ask this question: "What makes up the moral fiber of the nation? What makes up its inner strength? Some phantom spirit? Or is it the collective discipline of the individual that makes up that nation?" [2]

Recognizing the danger of pornography vis-à-vis the existence of fundamental rights, the courts have put the burden of responsibilities on the seller, not the reader.

3. *"What about the First Amendment?"*

Concerning First Amendment rights, the Supreme Court in *Miller* v. *U.S.* (and other cases) said: "This much has been categorically settled by the Court, that obscene material is unprotected by the First Amendment."

The moral climate of America belongs to the people. No one enjoys a right to pollute it helter-skelter.

Referring to television's "nouveau" smut ("Mary Hartman, Mary Hartman"), TV critic Kay Gardella said:

172

Our own view is that the First Amendment has been used as a shield for these special-interest groups who want the freedom to use the public airwaves in any way that they see fit and to be as shocking and outrageous as possible. Hollywood producers, who stand to make millions out of television—Norman Lear is already there —would love to brainwash a nation into believing that TV's a medium on a par with theaters, movie houses and other forms of entertainment. This is not true and the public should never forget it. Television is a unique and special medium that is government regulated. The Federal Communications Commission is the regulating agency of broadcasting; and the *airwaves*—to remind you once more—*belong to the people.* (Emphasis MM's.) [3]

4. "What about 'freedom to read' and libraries?"

In America, read what you like. Obscenity laws respect that right. Freedom-to-read was reaffirmed in the high court's *Stanley* v. *Georgia* decision.

Obscenity laws deal with the freedom to sell. Or, broader, the freedom to distribute (selling, loaning, or giving away). In democratic society, a citizen who distributes *any* material within society is answerable to the laws of that society. He may eat poisoned soup in the privacy of his own home; he may not sell, loan, or give it away. He's subject to FDA legislation, representing the will of the majority. The majority do not want poisoned soup peddled for public distribution. The minority, therefore (enjoying the nausea of poisoned soup), abide by that majority will. They cannot peddle their poisoned soup.

That's what it means to live in a democracy.

Confusion over "freedom to read" has crippled a basic right of parents to train children in a robust, moral atmosphere. If the Gallup and Harris polls are correct, most of America's 50 million parents want to protect their children from abusive sex. Specifically, they want to protect their children from seeing on covers (and on open display) bare-breasted, vagina-spread prostitutes and couples involved in sexual acts. Obscenity laws, specifying what may and may not be *sold*, affirm a parent's right to protect his and her children.

And such laws apply to (formerly) sacrosanct libraries.

Consider the library: A box of new books and magazines drop on a librarian's desk. He or she unpacks them and—with or without reading them—decides what goes on the shelves. There they are for children, for anyone, to pick up.

It's reverse censorship. Here, a single person doesn't decree what may not be distributed. No. Here a single person decrees what may be distributed.

That is changing. Citizens are recognizing that *their* right to read does not empower the librarian to use *their* tax money to single-handedly choose books and magazines to buy and place on open shelves.

The books are purchased by the public. They are distributed to the public (including children). But a private few have arrogated to themselves an ivory-tower authority to baptize books as "good for everyone."

Libraries are not immaculate, infallible or omnipotent. A dozen censors enjoy no right to say what shall and shall not be in a library. Neither does a duet of librarians.

"Imperial" libraries—like imperial presidencies—are inappropriate. Libraries—like legislatures—are answerable to the public they serve.

5. *"What about the Commission Report on Obscenity and Pornography?"*

Cited earlier in this book (ch. 1) are police cases taken from Commission records documenting the link between pornography and sex crimes.

The chairman of the Commission, however, a self-confessed American Civil Liberties Union leader, chose to ignore the police cases because *he* approved the public distribution of pornography. (Having an ACLU chieftain chairing the Commission Report on Obscenity and Pornography was like having the Imperial Wizard of the Ku Klux Klan chairing a Civil Rights Commission.)

Among people rejecting the report were the President, the Senate (by 60-5 vote), and syndicated columnists.

In one battle of opposing views aired in a newspaper, respondents said:

> *Statement:* Empirical research was used to justify the Commission's conclusions. You can't argue with that unless you're going to admit you're basing your case on feelings.

(1) "Empirical research" means that actual, true conditions are simulated in the laboratory. The actual conditions under which a person gawks at pornography are secret and surreptitious; privately, in his bathroom or bedroom, he hiddenly pores over its pages. The Commission's "research" on pornography was a circus. Slapping electrodes on a 19-year-old college student, they hoisted him on a public stool and tossed a fat deck of porn magazines in front of him. Everybody watched him watch pornography. Real secret. Real surreptitious. When electrodes diminished in stimulus vibrations, the Commission concluded that the paid spectacle-subject was satiated with pornography. The Commission thus concluded that rampant pornography in society will give people their fill.

The Commission might just as well have experimented by slapping a side of beef before a hungry prospect. Watch him engorge. Watch him vomit. Conclude that he no longer likes beef. The problem is that *tomorrow* he will *like* beef again. Sexual hunger, like food hunger, though capable of satiation at a particular moment, is a hunger that re-occurs and with greater and greater passion if perviously engorged.

(2) Empirical research means that primary or original materials are employed in the research. Commission members dealt with pornography at second hand: They did *not* personally and systematically scrutinize the pornographic materials flourishing on American

shelves and screens. They virtually ignored primary sources.

(3) Empirical research means that examining methods and tools do not interfere with the *normal, usual,* functioning of the subject being examined (the Heisenberg principle in physics). One would think that a covey of investigators staring at a paid subject (studded with electrodes) would hardly allow for an examination in which the subject's normal sexual reactions could erupt.

> *Statement:* This finding has been affirmed and reaffirmed by studies even more thorough than the Commission's. . . .

(1) What studies? Generalities do not support anyone's argument.

(2) The following, however, are two studies which specifically *belie* the Commission's conclusions:

(a) The Davis-Brauch report (a primary-research study available to the Commission but eschewed by them). Studying 305 people from seven different groups, the report concluded, "One finds exposure to pornography is the strongest predictor of sexual deviance. . . . "

(b) Lord Langford's committee report in Great Britain. Composed of 52 members including social scientists, housewives, educators, pop stars, and writers, this committee pursued research for 16 months examining pornographic magazines, interviewing pornography dealers, holding discussions with policemen, and reading 5,000 letters sent to the committee. Their conclusion: "Pornography creates an addiction leading to deviant obsessions and actions."

> *Statement:* The Commission's report—for those who listen—will help take a long, steady look at victimless crimes.

"Victimless crimes" do not exist. An 18-year-old girl, enticed by the quick-buck of prostitution, takes it up. Before she's 25, she's a violent hater of men, stripped of any chance of a husband, children, and an inclusive

family of loved ones. (Less than 1% of prostitutes successfully marry.)

Victimless?

A 60-year-old homosexual, instead of cooing grandchildren or embracing a life-long companion, hustles
fellatio for 25 cents a trick.

Victimless?

An 18-year-old boy ("legally" sanctioned to devour
pornography) reads the pornographic account of a gang
raping a virgin. It plants hard and deep on his libido.
He goes out and, someday, rapes his date. (The porno
magazine assured him that the girl *wanted* to be raped.)

Victimless?

6. "What about 'censorship'?"

In America, thanks to free press, representative government and responsive electorate, censorship is impossible.

Censorship means (1) prior restraint and (2) control
of visual and literary material by an autocracy or oligarchy.

Obscenity laws are not prior restraint.

Obscenity laws say: Print or publish whatever you
want. We're not putting prior restraint on you. But
once you circulate your material in society, you must
understand that the electorate has the right to give
or deny a legal blessing to your material.

In democratic society, legal blessings are expressed
through legislators or city councilmen (following public
petitions). Resulting laws, therefore, represent the will
of the people. If laws did not represent the will of the
people, they wouldn't be laws. That is the legal premise
upon which the framework of democratic society exists.
It is not the will of one (autocracy) nor the will of a
few (oligarchy), but it is the will of many which is reflected in democratic society. Since Harris and Gallup
polls say that 80% of America opposes pornography,
strong obscenity laws are, therefore, inevitable.

I should have said that censorship is almost impossible. It does exist, flourishing among those who tolerate
the abuse of sex. In the literature of censorship in the

20th century, nothing exceeds the FCC document on censorship in communication-media. (See Appendix 3.)

7. *"If the jury represents the 'average person' and the 'average person' does not want pornography, why don't we have more convictions?"*

The jury *does represent* the average person according to the June 22, 1973, decisions. And the average person does not want pornography according to Gallup and Harris polls.

But one large reason that we do not have more convictions is that the quality of judges is poor.[4] (See Appendix 4.)

8. *"Is legal progress being made on the problem of a legal definition of pornography? Where does the law now stand on it?"*

The legal definition of obscenity was handed down by the Supreme Court on June 22, 1973, in *Miller* v. *California.*

> The basic guidelines for the trier of fact must be: (a) whether the average person applying contemporary community standards would find that the work, taken as a whole, appeals to the prurient interest, (b) whether the work depicts or describes, in a patently offensive way, sexual conduct specifically defined by applicable state law, and (c) whether the work taken as a whole lacks serious literary, artistic, political or scientific value.

While that's not exactly a definition for which the Supreme Court ought to be crowned prophets of righteousness, it's far superior to the legal mish-mash formerly prevailing. Among other things, it means (1) under a: If the people of Los Angeles and New York give legal approval to street-corner masturbation and child-molesting magazines, the people in Austin or Detroit are not bound by that approval. It is up to the local community to decide. (2) under b: The plug has been pulled on the insane escalation in porno mags and flicks. Nearly any judge and jury would find contemporary pornography "patently offensive" and therefore "obscene" (and many have done just that since *Miller*). The trick is to get the piece of pornography before the courts so a judge and jury can actually *see* what pornography is. To get porno before the courts, citizens must scream so loud that, under fear of being lynched by an angry community, police, sheriffs, and district attorneys *will* make arrests. Arrests lead to trials and that gets porno before the courts. (3) under c: Literary or visual masterpieces which do contain sexual descriptions or depictions are protected from ranting crusaders and uptight puritans. The Bible, Shakespeare, Venus de Milo and a thousand other masterpieces depict or describe sex realistically, but they would hardly be judged obscene. The work is taken as a whole.

Pornographers, of course, have abused that provision. Writing steamy page after steamy page of incest, child-rape, or intercourse with animals, they then drop in a page or two of windy political opinion rescuing their work from obscenity. Public pressure dissuades courts from allowing pornographers that trick.

9. "We cannot legislate morality."

Consider: "We should teach nondiscrimination of blacks. We should preach nondiscrimination of blacks. But we should not legislate nondiscrimination of blacks. We cannot, after all, legislate morality.

"Whites must be free to use 'Whites Only' water fountains and restrooms and motels. And blacks must be free, if they choose, to use 'Coloreds Only' water fountains, restrooms and motels. We cannot force whites or blacks to use (or build) integrated facilities. Let them choose what they want to use without interference from other citizens, legislators, or the court."

With the crescendo of high-school freshmen in debate, porno-advocates slam down that cliche, "We cannot legislate morality."

What they mean is: We cannot legislate spirituality. You cannot make people love what is right. But you can make them obey it. That's what law is for.

Some people (including me) think it's morally wrong to discriminate against blacks. And *that* morality is expressed in public law. Even the bigoted have to obey it, though they don't like it.

Many people (and apparently fewer every day) think it's morally wrong to take something that doesn't belong to them. And *that* morality is expressed in public law. Even the greedy have to obey it.

Many people think that abusive sex is morally wrong. And *that* private morality is expressed in public law (obscenity law). Even those who will not discipline lust must obey it.

The history of the civil rights battle parallels the decency battle.

Some whites hate blacks (and vice-versa). They abuse them. No law will make them love blacks.

Hate expresses itself in action. Can blacks expect protection of law from bigoted whites? They can and they have. That is the way America works.

Some men hate women. They print and publish the sexual abuse of women.

No law will make them love women. Hate expresses itself in action. Can women (and everyone else appreciating beauty of sex) expect protection of law from abusive men? They can and they have. That is the way America works.[5]

Many whites did not want to give up discriminating practices against blacks because those practices brought financial gain. Many men do not want to give up their abusive practices against women because those practices bring financial gain. Blacks *demanded* protection of law for their rights. And that's what women (and others) are doing for decency rights. Blacks and women agree:

> It is not light that is needed, but fire. It is not the gentle shower, but thunder. We need the storm, the whirlwind, and the earthquake.[6]

10. *"Some cities have designated special sections for the legal sale of pornography. Is this satisfactory?"*

When a flood breaks into a city, regardless of point of entry, it washes over everybody. Ask the people of Boston if they find the "combat zone" satisfactory:

TWO HARVARD ATHLETES STABBED IN COMBAT ZONE

One Harvard University football player was "brought back to life" and another listed in "good" condition yesterday, after being stabbed during a brutal early-morning fight in the Combat Zone.

Fast action by Boston police and doctors saved the life of Harvard senior Andrew Puopolo, 21, of Mossdale Rd., Jamaica Plain, who was stabbed twice in the heart and once in the left lung. He was reported in "stable" condition last night, but his name remained on the danger list.

Thomas J. Lincoln, 23, of Richard Rd., Hingham, a senior, suffered superficial stab wounds of the abdomen during the melee between Harvard football team members and a group of black males. He was being treated at Massachusetts General Hospital.

Puopolo was a starting defensive back who played well in Saturday's Yale game, and Lincoln was a fullback.

The fracas began after the Combat Zone bars closed at 2 a.m. A black female prostitute allegedly stole a student's wallet and a small group of Harvard players chased her to try to get it back. Black males intercepted them.

Three men were arrested by Boston police, who swarmed onto the scene minutes after the trouble began.[7]

Two weeks later (two weeks too late), the UPI report from Boston said:

COMBAT ZONE THEORY "FAILING"

The concept of controlling prostitution and pornography by creating a special adult entertainment zone is failing, according to two law enforcement officials.

"This city's adult entertainment district—known as

the 'Combat Zone'—is a failure," said Assistant District Attorney Timothy O'Neill.

"The district attorney's office has never been in favor of a clustered Combat Zone. The clustering created an illusion of license that doesn't exist under state law," he said.

The Combat Zone is an area of sleazy bars, X-rated movie houses, and strip joints located on the fringe of the downtown shopping district. The area has been the center of public attention due to a number of recent violent incidents.[8]

One month later, Andrew Puopolo died.

11. "How about other zoning plans, like Detroit's?"

Detroit's zoning plan (porno shops cannot operate within 1,000 feet of each other, nor can they operate within 500 feet of homes) has been upheld by the Supreme Court, attracting the attention of many city fathers who see it as an answer to their growing and stinking porno problem.

Zoning is not the answer. "Zoning" pornography will not cure the problem any more than zoning the flu will cure the flu. Zoning is a superficial solution.

A physician treats the cause of the victim's flu. He doesn't simply "zone him away."

The pornography problem requires:

(1) Men's hearts to be changed by Jesus Christ, empowering them to pulsate with love, not lust.

(2) Men's actions to be controlled by clear, tough laws halting the distribution of all pornography.

12. "The store managers in our city said they'd take all the porno books off the shelves. I don't see any need to get a city ordinance passed now."

We cleaned the shelves of a big Texas city. Boycotts, petitions, public meetings, phone calls, letters—they worked.

I, and other citizens, submitted the Display Law to the city council. I left the city to take up decency work elsewhere. I was assured that citizens would push the law through.

They did not.

That city is again buried in open-shelf porno. The spiritual, civic, *and legal clout* work together—or they don't work.

CHAPTER 9
Pornography and the Media

Many media personnel tolerate pornography. They tolerate it because they are frightened by laws dealing with restrictions of the written or spoken word. Either they do not know or do not care about the Supreme Court's ruling on obscene speech.

The Supreme Court said that "a man has no more right to dispense obscenity in the name of free speech than he does to shout 'fire' in a crowded theater—in the name of free speech."

It is no mystery why the media eschews Supreme Court guidelines: (1) They see themselves as champions of "freedom of the press." (2) They see their jobs threatened by restrictions on pornographic print or pictures. (If sexual abuse, after all, was not allowed free circulation, talk-show gabbies would lose jokes and guests, and magazines would lose millions in advertising revenue.)

Fear of restrictions leads to prejudice and distortion.

Simon Leis[1] witnessed it firsthand. (See Appendix 3, Section B, p. 232.)

Media personnel often splash columns and interviews with pro-pornography colors. If interviewed, you can expect the following questions:

Q. *How do you define pornography?*

A. I don't have to define pornography. The United States Supreme Court has defined it. It is up to law enforcement to apply that definition.

Q. *Why would you want to take this away from adult mature people who want to see it?*

A. It's a matter of what the community wants. It is the *law*. The United States Supreme Court has concluded that society does not want pornography polluting the atmosphere. The Court "categorically disapproved" the so-called "consenting adults" theory, saying that while a man has the right to view whatever he wants in the privacy of his own home, that right does not extend to exhibiting pornography in public places. The Court went on to say (in *Paris Adult Theater*), " . . . Rights and interests other than those of the advocates are involved. These include the interest of the public in the quality of life and the total community environment, the tone of commerce in the great city centers, and possibly, the public safety itself."

One need only look to Times Square in New York City to see what pornography does to a physical area. Times Square always had a somewhat honky tonk aura. But, it was not until the adult theaters and the adult bookstores opened that the area began to be peopled by prostitutes, pimps, pushers. Pornography attracts other crime and leads to the deterioration of entire areas.

Q. *Don't psychiatrists say that pornography does some good since it presents an outlet, a release from tension?*

A. *Dr. Ernest van den Haag*, psychoanalyst: "Hunger is intensified rather than gratified by reading about or seeing food."

Dr. Frederic Wertham, psychiatrist: "There is no clinical justification for such an opinion. The 'outlet' theory is based on a misunderstanding of Freud, who never advocated that people indulge their aggressiveness either vicariously or actually."

Dr. Max Levin, psychiatrist and neurologist: "The falsity of the 'outlet' argument may be demonstrated by an analogy. . . . How would starving people respond to a movie of a Thanksgiving feast? Would it serve as an outlet and diminish their hunger? Not at all. It would only intensify it. So it is with aberrant sex impulses . . . sex impulses will only be intensified by pornographic films and books."

Q. *Who are you to tell me what I can see or read?*

A. *Professor Reo Christenson:* "Those who say this

are consulting their impulses rather than the larger interests of society. A socially responsible person will forego the indulgence of a desire if the policy permitting that indulgence jeopardizes the well-being of others."

Q. *Pornography is in the eye of the beholder, isn't it?*

A. Obviously false. Such an attitude is a denial of evil. Evil is committed by a person whether seen by another or not. It is evident that evil is *not* in the eyes of the beholder of the action, but rather in the person acting.

Q. *No girl was ever ruined by a book. Right?*

A. That flippant statement was made by a playboy major of New York City. Preposterous though it may seem, it is brought up as a serious argument by many extremists. If no girl was ever ruined by a book, was any girl ever helped by a book? What are books for, if not to inform, to stimulate and provoke thought? What are libraries for? What are schools for? If a book can improve a person's mind, certainly it can help deform the mind. Professor Irving Kristol of New York University said: "If you believe no one was ever corrupted by a book, you must also believe no one was ever improved by a book (or a play or a movie). You have to believe, in other words, that all art is morally trivial ... all education morally irrelevant."

Q. *Shouldn't one have an open mind?*

A. Agreed. But open sewers should be closed.

Q. *What is obscene to you may not be obscene to me. Agreed?*

A. You and I are not the determinants of what is obscene. We are a small segment of a very large community. The matter revolves around what the community determines is obscene, i.e., what the community chooses to set up as a standard of *public* morality. If that standard is threatened, the community has a right to legislate to protect itself from that threat.

Q. *Who is to judge what is obscene?*

A. According to the Supreme Court, the average person is to make this judgment. Legally, the court makes the determination, acting after the individual has made the decision as a member of a jury. Such a panel of citizens act as a representative of the community.

Q. *Where do you draw the line?*

A. The guidelines were drawn by the United States

Supreme Court in the *Miller* decision of June 1973: "The basic guidelines for the trier of fact must be: (a) whether 'the average person, applying contemporary community standards' would find that the work, taken as a whole, appeals to the prurient interest; (b) whether the work depicts or describes, in a patently offensive way, sexual conduct specifically defined by the applicable state law; and (c) whether the work, taken as a whole, lacks serious literary, artistic, political or scientific value."

Q. *We don't like to put straitjackets on people's minds.*

A. The Supreme Court guidelines are ideally suited for a democratic society in which free speech is paramount. Obscenity is not protected speech: the Supreme Court has said this and has ruled for the "social interest in order and morality" (*Roth*, 1957), and the "quality of life" (*Miller*, 1973).

Q. *If you don't like certain books or films, you don't have to read or see them, do you?*

A. The implication here is that all laws dealing with guidelines in mass-media communications should be repealed. If this is what the community wanted, then it would be done. However, there is no indication that the community wants this. In fact, the opposite is true, as is evidenced by a number of national polls where the majority support strict enforcement of obscenity laws. The community does not want obscene material polluting its atmosphere, for it leads to the degrading of society.

Q. *Do you think you can tell me what to read and what not to read? what to see and what not to see?*

A. Nobody is telling anybody what he can read or not read. The community is setting up standards for itself and protecting itself against the effects of pornography on society. Anyone is free to print, publish or film what he wishes. However, once it is released he is responsible before the law. The Supreme Court has said that a man has the right to view pornography in his own home. However, it said subsequently that this does not give another man the right to distribute or exhibit pornography. It reiterated in 1973 that the privacy right does not extend to places of public accommodation such as movie houses, etc.

Q. *Shouldn't each individual decide for himself what to read and see?*

A. This is true. However, this does not mean that

an individual is free to expose himself in a public place. We have laws covering this. Much less does a man have a right to film nudity or graphic sex and show it in a public place, since more people will be exposed to it.

Q. *Would you ban the Bible? It has many frank passages.*

A. The supposition is that we ban anything at all; we ban nothing. The question should be, would the *community* ban the Bible? Moreover, on its face value, this question is obviously absurd. There is nothing obscene in Scripture. If evil is in the Bible, it is presented as evil. In obscene material, the point of view given is that evil is presented as good.

Q. *The Sistine Chapel in the Vatican has nudes.*

A. There is nothing objectionable about true art depicting nudity. What is objectionable is exploitation of the naked human figure.

Q. *Isn't freedom of speech protected by the First Amendment?*

A. Yes, but the United States Supreme Court has said that obscenity is not protected free speech.

Q. *Aren't you acting as censors? Such censorship violates the First Amendment.*

A. Censorship is prior restraint. An individual can have complete freedom to print or portray anything he wants. However, once he does so, he is responsible to the community. This is not censorship; it is law enforcement.

Q. *Don't you think your thinking is the result of the Puritan era?*

A. This is a twist on name calling. You're a puritan, narrow-minded, blue-nose, prude, censor. Is anyone who stands for public morality in mass-media communications a puritan? Labels have a psychological effect on people—the majority intensely dislike being labeled.

Q. *Some people enjoy pornography. Aren't you infringing upon their freedom to have it?*

A. Some people enjoy drugs. The community has judged otherwise in both the areas of drugs and obscenity by enacting laws to protect society.

Q. *Shouldn't we keep up with the times?*

A. "This is the era of sexual revolution; the new morality is here. Sexual freedom is prevalent now; there-

188

fore, let's show it and let's portray it." The laws that regulate sexual expression are divine and are unchanging. The current attitude on sexual freedom is evidently a denial of sin. It says that once there was such a concept of sin, but that is no longer true. This is relativism and moral chaos.

Q. *No one has ever been able to prove that obscene material has harmful effects.*

A. This statement is false, as studies in the Hill-Link Minority Report of the Presidential Commission on Obscenity and Pornography indicate. There are extremely interesting, scientifically supported linkages between exposure to obscene material and sexual deviancy, promiscuity, affiliation with anti-social crime groups, and so forth. However, there will never be a one-to-one scientific proof that a particular film caused a man to commit a specific crime. Criminologists have never been able to isolate a single motive that causes an individual to commit a crime. Illegal activity is the result of a whole lifetime of experiences and judgments.

Q. *Aren't you trying to impose your moral standards on others?*

A. This attitude involves a misunderstanding of public morality as opposed to personal morality. Public morality is a common denominator, the quintessence of community sentiment. It is something the community as a whole agrees on. Therefore, federal, state or local obscenity laws in no way attempt to impose individual moral standards on others. There is no imposition. There is *consensus*.

Q. *Racial injustice, poverty, war. These are the obscenities.*

A. And the Bible condemns all obscenities—sexual abuse, slavery, poverty, etc.

Thus saith the Lord: for three transgressions of Israel, and for four, I will not turn away the punishment thereof; because they sold the righteous for silver, and the poor for a pair of shoes; that pant after the dust of the earth on the head of the poor, and turn aside the way of the meek: and a man and his father will go in unto the same maid, to profane my holy name: and they lay themselves down upon clothes laid to pledge by every altar; and they drink the wine of the condemned in the house of their god. (Amos 2:6-8)

Some reporters say they are with you. Some say they are objective. Some you can believe, some you can't. After the interview, don't be surprised to see what's printed in the paper.

Keep saying the positive and the message eventually comes through. If you quit, people never get the right message. And, no matter how a newspaper slants or distorts an interview, the very fact that *this is* an interview with a decency advocate says to the public: *Decency is significant.*

TV or radio talk-show hosts say (off-camera) they are with you. They say (off-camera) they are objective. Some you can believe, some you can't.

Be prepared for a talk-show host to say anything to you once a camera or mike is turned on. He may even slip in a surprise guest, some porno plugger. He didn't tell you ahead of time.

That's okay. You're right and he's wrong. Everyone knows that sexual abuse is wrong. Rip the offensive from him and keep it.

Decency advocates (including myself) have done this. Take a porno magazine on the set (don't let the host know you have it). When he or the porno plugger belches cliches about "right to read," "censorship," etc., pull out the magazine, open to the roughest picture, turn to the camera and say:

> Mom and Dad, you know porno is wrong, this station knows it's wrong, and these guys know it's wrong, and I'm going to prove it to you. I'm going to hold up before the monitor a porno magazine from one of our local, friendly drive-in stores. You won't see it, however, because they'll black me out.

You hold it up and they do black you out. When the camera returns, you say:

> Now if it's wrong to hold it up to the screen where everyone can see it, it's just as wrong to peddle it in stores where everyone can see it and buy it.

Then, turning to talk-show hosts and his porno guests, say: "Would you let your daughter pose for this picture?"

If you're reading from a sex-sick porno paperback, say:

> Mom and Dad, you know sexual abuse is wrong, these guys know it's wrong, and this station knows it's wrong, and I'm going to prove it to you. I'm going to read one paragraph from this book available at your friendly neighborhood drive-in store (or library, or supermarket, etc.). You won't hear the words because they'll beep me out.

You start to read and, sure enough, they'll beep you out. When the audio returns, you say:

> Now, if it's wrong to read this where everyone can hear it, it's wrong to sell it where everyone, including children, can buy, see, steal, and read it.

You turn to your talk-show host and his porno-guest and ask:

> Would you like your daughter or wife to participate in the scene I just read?

There are many other ways to crash the indifference, ignorance, greed, or deceit of talk-show hosts and their guest. I cannot put them here in print since this book will be read by porno advocates.

(If you wish more information, contact me for a workshop-training in handling the media, introducing legislation, handling objections, etc.; write me c/o Bethany Fellowship, 6820 Auto Club Road, Minneapolis, Minnesota 55438).

CHAPTER 10

Anti-Pornography Workshops

*1. "Who do you find giving you the most support
in anti-pornography workshops? And are all Christian
people actively involved?"*

Most of my workshops (which are by invitation only,
by the way. I never say, "Hey, let me come clean
up your town." People hear about this ministry, they
do all the leg work to set up a workshop, and then
I come.) are in churches, colleges, and conferences.
I know three Christians who have openly opposed a
workshop. Two were professors at a Christian college
in Tennessee whose remarks were coached and manipulated by an angry news reporter whom I publicly hu-
miliated for his lack of knowledge on obscenity law
(and I herein confess that sin; humiliation is not
conducive to truth). The other was a preacher's wife
on the West Coast who criticized my methods. Which
is fine. I need criticism and direction. Oh, one other.
A man (I think) sent me a long letter telling me everything I was doing wrong. He then told me he was deliber-
ately omitting his name. I don't call that opposition. Opposition means you're willing to glue name to convictions.

Expect criticism. Be prepared for abuse and attack
when you loudly and consistently protest porno. You'll
make mistakes. Sticking in my mind is the incident
I related earlier which has helped me keep going these
several years. In the very early days of this work,

only my wife and Tommy Clay (Christian book dealer in San Antonio) deeply and radically believed in my ministry. One day Clay received an anonymous phone call, shouting out a list of things for Clay to tell me about everything I was doing wrong. Clay's reply was: "You may be right but I prefer the way Neil Gallagher is fighting pornography than the way you are not."

Overwhelmingly, most people are "with" you on this issue. Baptists, Church of Christ, Pentecostal, Assembly of God, Mennonite, conservative Presbyterians, Lutherans, Methodists, Catholics and Jews have been supportive of this ministry.

Administrators in Christian colleges have sponsored workshops.

2. *"How do you respond to one reporter's accusing you of 'histrionics' in dramatizing the terror of the pornography problem?"*

I don't know what histrionics means. If it means a display of emotion unwarranted by the facts, then I am not histrionic. If it means a display of emotion warranted by the facts, then I am.

Take the Nashville case: I have been in every major U.S. airport and none exceeded Nashville for sexual filth. (It has been cleaned up since a workshop.)

Lining the *corridor* of the airport, which everyone must pass to reach departure gates, were neat rows of naked prostitutes—at arm-reach and eye-level of a four-year-old. Dozens of magazines flashed not only engorged, glistening nipples (the wet-lipped prostitutes pointing to them with one hand) but spread-eagled legs veiled behind white-lace panties (the prostitute pointing to her vagina with the other hand). Nearly every airport in the United States displays these magazines (except Rhode Island), but they contain them within newsstands or drugstores. (I *still* complain, however.)

In January, 1976, I caught a connecting flight through Nashville and it was too much. At the Nashville airport, porno lined the *corridor*. Neither children nor adults could escape the nightmarish wallpaper.

When I first saw them, I floated by in a zombie trance. I couldn't believe it. I couldn't believe it. I sat down, stared at the floor, and didn't blink for minutes. I kept thinking, rehearsing the names of Big Guns coming in and out of Nashville daily to and from churches, colleges, lectureships. Pentecostal, Baptist, Church of Christ, thousands of preachers, hundreds of thousands of Bible school teachers—all of them bubbling with Bible exhortations. And yet . . . and yet. . . . I took two of the worst magazines to the clerk. She said she didn't like them either but I was the first one to complain. She pointed to the airport police. I went to the airport police. They said they didn't like them either, but I was the first one to complain. The first? The first.

"Lord, show me what to do."

I sat down. I wrote a passionate article "Heart of Bible Land Airport Unfit for Children and Other Living Things." I circulated it until my money ran out. To their eternal credit, a group of West Nashville Christians, headed by Cliff Dobbs and Melvin Turner, said they were going to do something about it. They must have worked twenty-five hours a day for eight days a week because they set up a powerful workshop. Not only did they get Nashville's city councilmen and Nashville's mayor to endorse the workshop, they excited the interest of every TV radio station and newspaper in Nashville. When I hit the airport the night of March 24 for the workshop, the prostitutes were still on kid-level display and the media pens and cameras were trained.

And I did what Dr. Martin Abend, New York's television curmudgeon, advised me: catch and keep the media, be bold; shout, wave, bristle with conviction. I did what Christians in Nashville should have done years earlier: I grabbed magazines, strode to the center of the concourse, and yelled: "Ladies and gentlemen, listen to me! Are you going to continue to let this airport sell this filth where *even your kids* can pick it up? This is illegal under Tennessee law (I had done my homework.). It's up to you. Porno causes sex crimes. Your kids can't complain, but you must!"

I kept on waving the magazines. It was on the 10 o'clock news two nights in a row. It was on six radio stations and in two newspapers (photos included). And that's what we wanted. The airport (and dozens of Nashville stores since) cleaned up their racks.

Homosexuals (a small minority) and extremist wranglers of ERA (a smaller minority) swing legal clout because they scream. They picket, boycott, sit-in, and march. They grab the media. They're willing to "make fools" of themselves. And they get what they want.

I know. You say, "Oh, I could never do that. I'm too quiet, reserved, just a woman, just a preacher, too old, too young, too ugly. . . . "

Dramatizing the terror of pornography, for me, is hard. It's like using cold, naked fingers to rip a curb from the sidewalk.

But I learned long ago to claim Jesus' power to do it. Long ago I glued my gut to 2 Timothy 1:7: "For God did not give us a spirit of timidity, but a spirit of power and love and self-control."

Neil Gallagher *is* timid, weak, unloving and self-willed. (And an academic buff. My thing's philosophy and I much prefer the isolated, analytical classroom.) But every time I enter a public demonstration I say: "Okay, Lord, you know I'm exhausted and scared to death. I've been running around pulpitizing about your great power. Okay, I claim your power and your love and your self-control for me right now. I absolutely cannot do it on my own."

3. *"How long does a workshop take?"*
Usually three days.

Friday: A.M.—meeting with leaders of the local effort to rout pornography; press conferences, interviews. P.M.—mass rally. Speaking engagements—service clubs, colleges, etc.

Saturday (workshop, and I mean *work*): A.M.—organizing, organizing, organizing citizens—the pri-

195

vate clout, the public clout. P.M.—explanation of pornography legislation; the legal clout; how to introduce, how to enforce.

Sunday: A.M. & P.M.—speaking engagements in area churches.

I perform no miracles. I show people how to do it. I show what's worked in other cities. And then I leave. It's up to them.

CHAPTER 11
General Questions

1. "Haven't we always had smut around? How serious a threat to morality do you think pornography actually is now?"

Duration of evil never makes evil good. Murder's been around longer than smut and it's still murder.

The threat to morality (to civilized society itself) was addressed in a Cedar Rapids' article in December, 1975.

> How many who consider it harmless are aware of exactly what it is? So-called "adult" bookstores carry literature dealing with bestiality, child-molestation, and sadomasochistic materials. There is no type of perversion or violence off limits to them. This is the type of material they carry:
>
> Incest—books in which family members copulate with each other and family pets. Homosexuality—photos of nude boys in positions of sexual arousal and stories of children being picked up and forced into homosexual relationships. Child-molestation, incest, sodomy, oral copulation—all with children. One particularly vile example depicts a Girl Scout selling cookies, who is seduced by a grown man into all sorts of perversions. Bestiality—copulation between humans and animals—one example, child molester gets victim and takes her to sex with ape. Sado-Masochistic—torture including whipping, beating, burning women with cigarettes, branding them, forcing them to eat human excrement, sticking pins through various parts of the body, mutilating sexual parts of the body.[1]

2. *"Why don't more churches speak out?"*

Two reasons: (1) Churches don't speak out. Individuals do. (2) And individuals (priests, preachers, nuns, bishops, and lay people) do speak up. But their comments rarely appear in the morning paper or nightly news of the secular press.

More church-goers recognize that God condemns any oppression of people: sexual, financial, or political. Again:

> Thus saith the Lord; For three transgressions of Israel, and for four, I will not turn away the punishment thereof; because they sold the righteous for silver, and the poor for a pair of shoes; that pant after the dust of the earth on the head of the poor, and turn aside the way of the meek: and a man and his father will go in unto the same maid, to profane my holy name. (Amos 2:6, 7)

Individual church members *do* speak up:

WAR IN TORONTO
(Catholic)

In a move that made front-page news in the city's papers and dominated newscasts early last month, Roman Catholic archbishop Philip Pocock of Toronto launched a full-scale attack on pornography. The spiritual head of Canada's largest English-speaking archdiocese called on the 900,000 faithful to boycott all publications, theaters, and businesses that "encourage the pornographic."

He issued his call to arms in advertisements in all three Toronto dailies. They were paid for by the Knights of Columbus. In the ads, Pocock said the prime motivation for the current "amazing proliferation" of pornographic material is financial profit, but the ultimate result is "the destruction of the moral fibre and virtue of our people, especially the young."

Priests in the 200 congregations of the archdiocese were ordered to read the letter at masses and to preach against pornography. Parents were urged to protest the sale of smut at neighborhood stores and ask that "adult" publications, if they must be carried, be kept out of sight.

In an unprecedented display of unanimity, major

Protestant leaders voiced their support and urged their church members to support the anti-obscenity drive.[2]

MM MAN OF THE MONTH
Bishop Floyd L. Begin

Early in May, a full or half-page paid advertisement appeared in all the newspapers—secular and religious—of Oakland, California. The ad was headlined: "An Open Letter of Concern from Bishop Floyd L. Begin."

The Most Reverend Floyd L. Begin is the Roman Catholic Bishop of Oakland. A native of Cleveland, he has been bishop of Oakland since the creation of the diocese in 1962; was a member of the Administrative Tribunal of Vatican Council II; a member of the administrative board for the National Conference of Catholic Bishops; and is vice-president of the California Catholic Conference.

The Bishop publicly expressed his concern about the traffic in pornography, and then sent the same letter to all religious leaders in his area, all media outlets, and all Catholic elementary and high schools and colleges.

In addition to the letter, he had printed hundreds of thousands of cards containing a prayer and pledge of decency, and distributed them widely.

Following is the text of Bishop Begin's open letter: "As a spiritual leader in our community I wish to address an area of increasingly grave concern. It is the rapid growth of the pornographic and nearly pornographic in the society around us.

"There seems to be an almost constant barrage of the immodest and indecent through motion pictures, stage productions, magazines, newspapers, television and even on the streets of our cities. So universal have these things become that too many of us have accepted them almost as a way of life, as an inevitable consequence of modern society. Sensitivities have been dulled, right and informed consciences stilled, and moral objections silenced.

"I feel it not only appropriate, but urgent, to speak out against this amazing proliferation. Its prime motivation seems to be financial profit, but its ultimate result, too often, is the destruction of the moral fiber and virtue of our people. I write this, not out of a sense of prudishness or latter-day puritanism, but with what I trust is sensitivity to what the gift of human sexuality is all about.

"It is through our God-given sexuality that we as human beings can reach out to one another in love. It is in sexual union that a couple can express to one another tenderness, intimacy and permanent fidelity. The public and profitable exploitation of the sexual, so common around us, is a direct betrayal of the basic values of sexuality itself. What is sometimes referred to as the 'playboy philosophy' of sexually using and discarding another person with 'no strings attached' is not a form of freedom but of enslavement. What was intended to be most precious becomes almost trivial. What was created to be most deeply personal is dehumanized.

"Pornography of any kind is gravely wrong and the abuse of the gift of sex remains wrong no matter how common or well publicized it becomes.

"I call on concerned people, and particularly on my fellow Catholics, to refrain from patronizing those publications, theaters and places of business which encourage the pornographic. I ask their support in affirming what is positive and wholesome in the media and opposing publicly what is not. I urge them to pray for decency in the community and the country.

"Finally, I ask citizens everywhere to promote what is wholesome and good in our society and to encourage reverence for humanity and sexuality at all times."

Bishop Begin's public statement elicited tremendous response in the Oakland area. Such statements from religious leaders of all faiths in all areas of the country could generate the vocal community expression needed to solve the problem of pornography.[3]

CARDINAL ATTACKS LAX SEX ATTITUDES

BOSTON (UPI)—The "moral nakedness" of sexual permissiveness has "catapulted our civilization into the dark caverns of hedonistic confusion," according to Cardinal Humberto Medeiros.

Medeiros, the spiritual leader of the archdiocese of Boston's two million Roman Catholics, said in his annual Lenten message published yesterday that modern culture is "seriously lacking in its ability to give a vital, personal and vibrant meaning to sex. The accelerating pace of

200

sex corruption continues under the guise of sexual
freedom," he said.

The cardinal's message, entitled "Growing Together
in Holiness," is the first response he has made to a sexual
ethics document issued earlier this year by the Vatican's
Congregation for the Doctrine of the Faith.[4]

PORNOGRAPHY PROBLEM CAN BE
SOLVED IF CHRISTIANS WILL DO
THEIR PART
(Methodist)
By Betty L. Bundy

In one who has been working for over a year with
increasing success to alert Christians to the perils of
the anything goes attitude of the "new morality," your
editorial in the Sept. 24 issue, "Protest Can Be Counterproductive" aroused mixed emotions.

In part, it was a welcome, if trifle small and very
late comfort. Indeed, Christian action is called for—and
where is it? Do we not as stewards of the Lord's Kingdom
have a responsibility to stand and fight the worst pollution
that man can bring to the world? Compared to this
moral pollution through which we must daily wade and
in which we must raise our children, the fouling of our
waters, our air, and our countryside is insignificant. Yet
Christians rail against the latter and try to ignore the
former. We must be reminded that sin is not only in
acts of commission but just as often in acts of omis-
sion. It is past time for Christians to defend Christian
morality; for if they don't, who will?

I agree that sometimes protest can be counterproductive, but we must be willing to take some risks. At
its worst, it is not nearly as counterproductive as the
inaction and abdication of responsibility inherent in si-
lence which by its very nature implies acceptance. There
is much to be done and it is time for you of the religious
press and the members of the clergy to start doing it.
You must lead from the pages of your papers and from
the pulpits of your churches and show others what they
can do and how. Where are our Christian leaders?

I would call your attention to the example of Bishop
Floyd L. Begin, a Roman Catholic bishop of the Oakland California Diocese. Early in May he purchased half
page and full page ads in all the newspapers, both secular

and religious headlined, "An Open Letter of Concern from Bishop Begin." He then sent the letter to all religious leaders, all media outlets and all Catholic schools in Oakland. (Mrs. Bundy then quotes Bishop Begin's letter.)

Bishop Begin's statement elicited a tremendous response in Oakland. Such statements from religious leaders of all faiths from all areas of our country could generate the vocal community expression needed to solve the problem of pornography. The legal means are available, restored in recent Supreme Court decisions. Pornography is not free speech; it is not protected by the Constitution; it can be silenced. I hope you will do your part to start this important work for the Lord.

(Baptist)

"Pornography is an open sewer flowing through our streets."—Dr. Billy Graham

LDS PRESIDENT DECRIES IMMORALITY
(Salt Lake City, Utah)
(Mormon)

President Spencer W. Kimball, leader of the 3.6 million members of the Church of Jesus Christ of Latter-day Saints admonished followers to avoid temptations of the flesh by adorning an "armor of righteousness." His remarks were heavily weighted with concern about the moral temptations of pornography, abortion, shoplifting, hijacking and general thievery.

He cautioned that billions of dollars are being spent on obscene motion pictures and literature. He urged Latter-day Saints to get involved as citizens to fight obscenity.

"Members of the Church everywhere are urged to not only resist the widespread plague of pornography, but as citizens to become actively and relentlessly engaged in the fight against this insidious enemy of humanity around the world," President Kimball said.

CURRENT RELIGIOUS THOUGHT
(Evangelical and "Liberal" Leaders)

Even "liberal" thinkers are beginning to change views on pornography:

Today there are serious second thoughts upon the subject, reflected especially in a changed editorial thrust in liberal theological journals. As late as April 30, 1975, the *Christian Century* editorialized strongly against any attempt to curb the spread of blatantly obscene literature. The arguments were the usual ones: control implies some form of absolute judgment upon what is "truth" in publication; censorship deprives the public of dimensions of social understanding essential to society; pornography survives only as a result of the opposition to it.

The editor of that journal urged all who favor restrictions upon pornographic literature to cease their efforts and "let such material die of its own shallowness." Fifteen months later the same editor admitted that porno has not died but has extended itself to a point at which some form of limitation is probably desirable (issue of July 7-14, 1976).[5]

ARCHBISHOP TO FIGHT SEX FILM
ON JESUS
(Episcopalian)

LONDON (AP)—The Archbishop of Canterbury said yesterday he will oppose "with every power in my being" plans to make a film in Britain on the sex life of Jesus Christ.

The Most Rev. Dr. Donald Coggan, head of the worldwide Anglican Communion, told reporters England's old law of blasphemy might be invoked to prevent Danish director Jens Joergen Thorsen from showing the film if he could not be prevented from making it.

Dr. Coggan said Thorsen "would have to face the wrath of the majority of the British people" if he tried to show the film.

"If the person of our Lord is very dear to you, you are not going to have it held up to scorn," the archbishop told newsmen at the U.S. Embassy. The news conference was called to discuss his visit later this month to the United States.

Reporters sought Dr. Coggan's views on the film after the leader of British Roman Catholics, Archbishop Basil Hume, denounced the project Wednesday in a letter to the Times of London.

Archbishop Hume said he had learned the film would be "sensational, pornographic and, in terms of truth, entirely speculative."

Dr. Coggan said that anyone with "an atom of New Testament scholarship knows that there is not an atom of evidence for the kind of things that are to be depicted if this film is made."

3. "How do I stop pornography—which I did not order—from being mailed into my home?"

File Post Office Form 2201. This instructs the post office to inform publishers of pornography that your name is *not* to be part of their mailings. If pornographers *then* mail pornography to you, they are prosecuted.

NOTE: You need not wait until they mail pronography to you. You may file 2201 in advance, insuring that no pornography ends up in your mailbox where even children could pick it up.

4. "Pornography will eventually go away. Look what happened in Denmark—it's decreased."

The vigorous circulation of frosty bottles of Coke intensifies people's desire for Coke. It *intensifies* it. The more we see, the more we want. Consider Denmark and its porno problem:

Scandinavian countries, including Denmark—in film, literature, and behavior—are equally famous for suicide rates. The more people are assaulted with sex, the more jaded and gloomy they become. Human beings intuitively sense that sexual gratification is not the goal of life. They crave meaning, purpose, worth, a sense of service and nobility in their lives. When these qualities shrink because of the assault of sex, people despair. Bombardment of sex robs their lives of glimmer and gusto. Hating the resulting pessimism and bleakness, they choose death. *Playboy's* first "playgirl," Marilyn Monroe, later earning $10,000 a week in Hollywood exploitation of sex, committed suicide.

Yes, pornography is dying out in Copenhagen. And, according to the October 27 AP report, here are the reasons: (1) Other countries, notably the United States and France, push kinkier sex than Denmark's. You don't have to buy something rotten in Denmark anymore. You can buy it right here in River City. People buy less Denmark porno because they can get worse at home. (2) Porno and its spin-offs became so severe that the Denmark police cracked down. With a crackdown, sales dropped. The AP news report said:

> The most important factor [in the Denmark decline] according to Police Inspector Brun Rasmussen, head of Copenhagen police's 10-man squad, was the decision more than a year ago to close down the shows in which sexual acts were performed before an audience.

5. *"Sex crimes decreased in Denmark with rise of porno."*

They did not. They simply were not reported. As porno rose, police simply ignored sex crimes and eventually some sex crimes (e.g., exhibitionism) were taken off the books.

The same number (or greater?) of sex crimes are committed, but in print it appears less, simply because they're not reported.

6. *"Does pornography have therapeutic value? Doesn't it have a catharsis effect?"*

You don't cure an alcoholic with alcohol, or drug addict with drugs, or a gambler with chips. Feed lust or greed, and the appetite increases, demanding more and more. The more we see, the more we want.

Pornography is an insatiable cancer: it stalks and devours, ever increasing its appetite. Like heroin, the more one ingests it, the more one lusts for it. And with greater indulgence, greater appetite increases. And with greater appetite comes greater lust, provoking, in turn, greater indulgence and, again, a greater appetite. It is like unleashed sex entrapping a pitiable teenage boy. He starts with parking. He's got to have more. French-kissing follows. Fire fills him. He's got to have more. Petting follows, and feeds the fire. He's got to have more. Genital fondling follows. He "needs" her body. He groans and craves and demands it—like a fix. "Give me your body, baby," he says, "because I love you." King Lust kills when allowed to reign.

7. *"If pornography is that bad, why the increasing popularity of it?"*

It depends what you mean by "popularity." Heroin has become increasingly popular over the last ten years. And so has the Living Bible. The *reason* behind the "popularity" counts.

It has never been difficult to circulate a product pandering to people's greed, lust, or vanity. We are weak creatures.

Many turn to pornography simply because they do not know the robust sex available to them in marriage. It has always been "popular" to give in to lust rather than work hard at building a lifetime of love in marriage. Many of us cave in.

W. C. Fields was right: No one ever went broke underestimating the taste of the American public.

8. *"I can't get involved in fighting pornography. My family needs me and I can't afford to be financially or physically hurt."*

This is a healthy statement, showing that the questioner is nervous about routing porno. He's probably witnessed that his complaints to managers, legal complaints to police, his picketing, boycotting, etc., have caused porno to melt from the shelves. "They're not going to take this lying down. They're going to retaliate." He's getting worried.

When—in 1973—these thoughts hit me, I didn't get worried. I got scared. My heart banged out blood faster than a jackhammer, bambambam—bambambam—bambambaming into a sidewalk slab. The palms of my hands burst into cold, wet sheets. I received veiled threats and obscene calls. I panicked. I planned to pack just whatever we (wife and two children) could carry and slide out of town after midnight.

I prayed, and three things became clear to me:

If thugs really came after citizens who routed pornography, then there ought to be *at least* three persons dead or horribly injured: Charles H. Keating, Jr., attorney, businessman and founding president of Citizens

206

for Decency Through Law; Morton Hill, Jesuit scholar, founder of *Morality in Media*; and Harold Doran, Pawtucket, Rhode Island, electrician and father of the Display Law, the nation's strongest anti-smut law.

I also remembered what John Quinlan III, assistant criminal prosecutor, San Antonio, told me about porno and organized crime. He said that the organized crime-porno-peddlers "hit" only *other* organized crime-porno peddlers.

If they ever "hit" the average decent citizen, community rage and police bloodhounds rushed in. And that the porno gangsters didn't want. For three reasons: First, they don't want to get caught.

Second, they want to preserve the image that pornographers are, after all, respectable businessmen who —with wife and children to support—simply chose to earn their livelihoods by servicing the public with adult bookstores and theaters. A gangland "hit" on a respectable citizen would shatter that public-image lie.

Third, they want to hide from the public the connection between pornography and organized crime. A porno-gangster "hitting" another porno-gangster makes one of the pages in the city where the slugging occurred. But a porno-gangster's bombing of a decency-spokesman blows the cat out of the bag. *That* story (no matter where it happens) hits the front pages of the New York and London Times tomorrow.

It further became clear to me that I could not face my children if I split. Fifteen years hence—when bestiality was on TV—and my son or daughter said, "Daddy, how did that sick stuff get so bad; how come people didn't stop it long ago?" I could not have looked at his or her eyes.

9. *"Pornography is boring. Let it die."*
Drugs are boring too. You take the first dose of heroin. And that dose gets boring—so boring you demand more.

10. *"Do anti-porno campaigns generate the kind of*

*puritanical thinking that is embarrassed by human sex-
uality and by sex in the Bible, etc.?"*

In my workshops, tracing the rise of pornography
and teaching civic and legal tools to curb it, I sometimes begin by saying, "Hi, I'm Neil Gallagher and
I enjoy sex." If she's with me, I have my trim, Texas
wife, Gail, stand up, Breck-blonde hair spilling over
her shoulders, and say, "And this is my wife, Gail."
(I used to say, "And this is my lover, Gail," but she
blushed so I stopped it.)

Quite often I say (and this really slams the brains
of secular audiences, thinking that Christian living is
anti-sex): "Hey, I wanna give you a little quiz. Here
it is: Where's this piece of sex-wisdom given? 'The
body of the husband belongs to the wife and the body
of the wife belongs to the husband.'"

I tell them that's the sexiest, clearest marriage advice ever given. "And where's it found?" And they
guess: Masters and Johnson? Freud? David Reuben?
Nope. It's in the Bible. Huh? Yup, 1 Corinthians 7:4.
Look it up. (Most of them don't carry around Bibles
so I whip out mine and look it up for them and read
it right then, so they know I'm not kidding.)

Dr. Bill Banowsky, president of Pepperdine University, pointed out that the puritanical view (sex is
hush) is as unbiblical as the *Playboy* view (sex is
heaven). The reason many Christians and others don't
enjoy the Bible's robust, passionate view of sexual
freedom in marriage is boringly simple: They don't
read the New Testament. Thus, they don't know the
lordship of Jesus over their entire lives.

I'm guessing that some Christian men have not been
claiming the lordship of Jesus over their sexual lives.
David Reuben has sold over 16 million books to orgasm-
starved, married women, some of whom have Christian husbands who have not helped their wives enjoy
their sexual potential. Fellows, 1 Corinthians 7:4 says
that your body is for her pleasure, and vice-versa. If
all American husbands and wives gave to each other
the seductive tenderness and robust sex God intended,
there'd be very little market for porno.

Appendix 1

DEFINITIONS

Bestiality—(1) The condition or status of a lower animal.
(2) Display or gratification of bestial traits or impulses.
(3) Sexual relations between a human being and a lower animal.

Cunnilingus—One who licks the vulva; act of licking; oral stimulation of the vulva or clitoris.

Fellatio—Oral stimulation of the penis.

Homosexuality—Of, relating to, or exhibiting sexual desire toward a member of one's own sex.

Lesbian—A female homosexual.

Masochism—Abnormal sexual passion characterized by pleasure in being abused by one's associate; any pleasure in being abused or dominated.

Masturbation—Stimulation of the genital organs or orgasm achieved by manual or other bodily contact exclusive of sexual intercourse.

Necrophilia—An erotic attraction to corpses.

Pederastry—Unnatural sexual relations between two males, especially when one is a young boy.

Pedophilia—Sexual desire in an adult for a child.

Pimp—Procurer, panderer of prostitutes.

Prostitution—(1) The act or practice of indulging in promiscuous sexual relations, especially for money.
(2) The state of being prostituted: debasement.

Sadism—(1) The infliction of pain (as upon a love object) as a means of obtaining sexual release.
(2) Delight in cruelty; excessive cruelty.

Sadomasochism—The derivation of pleasure from the infliction of physical or mental pain either on others or on oneself.

Sodomy—Carnal copulation with a member of the same sex or with an animal; noncoital carnal copulation with a member of the opposite sex.

Appendix 2

CIVIC ACTION MATERIALS

Organize, organize, organize. Get supporters of decency together. Nail down commitments. Organize a work force, identifying who will do what.

Here's a portion of a mailing list from a decency group in one city. When letters, phone calls, and lots of leg work were needed, we knew whom to call.

SAMPLE MAILING LIST

Numbers indicate volunteer is willing:
- 1—to serve on telephone committee
- 2—to help prepare newsletter
- 3—to help distribute newsletter
- 4—to write to officials

Name, Address, Occupation	1	2	3	4
Alvarez, Mrs. Danna 104 W. Layndale Ave. (672-1383) Housewife				X
Anderson, Jim 3401 Marion (318-1382) Technician			X	X
Arnold, Jeff 608 N. Pine (275-4235) Evangelist		X	X	X
Arnold, W. C. 506 W. Loring Ave. (261-2746) Brick Mason	X	X	X	X
Azle, Lila (Mrs. Garland) 2102 Sam Houston (679-1042) Home Housewife	X	X	X	X
Boepple, John, Jr. 203 Baker Rd. (678-1752) Alcoa	X	X	X	X
Boepple, Mrs. John 203 Baker Rd. (678-1752) Housewife	X	X	X	X
Bourland, Bob Box 6032 (873-8926) Pastor	X	X	X	X
Brock, Keith 4406 E. Dan Wilson (348-1927) Business		X	X	X

(348-3132) Home
Sales
Brooks, Jesse E.   X X X X
    104 Landby St. (273-3549)
    Welder
Bryan, W. H.   X X X
    Rt. 1, Box 22-A (671-1624)
    Security Guard
Bunting, T. C.   X X X X
    3302 Bon Aire Rd. (278-3655) Business
    (275-2144) Home
    Accountant
Burton, Harvey   X X X X
    2002 Rosewood Dr. (672-3131)
    Student
Burton, Jim   X
    Same
    Dupont
Burton, Mrs. Jim   X X X X
    Same
    Housewife
Etc.
Etc.

SAMPLE LETTER SENT TO RETAILERS

Dear Sir:

We have discovered that many dealers here do not really know the kind of material that jobbers leave in their stores.

We have checked every store. You sell either one or several of the publications on the enclosed sheet. These magazines depict *at least* fully nude (frontal views) men and/or women. Many are worse: sodomy, fellatio, intercourse, sexual torture and more were in publications we collected.

We have further discovered that many dealers do not realize that obscene publications

    (1) invite organized crime into a city. (90% of smut is linked to Mafia)

    (2) lead to sexual distortions in adults and children, plus

    (3) lead to sex crimes (Davis-Brauch report) (Langford's report).

We know that the enclosed publications bring a high margin of profit. That's why these publications invariably invite participation by syndicated crime.

We also know of an increasing number of spiritual retailers who have decided that the moral and civic gains in *not* selling these publications outweighs the financial. (Some retailers, incidentally, have had *increased* patronage since they've taken the smut off their shelves.)

Not only the average citizen recognizes the danger of smut, but high-court officials do. That's why smut is illegal (June 21st Supreme Court Decision, Penal Code 43-23, City Code 14-24).

Would you be so kind as to carefully look through your publications and entirely remove those on the enclosed list? When you have finished, could you please call us or write us? In our next newsletter and next mass meeting, we want to publicly commend you and urge the community to patronize you as they are currently doing with retailers who have cleaned their shelves.

Cordially,
Neil Gallagher, Chairman
Citizens for Decency

SAMPLE LIST OF PUBLICATIONS ON OPEN SHELVES

Magazines

1. Adam
2. Adam Film World
3. All Man
4. Bachelor
5. Best For Men
6. Cabaret
7. Cavalier
8. Daring Special
9. Escapade
10. Fling
11. Follies
12. Gala
13. Gallery
14. Gem
15. Genesis
16. Jaguar
17. Knight
18. Male
19. Man's Pleasure
20. Man To Man
21. Men's Digest
22. Modern Man Deluxe
23. Mr.
24. Night and Day
25. Oui
26. Penthouse
27. Playboy
28. Playboy Holiday Album
29. Playgirl
30. Rascal
31. Rogue
32. Rogue Inter Annual
33. Sir
34. Swank
35. Tab
36. The Swinger
37. Tiger
38. Venus
39. Viva
40. Vue
41. Wildcat

Newspapers

1. National Informer Reader
2. Rampage

(Not all stores who carry objectionable material carry all the above-mentioned material, but they carry at least one —in some cases as many as 25—of the above magazines.)

Dump Ground

SAMPLE DIRECT-MAIL FLYER

It's all here—in your local drive-in grocery store, department store, drugstore, and theater—available to *children* and *adults* alike.

The Facts

1. More pornography, more rapes, and other sex crimes.
2. Pornography destroys a teenager's normal sexual maturing.

3. Pornography fills its readers with insatiable and distorted sexual fantasies.

What Can You Do?

1. Encourage local officials to enforce existing obscenity laws.
2. Talk to local dealers about their books and films.
3. STOP trading with ANY business (store or theater) peddling pornography.
4. Pray, pray, pray that our city will be rid of the smut on the screens and the magazine racks.
5. Attend the next meeting of Citizens for Decency, Thursday, January 17, at the First Baptist Church in Victoria, Texas.
6. We are publicizing heavily to drive smut from our city. Please send donations to: (local address)

YOU ARE WHAT YOU READ!

Bombardment

SAMPLE DIRECT-MAIL FLYER

1. And the shells are being shot from *within*. Pornography dealers, reluctant to let any of their $3 *billion* industry diminish, wreak havoc on America's moral fiber while they reap their fantastic financial profits.
2. When will America wake up? We have taken sex out of the rapturous, romantic marriage-bedroom and plastered it in garish, ugly detail on movie screens and slick magazines.
3. America: Is it now home of free sex and land of bestiality? Or do we still want it land of the free and home of the brave?
4. Let's join national, state, and city officials in enforcing the laws which flatly state that obscenity is illegal (June 21st Supreme Court Decision, Penal Code 43-23; City Code 14-24).
5. We don't want heroin-selling on shelves, over the counter, under the counter, or *on the roof*—to children or adults. Neither do we want pornography-selling. We want America clean and strong and true.

"YOU ARE WHAT YOU READ"

SAMPLE DISPLAY LAW DECISION
State of Rhode Island and Providence Plantations

PROVIDENCE, Sc.   SUPERIOR COURT
Filed July 13, 1972, Louis A. Carlone, Clerk

STATE OF RHODE ISLAND
vs.   IND. NO. 72-269
NORMAND JOSEPH CARDIN

STATE OF RHODE ISLAND
vs.   IND. NO. 72-281
JOSEPH MARKOVITZ

Decision

MACKENZIE, J. This matter is before the Court on the defendant's Motion to Quash the Indictment. Indictment No. 72-269 charges Normand Joseph Cardin with a violation of *11-31-10* of the *General Laws of Rhode Island, 1956,* as amended, which concerns the sale or exhibition to minors of indecent publications, pictures or articles. Indictment No. 72-281 charges Joseph Markovitz with a violation of the said

11-31-10. The alleged violations of *11-31-10* took place on September 28, 1971, at the Fairlawn Spa, 757 Mineral Spring Avenue, Pawtucket, Rhode Island. The Attorney General and both defendants have stipulated that the only evidence in this case is a publication entitled *Modern Man DeLuxe Quarterly,* Winter, 1972, Vol. 69 (110).

Both the motions in this matter are similar in content. They read:

> Now comes the Defendant in the above entitled matter and moves that the indictment be quashed and for reason therefore states that said indictment is vague and uncertain and therefore unconstitutional, and further, that said indictment subjects said defendant to jeopardy for the commission of a felony when in fact the allegations contained within the framework of said indictment is (sic) not within the definitions set up by *Roth v. U.S.,* 354 U.S. 476, 77 S. Ct. 1304 (1957), and therefore is in conflict with the first amendment of the United States Constitution. The allegations contained in the indictment refer to a violation of Title 11, Chapter 31, section 10, of the General Laws of Rhode Island, 1956, as amended, and the language of this statute is vague, indefinite and the definitions contained therein are not within the meaning of obscenity as set forth by the Rhode Island Supreme Court in the case of *In Re Seven Magazines,* 268 A2 707, and therefore, said statute is unconstitutional and said indictment should be quashed and dismissed.

Initially, it is to be remembered that a statute is presumed to be constitutional and when the constitutionality of a statute is questioned, " ... every reasonable intendment will be resolved in favor of its validity unless and until the party raising the constitutional question proves beyond a reasonable doubt that the statute is invalid."

State v. Domanski,
57 R.I. 500, 190 A. 857
State v. Raposa,
_____R.I._____, 271 A.2d 306, 307, 308 (1970)

The defendants contend that the statute is vague and indefinite. The vague and indefinite argument, so-called, concerns itself with the due process clause of the Fifth Amendment as applied to the states through the Fourteenth Amendment of the United States Constitution. Basically, the "vague and indefinite" argument stands for the proposition that a statute which imposes a criminal penalty must sufficiently define the prohibited conduct so that a man of common understanding does not have to guess at its meaning.

Coates v. City of Cincinnati,
402 U.S. 611, 91 S. Ct 1086 (1971)
State v. Jamgochian,
____R.I.____, 279 A.2d 923 (1971)

This Court is more than satisfied that the statute in question is sufficiently definite to withstand constitutional challenge on grounds of vagueness.

The Court now turns to the content of the statute itself. It seems to the Court that the content of this statute is the end product of legislation enacted in accordance with the holdings in *Roth* v. *U.S.,* 354 U.S. 467 (1957), and *Ginsberg* v. *New York,* 390 U.S. 629 (1967). There does not seem to be anything in this statute which conflicts with the decisions of the United States Supreme Court or the Rhode Island Supreme Court.

In Re Seven Magazines,
____R.I.____, 268 A.2d 702 (1970)

It is to be remembered that *11-31-10* is concerned with the distribution of indecent publications to minors. The instant case appears to be governed by *Ginsberg* v. *New York,* 390 U.S. 629 (1968). In that case, the defendant and his wife operated "Sam's Stationery and Luncheonette." Appellant was prosecuted under two informations, each in two courts, which charged that he personally sold a 16-year-old boy two "girlie" magazines on each of two dates in October 1965, in violation of 484-h of the New York Penal Law. The constitutionality of the New York law was challenged.

This case presents the question of the constitutionality on its face of a New York criminal obscenity statute which prohibits the sale to minors under 17 years of age of material defined to be obscene on the basis of its appeal to them whether or not it would be obscene to adults.

Ginsberg v. New York, supra, 631

The United States Supreme Court upheld the constitutionality of the statute and, in doing so, enunciated holdings apropos to the instant case. First, the court held that the "girlie" picture magazines involved in the sale were not obscene for adults.

Ginsberg v. New York, supra, 634

Next, the court said:

We do not regard New York's regulation in defining obscenity on the basis of its appeal to minors under 17 as involving an invasion of such minors' constitutionally protected freedoms. Rather 484-h simply adjusts the definition of obscenity "to social realities by permitting the appeal of this type of material to be assessed in terms of the sexual interests . . . " of such minors. *Mishkin v. New York,* 383 U.W. 502, 509; *Bookcase, Inc. v. Broderick, supra,* at 75, 218 N.E. 2d, at 671. That the state has power to make that adjustment seems clear, for we have recognized that even where there is an invasion of protected freedoms "the power of the state to control the conduct of children reaches beyond the scope of its authority over adults . . .". *Prince v. Massachusetts,* 321 U.S. 158, 170.

Ginsberg v. New York, supra, 638

Finally, the United States Supreme Court spoke of the standards contained in 484-h. In upholding the standards, the court said:

The state also has an independent interest in the well-being of its youth . . . Judge Fuld, now Chief Judge Fuld, also emphasized its significance in the earlier case of *People v. Kahan,* 15 N.Y. 2d 311, 206 N.E. 2d 333, which had struck down the first version of 484-h on grounds of vagueness. In his concurring opinion, id., at 312, 206 N.E.2d at 334, he said:

"While the supervision of children's reading may best be left to their parents, the knowledge that parental control or guidance cannot always be provided and society's transcendent interest in protecting the welfare of children justify reasonable regulation of the sale of material to them. It is, therefore, altogether fitting and proper for a state to include in a statute designed to regulate the sale of pornography to children special standards, broader than those embodied in legislation aimed at controlling dissemination of such material to adults."

Ginsberg v. New York, supra, 640

Turning to the instant case, this Court is satisfied that *11-31-10* sufficiently defines the prohibited conduct. Furthermore, in the light of *Ginsberg* v. *New York,* 390 U.S. 629 (1968), this Court is satisfied that *11-31-10* does not violate the First Amendment of the United States Constitution. For these reasons, the Motion to Quash, in each case, is denied.

The defendant's exception to the Court's ruling is noted in each case.

Appendix 3

CENSORSHIP IN COMMUNICATION

Appendix 3, Section A

Citizens for Decency Through Law

OPEN LETTER

November 26, 1975

Mr. Richard E. Wiley, Chairman
Federal Communications Commission
1919 M Street, N.W.
Washington, D. C. 20554

Dear Mr. Wiley:

I am again registering a formal *Fairness Doctrine* complaint with the Federal Communications Commission against several network talk shows, documentaries and public affairs programs, and all of the major nationally syndicated variety-talk shows—i.e., The Mike Douglas Show, The Dinah Shore Show, The David Susskind Show and Barbara Walters' Not for Women Only.

As the National Spokesman of our nation's largest anti-pornography organization, Citizens for Decency Through Law, I have tried unsuccessfully over a two-year period to beg, reason or cajole an appearance on all or even one of these influential forums to respond to attacks against decency, Judeo-Christian ethics, the U.S. Supreme Court anti-pornography decisions of June, 1973, and June, 1974, and unfair criticism of my organization and/or its founder, Charles H. Keating, Jr. Keating, a member of the Presidential Commission on Obscenity and Pornography, has never been afforded an opportunity on TV, other than five minutes on the Today Show, to expose that Committee's disgraceful squandering of public funds and, even worse, the deceitful suppression of its own research. I emphasize that my requests for appearances were in *all* cases not merely attempts for anti-pornography advocacy (a perfectly reasonable desire since prosecution of pornography is a controversial social issue of intense public interest), but rather attempts to answer *direct* attacks on CDL or Keating *by name*, or direct attacks also by name on Chief Justice Warren Burger and the four other Supreme Court Justices who had made up the majority on the above-mentioned decisions against pornography. In other cases, I requested that I or some other spokesperson for traditional decency be allowed to counter discussions denigrating Mosaic Law, marital fidelity, virginity, modesty, etc. In two cases, Fr. Morton Hill, S.J., founder of Morality in Media, Inc., wrote to network owned and operated stations in New York City to ask that I be allowed to respond to vulgar remarks about him by Gore Vidal on several national talk shows. At that time, almost a year ago, Fr. Hill was recovering from a broken arm and could not appear himself. To my knowledge, he did not receive the courtesy of a reply, nor did I.

These rebuffs by national shows are in sharp contrast to the local news/talk/public affairs presentations across the country. On the local level, in every state, in virtually every ADI market, our requests for Fairness Doctrine courtesy have been met instantly with both fairness and courtesy. Even where station management or the production staff of a show is biased toward the viewpoint of a recently presented prostitute, homosexual, lesbian, sex clinician, pornographer or porno-attorney, that station welcomes the opportunity to hear our side because (1) they know it's good programming; and (2) they seem to feel that our position on decency (sometimes they call it "the old-fashioned moralist viewpoint") is the majority audience position and airing both sides holds down a whiplash of citizen complaints to station and sponsors. But with the national shows, there is an arrogant and total disregard of the Fairness Doctrine, or a blasé "Don't call us, we'll call you" brushoff. No attempt to balance whatsoever, other than the infrequent appearances of Pat Boone, an outstanding advocate of family life and Christian ethics, who always holds his own against three or four guests smirking about his "squareness" and milk-addiction.

Mr. Wiley, I watched with fascination your recent appearance on Bill Buckley's "Firing Line." You gave the impression that you believe the Fairness Doctrine is generally respected by the major talk shows. This shocked me, because I respect your scholarship and completely support your helmsmanship of the FCC, I can only assume you are not a regular viewer of the shows in question.

Since I will be making this complaint public and will be sending carbon copies to the other FCC commissioners and to all of the networks herein mentioned, let me briefly discuss for the edification of media executives and their producers some broadcasting guidelines that you and your commissioners obviously know inside out and backwards.

In the 1934 Communications Act, your authority was restrained by the words, "Nothing in this Act shall be understood or construed to give the Commission the power of censorship ... and no regulation or condition shall be promulgated or fixed by the Commission which shall interfere with the right of free speech. ... " Great. Great for the networks, but what about their interference with my right of free speech, CDL's right of access to a limited marketplace, the marketplace of ideas that establishes the agenda of discourse for the nation? To paraphrase the famous vague line from that same 1934 Communications Act, how are the networks "serving" "the public interest" in moral decay (maybe *terminal* moral decay); the "convenience" of reaching millions of U.S. citizens with a positive message of communities defending themselves against moral pollution with laws backed up by the U.S. Supreme Court; and lastly, the "necessity" of an informed public having all the facts and viewpoints available about social cancers that may bring about the destruction of Western civilization?

Fairness should be the hallmark of national broadcasting and it simply is not. This is particularly so in news/documentaries/public affairs/talk programs, where the absolute obligation to give viewers accuracy, honesty and BALANCE cannot be overemphasized. If the obligations of the networks are great, so are their profits.

In 1949, the FCC announced its Fairness Doctrine. The language was and *is still* as clear as is humanly possible:

> When a broadcast station (or network) presents one side of a controversial issue of public importance, reasonable opportunity must be afforded for contrasting views."

Beautifully put. But let's analyze what's happening with discussions involving decency. Is pornography and all the related problems of moral decay "a controversial issue of public importance"? Absolutely! Just ask your friends. Walk along Times Square in New York, the once Great White Way turned into instant human sewer. Walk down Hollywood Boulevard in California, the once walkway of the stars turned into a human zoo of sleazy massage/masturbation parlors, cruising pimps, perverts and prostitutes, with sidewalk-racks selling sick tabloids that glorify weird people obsessed with urine, excrement and the molestation or torture of children.

Are "reasonable opportunities being afforded for *contrast-*

ing views" on national TV shows? Absolutely not!

The end result is that, where television discussion and debate could help citizens arrive at solutions to eliminate or at least alleviate a social evil, "television talk" instead becomes part of the problem.

Mr. Wiley, think of how angry the citizenry of this country would become if people were aware of the extensive domination of pornography distribution by the Mafia. But this nexus between organized crime and the pornographic corruption of the marketplace has never to my knowledge been discussed on the tube at any time from Cronkite to Carson. Nor have the networks covered the tragic UPI and AP stories about "snuff" films, the underground 8mm movies of actual sadistic sex-murders, "snuffing" out the lives of pornography performers by slitting their throats during the climactic moment in orgy scenes. A news editor at a network owned and operated radio station in Los Angeles told me he didn't use the UPI story—suppressed it—because he personally didn't believe it. *He* didn't believe it! Now that's censorship.

The following are just *a few* examples of how CDL's requests for fairness have been stalled, rebuffed or ignored by national shows. This has involved incessant hours of letter writing, many fruitless trips to New York City, and countless expensive long distance telephone calls. The networks are constantly *"upping the ante"* on vulgarity, violence and suggestive dialogue, so I'll begin with them in alphabetical order.

1. ABC: One hour "Special" on Hefner/Playboy

A few weeks ago, ABC presented at 9:00 PDT a shallow, so-called documentary on the Playboy world of the "Sultan of Soft Core," Hugh M. Heffner. I suppose the justification for running in prime time this hour-long glorification of a "peddler of skin magazines" (*Time* magazine's description of Hefner) is that "he is there." Well, then, ABC should have analyzed fairly what Hefner's *legal fund* has done to public morality for years by backing hard-core pornographers. In *fairness*, ABC should have given *both sides*, and truly analyzed the "new morality." Why puff up with lies an advocate of hedonism whose fortunes are fading fast? Ironically, Hefner is in financial trouble because more graphic and depraved skin magazines are tearing up his pathetic market. Witness *Playboy* magazine's panic-reaction. The October cover displayed for the first time two lesbians. Then, the all-time *Playboy* low, the November cover! It displays a frontal picture of a young girl, legs wide apart, as she masturbates while watching one of the latest "R" or "X" or "XXX" rated films which are graphically reviewed inside.

CDL REQUEST FOR FAIRNESS
DOCTRINE BALANCE

Our request was rejected. An ABC network producer actually told me the Hefner puff-piece was "hard news"!

2. ABC: Pornography Performer on "Goodnight America"
On one of the recent segments of this youth-targeted, talk-variety show, the host, Geraldo Rivera—with much smirking and feigned awkwardness—presented to his giggling audience a so-called "porno-queen," Marilyn Chambers. This term, porno-queen, is, of course, a euphemism for exhibitionist-prostitute. These people, as in prostitution, take money for sex acts, but, unlike most whores, they perform their acts in front of cameras in public with multiple partners.

CDL has available an audio-tape of this program in order to document our claim for balance.

CDL REQUEST FOR FAIRNESS
DOCTRINE BALANCE

Here is a sample of the way we were brushed off. A producer said, "I admit Marilyn Chambers is controversial. We do want your viewpoint. Definitely. We got several complaints. Our host is quite liberal on victimless crimes. But, the show is through taping for a while. We'll get back to you." We, at CDL, won't hold our breath.

3. ABC: Pornography-Performer on KABC Radio, Los Angeles
Linda Lovelace, another notorious film-prostitute, i.e., porno-queen, joined an inane talk-program host in the early evening hours to discuss, among other immoral subjects, breathing methods for some of her sex acts. One youth who phoned in stated she was 15 years old, and the first phone-in after Lovelace left the studio was an awed 10-year-old child. Outrageous! The inept host handled it all with the poor taste expected of a program that would invite as a guest the tragic "star" of the infamous hard-core stag film, "Deep Throat." I know radio has experienced a problem with the "drooling Bill Balance school" of dirty innuendo, but this was reprehensible.

CDL REQUEST FOR FAIRNESS
DOCTRINE BALANCE

KABC Radio's response was: "No. Our programming is already balanced. We have a conservative host who takes opposing views." He was on from midnight to 5 a.m. What a farce. There is only a fraction of audience left at midnight. A demographic rip-off! We appreciated the prior FCC commissioner blocking the plunge into filthy talk radio with his succinct warning, "Some of you guys on the way to the bank have crawled through the gutter." This simple statement, combined with the fining of an Oak Park, Illinois, radio station, accomplished wonders. You see, Mr. Wiley, we need you. Linda Lovelace's appearance on KABC-AM is just one example of a vicious abuse of the public airways that was never balanced.

4. ABC: Gore Vidal on "The Dick Cavett Show"
Gore Vidal, although sometimes a very gifted writer, is a vitriolic, admitted bi-sexual (more often than not homosexuals claim to be "bi" for cosmetic reasons, to appear "butch" as they say, when in truth the mere touch of a woman makes them "f'wo up"). Suffice it to say, Vidal snidely demeaned everyone who attempts to defend traditional morality. He attacked the Supreme Court, all five anti-pornography Supreme Court Justices by name; priests; ministers; Billy Graham; President Ford; CDL; its founder, Charles Keating; etc. Vidal's interchanging of the justices' names as synonyms for sex organs and acts of sexual perversion is a constant vulgar "routine" in all of his frequent television and radio appearances.

CDL REQUEST FOR FAIRNESS
DOCTRINE BALANCE

Stalling. Stalling. Finally, an ABC executive told me, "Sorry, Cavett's show is going off the air. Call CBS." Musical chairs but no fairness.

5. ABC: Masters and Johnson on "A.M. America"
For ten hours last September (7 to 9 a.m., Monday through Friday), Masters and Johnson, the husband-wife "sexologist" team from St. Louis, co-hosted the ABC network show, "A.M. America." Although ABC may think that this sex clinic team is now "mainstream," many Americans still consider them

224

bizarre and anti-Christian. Their modus operandi of photographing the insides of female genitalia with weird, glass penis-cameras, while these devices are used to masturbate the "patients" is—well, many people still think that's morally *sick*. The same for the "training" (i.e., "correcting male dysfunction") of their male patients (why only male?) with prostitutes (they call them "surrogate partners"). These so-called "sex clinicians" said on A.M. America that "95 percent of the proliferating sex clinics around the country are rip-offs." 95 percent! Interesting opinion. Well, CDL agrees but also thinks Masters and Johnson are a moral rip-off—and irreligious. And we have a right to express our opinions on the public airways in counterbalance, at least for ten minutes versus ten hours.

CDL REQUEST FOR FAIRNESS
DOCTRINE BALANCE

So far, nothing. Several letters and personal phone calls to ABC executives have yielded only one letter flatly denying a fairness obligation. The letter stated that Masters and Johnson "are no longer controversial." One executive on the phone said Bob Dornan sounded like "an articulate and reasonable person." That's nice. *But* still no guesting for even *five* minutes to balance TEN HOURS! Meanwhile, this show has had a complete change of personnel and has been retitled, "Good Morning, America."

6. *CBS: The Norman Lear Prime Time Situation Comedies—"Maude," "All in the Family," etc.*
I know. I know. How do you apply the Fairness Doctrine to scripted fiction shows? Witness the flap over the arrogant CBS re-run of the pro-abortion "Maude" program. Well, I guess you just don't get fairness in this category. So, with the situation comedies, Lear wins and Judeo-Christian ethics lose. Lear claims to have more influence on mass audience thinking than anyone since Christ. But he is not satisfied to let his nest of writers propagate their philosophy and political editorial comment through his shows. Now, he's using the stature gained from his national programs to become a prime guest on the TV talk show circuit. What chance will CDL have to rebutt him? The beat goes on—but no fairness.

7. *CBS: Henry Miller and Erika Jong on "Sixty Minutes"*
Many citizens from around the country wrote to CDL and

asked if we could respond to these two advocates of soft-core pornography. "Sixty Minutes" is one of the finest shows on the air, so we wrote to CBS Headquarters in New York with some optimism.

CDL REQUEST FOR FAIRNESS
DOCTRINE BALANCE

No written response from CBS whatsoever. Ever try to get Mike Wallace on the telephone? Forget it.

8. NBC: Gore Vidal (and similar Hedonists ad nauseum) on "The Tonight Show"
Same as above with "The Dick Cavett Show." Vidal spewing venom hither and yon, while Carson shifts from brilliant wit—which he is—to naughty schoolboy, his most annoying affectation, as he eggs Vidal on with loaded questions. What a waste of God-given talent. Carson's *and* Vidal's.

CDL REQUEST FOR FAIRNESS
DOCTRINE BALANCE *AND* OUR RIGHT
TO ANSWER DIRECT
PERSONAL ATTACK

This rebuff is a CLASSIC! Because CDL has an office in Los Angeles and because CDL's National Spokesman lives there, we tried phoning "The Tonight Show" staff in Burbank. With my own TV talk show, broadcast for years in Southern California, "The Robert K. Dornan Show," all that was necessary for someone to request an appearance to answer an attack was to phone us. Actually, with my show, *we called* the person or group discussed and always *offered* them the opportunity to defend themselves. Besides a sense of fairplay, we were *required to* by The Fairness Doctrine! Right? But not Johnny Carson! And CDL intends to keep pressing for an answer to the simple inquiry, "*Why not?*"

So, we phoned. We received no return calls. So, we wrote. We got one reply from "The Tonight Show" producer, Fred de Cordova. From personal experience, I know Mr. de Cordova is a fine gentleman who believes himself to be a fair person, but his answer to our fairness request was a ridiculous and classic, improper rejection. "The Tonight Show" producer penned the following amazing lines showing an abysmal ignorance of the Fairness Doctrine, and a total rejection of plain common sense.

(1) "If we ever decide to present 'the other side' (to Gore Vidal), you (Bob Dornan) are on the top of our list.

(2) "We are well aware of your ability, Mr. Dornan. You are an articulate advocate of your viewpoint.

(3) "But *Johnny Carson* did not attack anybody. *Mr. Vidal* did. So, we feel no obligation for Fairness Doctrine application."

Analyze those statements from one of the nicest, one of the best of the TV producers. Sad!

Statement No. 1: It acknowledges *there is* "another side." (The emphasis quotes were theirs.) They have merely decided not to present it. Censorship?

Statement No. 2: Thanks for the compliment, Mr. de Cordova, *but* I thought the national talk shows were always hard up for *new* "articulate" voices. I can still picture Dick Cavvett and David Susskind musing on the latter's show last year about the derth of "conservative" advocates. "Only two, really," little Dickie sighed, "Bill Buckley and Bill Rusher!" Bull.

Statement No. 3: Get these words. *"Johnny Carson* did not attack. . . . " I see, you can have an anti-semite bigot on every night of the week, or a Ku Klux Klan kook sneering about lynching Negras for a whole month of shows, and as long as *Johnny doesn't join in,* then the Anti-Defamation League or the NAACP can wait until NBC "decides to present *the other side!"* This is very wrong. *Besides, Carson did not sit idlely by. He egged Vidal on and joined in with inaccruate criticism of the U.S. Supreme Court.*

CDL has it all on tape. Carson quote: "The Supreme Court said a local community could ban anything." Wrong. The Court never said that. Carson quote: "The Court never has defined pornography." Wrong. Misleading. Unfair statement. (Ref: the eight 1973 decisions, Miller, et al.)

Since the June, 1973, decisions, Carson has repeated these false statements with other guests—Shelly Winters for one. When and how can we correct these false statements to Carson's massive audience?

9. NBC: "The Tomorrow Show"

Tom Snyder and his staff have put more offensive sexfreaks on the air than any other show in television history. One night they presented a pathetically dumb Detroit prostitute whose teeth were either rotting or missing. The show's cocky host explained that the prostitute had sent a telegram, just *two* nights before, asking to come on television and discuss how she had sexually satisfied the entire Detroit Lions professional football team. (Vicious slander about athletes—and most of them are married.) Hard to believe, isn't it, Mr. Wiley? I sent a telegram that night begging for rebuttal time. No answer. Looks like a whore gets more respect than a spokesman for hundreds of thousands of decent Americans.

Seven months prior to this program with the prostitute, "The Tomorrow Show" did have on CDL's National Director, together with a spokesman from Morality in Media, Inc. The side for tradition gets one shot, while the slimiest, moral indigents appear month after month to argue their hedonist philosophy without opposition. Were we given the same opportunity to speak unchallenged? Hardly! As usual our appearance was in a panel format stacked 2 to 1 against us. That panel also included two pathetic hard-core porno performers, giving the program a freak show atmosphere.

CDL REQUEST FOR FAIRNESS
DOCTRINE BALANCE

I am now phoning NBC long distance—Los Angeles to New York City—on a weekly basis. I intend to hammer away until this show respects our right of access to the public airways, *our* airways.

NBC's "Today Show" and "Not for Women Only" have not done much better than their sister shows. Mr. Keating and Fr. Hill from Morality in Media got a little over a smashing five minutes each on the "Today Show." Keating in September of 1970 and Hill in June of 1973. Big deal!

10. National Syndicated Program—"The Mike Douglas Show"

Gore Vidal again! Naturally. And, of course, bi-sexuality is again a staple for afternoon or morning variety shows. CDL asked for fairness but get this: *I, Robert K. Dornan, have actually been booked, confirmed, "set" for three—count 'em—three "Mike Douglas Shows" and been cancelled all three times. Unbelievable!*

I have to believe Mike Douglas himself is not aware of this disgarceful runaround. I suspect Mike would appreciate presenting "the other side" because he appears to be a concerned parent.

First postponement: I was booked for "The Mike Douglas Show" on April 7, 1974, to answer Vidal plus others. A few days before the taping, an associate producer phoned California and told me that the co-host for the week, Bea Arthur (Maude), didn't want to appear with any "decency spokesman." They reset my taping for May 10, 1974. Since when do co-hosts blackball guests?

Second postponement: Two days before I was to fly to Philadelphia (They had my pre-paid airline tickets already waiting for me at the L.A. airport.), I got a phone call from another producer who told me that a six- or seven-year-old performer, Mason Reese, would be on the May 10th taping and they didn't want to discuss morality and/or immorality in front of a young child. I reminded them *which side* I was on but agreed to another postponement.

Now get this! *I was replaced on that May 10, 1974, taping —the show with that little boy—by a completely immoral weirdo who had run naked before the "live" TV cameras during the 1974 motion picture academy awards.*

(My cousin, Jack Haley, Jr., produced that Academy Awards show, and told me he had ordered this "creep streaker" arrested for cutting his way onto the stage through a $30,000 cyclorama backdrop. This type of massive blue cyc is the most expensive background in TV.) This exhibitionist was later arrested for running naked through a Los Angeles City Council Chamber at a fully attended legislation hearing (800 people). *He* was okay, as far as "The Mike Douglas Show" staff was concerned, to guest with a little six-year-old child, but not the National Spokesman for the nation's largest anti-pornography organization. Disgusting logic.

Third postponement. Maybe the longest put-off in TV history: A few days after my third taping date was set, I got a final telephone call *from* "The Mike Douglas Show" staff. (Since then I have originated many calls *to* them.) I was told that again a co-host had objections to me. Joan Rivers, a comedienne, did "not want to do a show with Bob Dornan." Strange. Speak up for Judeo-Christian ethics and you suddenly become a pariah. What's that New Testament quote by Jesus? "They will hate you in My name."

CDL REQUEST FOR FAIRNESS
DOCTRINE BALANCE

We have regularly placed reminder calls to the Douglas

staff in the last year and a half, particularly after Vidal's latest diatribe, but all to no avail. I'm still waiting for that *fourth* booking.

11. National Syndicated Program—"The David Susskind Show"
Better than most at balance, but not in the area of sexuality. Once more the scales are dumped totally in favor of the bizarre, the freakish, the hedonist, the anti-monogamous viewpoint.

CDL REQUEST FOR FAIRNESS DOCTRINE BALANCE

Not a single answer from them in two years. Not even in response to a personal visit that I made to the Susskind offices at 747 Third Avenue in New York City. Unfortunately, most of the young staff members on the larger TV shows are so liberal or radical or "sexually avant guard" (more talk than life-style) that I feel our letters get ash-canned before anyone with mature judgment even evaluates them. That's why I try to personally stop by the production offices. But even "the personal visit" seems to fail.

12. National Syndicated Program—"The Dinah Shore Show"
Suffice it to say, the same run of guests including Gore Vidal, Bobby Blake, Warren Beatty, et al., mouthing the same lightweight assaults upon Judeo-Christian ethics in the area of sexuality and voyeur violence-as-pleasure. Of course, these guests are all big on traditional morality as applied to napalm or Watergate.

It was tragic to see Warren Beatty hyping his "R"-rated film, "Shampoo," on this family type show. Dinah Shore, "the all American lady" (bookend to Mike Douglas' "the all American guy-next-door"), even giggled a bit over "that line" in "Shampoo" that has hit a new low in dialogue for "R" films—i.e., the gutter line of Julie Christie as she tries to remove Beatty's trousers at an elegant restaurant dinner party while screeching, "I want to s— his c—!"

This low level of discussion about morally decadent subject material is particularly offensive on syndicated shows because these programs appear in most markets during the morning or afternoon hours. Great for exposing young kids during the summer and on school holidays to the likes of

Gore Vidal. Also, those in their middle teens can be informed all about the latest "R" films that only two years ago would have been rated double "X" (i.e., "Lisztomania," "Shampoo," etc.)

CDL REQUEST FOR FAIRNESS DOCTRINE BALANCE

We got a curt "No, thank you." The staff member continued, " 'The Dinah Shore Show' doesn't do controversy."

13. Other National Syndicated Programs
A good word is in order for four shows that have had me on at least once, although that's not really "fairness" considering the parade of freaks who march across our "electronic bay windows to the world." The fair four are:
"The Merv Griffin Show"—April 6, 1973 (over 2 1/2 years ago)
"The Irv Kupcinet Show"—October 5, 1973 (over 2 years ago)
"The Phil Donahue Show"—July 19, 1974
"The Lou Gordon Show"—November 22, 1974
By the way, in case you were beginning to think that the National Spokesman for CDL is rejected by some of these TV shows because he is a drooling troglodyte, I submit as evidence that I am a better-than-average TV guest, the tremendous audience reaction to my appearances on those last four mentioned shows.
Several producers have put in writing that my TV debates and/or solo appearances have generated more favorable mail and phone calls than "any guest in years."
Well, Mr. Chairman, get the picture? Other than "dirty radio," things keep getting progressively more vulgar. It is impossible to believe that the spiritual antecedents of our once healthy culture can be defended and reinforced by the religious "time ghetto" of Sunday morning television when the big numbers just aren't there. Just as hopeless is the belief that the concept of "Family Viewing Hour" (distorted by four different time zones) is going to influence those who keep pumping out the voyeur violence and upping the ante of hedonism. I am personally opposed to the "Family Hour" because this "adults only" approach is only an attempt at quarantining a communicable plague. Interesting that the quarantined hedonism and brutality get the lion's share of

prime time at a 2 to 1 ratio. Also, this concept puts government into the improper position of judging the 'quality' of entertainment and public affairs, instead of government's proper function of insuring *fairness* in a controlled, limited-access medium of communication. By the way, if this Fairness Doctrine isn't enforced soon, we will lobby for its elimination so that citizens will at least be put "on guard." "On guard" that the "Manhattan Triopoly" of ABC-CBS-NBC can only be balanced by the free market concept of economic pressure and boycott, not by an unenforced governmental 'Doctrine' that is sneered at by those it purports to regulate.

Mr. Wiley, please forgive the length of this epistle, but it is still only a partial synopsis of years of personal experience with thoughtless and often arrogant bias in broadcasting.

Please advise Citizens for Decency through Law, Inc., what steps we can take with your guidance and assistance to see that we get our Fairness Doctrine rights.

Also, would you please advise us of your interpretation of that phrase in the Doctrine which reads, "with equal forcefulness." We take it to mean that, when a program is presenting "the other side," the program's staff cannot consistently select a Donald Meek, a Wally Cox, 'a mouse' to present that opposing viewpoint. Occasionally, "fairness" demands that they relinquish "their" platform to a *forceful* opposing advocate.

Respectfully and forcefully yours,

Robert K. Dornan[1]
National Spokesman

RKD:kmc

Enclosures

cc: FCC Commissioners:
       Messrs. Robert E. Lee,
       Benjamin L. Hooks,
       James H. Quello,
       Glen O. Robinson, Jr.,
       Abbott Washburn
       Ms. Charlotte F. Reid

cc: Mr. John Coleman, Chairman

232

Board of Directors
American Broadcasting Company

Mr. Leonard H. Goldenson
Chairman of the Board
American Broadcasting Company

Mr. Elton H. Rule, President
American Broadcasting Company

Mr. Frederick S. Pierce, President
ABC Television Division

Mr. Anthony L. Conrad
Chairman of the Board of RCA

Mr. Julian Goodman
Chairman of the Board
National Broadcasting Company

Mr. Herbert S. Schlosser, President
National Broadcasting Company

Mr. Robert T. Howard, President
NBC Television Network Division

Mr. William S. Paley
Chairman of the Board
Columbia Broadcasting System

Mr. Arthur R. Taylor, President
Columbia Broadcasting System

Mr. John A. Schneider, President
CBS Broadcast Group

Mr. Robert D. Wood, President
CBS Network Television Division

Certified Mail—Return Receipt Requested

Appendix 3, Section B

Letter Alleging New York Times Editorial Bias

Simon L. Leis, Jr.
Hamilton County Prosecuting Attorney
Hamilton County Courthouse
Room 420
Cincinnati, Ohio 45202
Area Code 513-632-8542

April 18, 1977

Mr. Arthur Ochs Sulzberger, Publisher
Mr. A. M. Rosenthal, Executive Editor
Mr. Max Frankel, Editorial Page Editor

The New York Times
229 West 43rd Street
New York, N.Y. 10036

Gentlemen:

Several weeks past I received a telephone call from Phillip Drysdale, a member of your Editorial Department, asking me whether or not I would like to defend myself for my actions in the Hustler case through means of an editorial. I was shocked, and responded that since when does a Prosecutor have to defend himself for doing his duty? Recognizing his mistake, he somewhat backed off the statement and suggested that since I had been criticized by the media because of the *Hustler* magazine case I might like to write an editorial stating my position. I hesitated because it was not my intent to reduce the level of a judicial decision to that of a carnival atmosphere by responding to all the criticism that has taken place. I told Mr. Drysdale I would let him know the following day as to whether or not I would accept that invitation.

After much deliberation I concluded that maybe the proper approach to this media criticism was to write an editorial stating our position. Accordingly, I notified Mr. Drysdale I would write the editorial he requested, and the attached document was transmitted to Mr. Drysdale several days later.

On March 16, 1977, Mr. Drysdale called my secretary and stated he liked the article, and some of the people at the paper to whom he showed it also liked it. However, he stated that the article was written as a rebuttal to editorials in general, and the policy of the New York Times was not to print any rebuttal to an editorial as such. He claimed they wanted to use the article, and therefore suggested three alternatives:

> 1. Revise the article so it will not be an actual rebuttal—change its wording but clear with me before running it.
> 2. If I did not want it revised they would abide by my decision and not use it.
> 3. Submit it to the letters editor, who may cut it a bit, but would not revise, and submit for my approval.

Subsequent to that call I personally talked to Mr. Drysdale and suggested that course number one be followed. To this date I have heard nothing from him, and as far as I know the editorial has never been published.

When I was asked to write this editorial there were no conditions whatsoever placed upon its content except for word limitation. It is rather obvious to me that your paper is embarrassed to run this editorial because it clearly points out the error your paper, and other papers, have committed by embracing the publication and its publisher. This is another clear example of intellectual dishonesty.

I have read this editorial to many groups here in this community and the reaction has been the same as my thoughts set out above. The dealing of your newspaper in this episode is certainly one in a long line of reasons why the public has become disenchanted with the media.

Yours very truly,
Simon L. Leis, Jr.
Prosecuting Attorney

UNPUBLISHED EDITORIAL

HUSTLER CASE—THE PROSECUTOR'S REPLY

In many sections of the country, including Cincinnati, a majority of the media has been generally critical of the Hustler case. The media has attempted, through editorials and articles, to misdirect and misguide the public. Their claim is the First Amendment to the Constitution was violated—freedom of the press. Obviously these editorials and articles are written from a selfish standpoint in that the media is somewhat concerned that the protection afforded them under this Amendment is being eroded. This fear is totally without any foundation in fact or in law.

To begin with, the Supreme Court of the United States has repeatedly pronounced obscene material is not protected under the First Amendment, and therefore states have the right to regulate its publication and dissemination. In Ohio the law does just that, and under it eleven issues of the *Hustler* magazine were judged to be obscene by a jury consisting of twelve members of this community (Cincinnati).

These critical editorials and articles have brushed aside the fact that the *Hustler* magazine and its publisher have been convicted of a crime. They have personally attacked me, as prosecutor, for adhering to my oath of office to enforce the laws of this state. These editorials and articles, by their very nature, are defending crime, which I find to be utterly amazing in view of the media's repeated air of self-righteousness. How can one construe prosecution of an admitted smut peddler as infringing upon the rights of those involved in legitimate news dissemination?

Criticism has been expressed because the magazine publisher has been convicted not only with publishing obscene material, but was also charged and convicted of organized crime, an offense carrying a more severe penalty than that of publishing obscene material.

It should be noted that the Legislature of the State of Ohio in 1974 passed the organized crime statute. This statute merely defines organized crime as a group of five or more people who violate a law for purposes of profit. It was not solely directed at the so-called "mafia" type of organized crime. It was a tool provided prosecutors to give the law some teeth in their fight against crime. As in many professions, including the media, every resource is utilized to accomplish a goal. In this case we did just that.

Pornographers could care less about a violation of law which carries a minor penalty, as obscenity does. They could withstand prosecution under the obscenity statute day in and day out, and still go about their business of distributing their obscene magazine. Little would be accomplished in the enforcement area if the obscenity statute alone were used. Because of the severity of the penalty under the organized crime statute, publishers will take a second look as to whether or not they will assume the risk of continued distribution of their obscene magazine.

The critics also claim that through the conviction of the publisher of *Hustler* magazine, Cincinnati is attempting to force its moral standards on the rest of the nation. We find this to be a weak and ridiculous argument. Today the magazine is still being sold in other parts of this state, as well as in many parts of this country.

To avoid this alleged secondary effect it has been suggested that the distributor should have been prosecuted rather than the publisher. Why should a publisher, who is the individual reaping enormous profits in degradation of the female body, be allowed to hide behind a local distributor? His responsibility as the publisher is much greater than that of the distributor, and therefore should be accountable for what he prints.

Apparently the majority of the media feels there should be no limitation as to the printed matter. Rather than attacking a prosecutor doing his duty, I suggest their attention should be directed to their respective legislative bodies, petitioning them to do away with the obscenity laws. Personally, I hope this never happens, for I have seen the effects of pornography. Times Square, once a lovely tourist attraction, is now a jungle because of the many adult bookstores, bawdy houses, adult movie houses and massage parlors dotting its streets.

In Cincinnati, because of our enforcement policy in this area, we have a clean, wholesome and vibrant city. Visitors and residents are able to walk our downtown streets. Recently Cincinnati was judged one of the ten most livable cities in the nation. I believe part of the reason for this is the community attitude against pornography. We are proud of this, and as Prosecuting Attorney I will continue my endeavors against obscenity to maintain this healthy atmosphere.

Appendix 4

JAMES CLANCY[1] PORTRAYS THE PROBLEM OF POOR JUDGES

The critical factor in [court] cases is and has always been the "quality" of the participating justices. Alexis de Tocqueville, a 19th-century political philosopher, made the following shrewd forecast concerning the future of these United States in his treatise *Democracy in America:*

> The peace, the prosperity, and the very existence of the Union are vested in the hands of the judges of the U.S. Supreme Court. . . . But if the Supreme Court is ever composed of imprudent men or bad citizens, the Union may be plunged into anarchy or civil war.

Speaking of the judges on the lower courts, he wrote:

> They must not only be good citizens, and men possessed of that information and integrity which are indispensable to magistrates, but they must be statesmen—politicians, not unread in the signs of the times, not afraid to brave the obstacles which can be subdued.

I have read just about every obscenity opinion reported during the past twenty years, and with this background have no hesitancy in saying that our greatest difficulty is with the "quality" of our judges. They just do not meet De Tocqueville's standards. In many instances they are not men "possessed of integrity," "statesmen" and "politicians read in the signs of the times." Let me cite a few examples:

1. In Fanning County, Texas, a justice of the peace admitted to reporters and grand jurors in Beaumont that he was paid $300 to sign court documents falsely certifying that jury trials were conducted in his court and that the juries found twelve different sexually explicit movies not obscene.

The justice of the peace resigned, but the resignation came too late to remove his name from the ballot and he was thereafter re-elected!

2. A Tennessee Court of Criminal Appeal Judge Charles Galbreath addressed a "fan" letter to *Hustler* magazine on official court of appeals letterhead, in which he stated that he enjoys reading pornographic literature. *Hustler,* a hardcore pornographic magazine, published the letter. When his fellow justices called for an investigation, the editor and publisher of *Hustler* agreed to pay Galbreath's salary for life

if he was impeached, and Galbreath said that he would take him up on it.

3. In Milan, Missouri, a police judge was elected on a platform of lawlessness and is reported as saying: "I told the people I wasn't going to enforce the laws and I'm going to keep that promise."

4. A Los Angeles Superior Court judge was arrested at a Hollywood theater and charged with an act of sexual perversion and lewd conduct with another man. He pleaded "no contest" to a lesser charge of trespassing and was put on probation with the admonition to avoid areas frequented by homosexuals and the suggestion that he seek psychiatric counseling.

5. A Michigan Supreme Court justice (former governor) resigned from the Michigan Supreme Court five days after being convicted of lying to a Federal Grand Jury in connection with an investigation on a charge that the judge was part of a $30,000 bribery conspiracy that involved getting a new trial for a convicted burglar.

6. The chief justice of the Michigan Supreme Court appeared on a television interview show and declared that marijuana, pornography, and prostitution should be decriminalized.

7. Within a span of little over one year, three justices on the Florida Supreme Court resigned while being investigated by the state's Judicial Qualifications Committee.

8. Two Illinois Supreme Court justices resigned while under investigation by the Better Government Association.

9. Two Oklahoma Supreme Court justices were thrown off the Oklahoma Supreme Court and one sent to prison for activities while on the Oklahoma bench.

10. In a major city in Florida, the mayor and two circuit judges and three others were indicted on bribery charges.

The examples I have given above do not paint a pretty picture—but it is a realistic one. Judges are not gods. In scrutinizing our difficulties with obscenity in the courtroom, we must be ever mindful of that fact. If judges allow pornography to become a part of the scenery in the community, then the community has got to start taking a hard look at the "quality" of its judges and determine whether it can afford to permit those judges to continue to sit.

This is not the first time this nation has had its serious moral problems. During World War I, prostitution presented a national problem and the high court with a similar crisis involving federal power. Those justices responded by up-holding the federal power to deal with prostitution on an interstate basis. The language used by the justices in those cases was exceptional. In *Caminetti* v. *United States,* the United States Supreme Court upheld convictions of two de-fendants under the Mann Act for transporting two women to become the defendants' concubines and mistresses. Com-menting on the persons who for hire or without hire offer their bodies to indiscriminate intercourse with others, the court said:

> The lives and examples of such persons are in hostility to the idea of the family, as consisting in and springing from the union for life of one man and one woman in the holy estate of matrimony, the sure foundation of all that is stable and noble in our civiliza-tion, the best guarantee of that reverent morality which is the source of all beneficient progress in social and political improve-ment.

In the year 1976, those words, uttered sixty years ago, seem strangely out of place. My hope is: (1) that they are not out of place and (2) that they may be heard again in some form in the decisions of this high court in the *Smith* and *Marks* cases.[2]

Appendix 5

REACTION IN MEDIA
TO ANTI-PORNOGRAPHY CAMPAIGN

"Letters to the Editor" in the *Victoria Advocate*, Victoria, Texas, January-February 1974 (used by permission of the Associated Press and the *Victoria Advocate*. Names changed to protect the innocent).

MORALITY GROUP HERE CHALLENGED ON AD

Editor,

I wish to take issue with an advertisement placed in Sunday's paper by a local morality in media organization. The advertisement indicated that the "dam" holding back pornography has broken, and that something must be done by citizens to remedy the situation. It seems that only half the story has been told here; both sides of the issue must be aired in order for the citizenry to make a just decision in this important matter.

First of all, I would like to compare the pornography issue with other recent trends in our society. In our Federal government, gross violations of civil rights have been disclosed, most notably in the Ellsberg case, in certain practices of the FBI, and in certain aspects of the Watergate scandal. Nearly every informed person—whether liberal or conservative—is outraged at these violations, and nearly everyone is demanding restoration of our fundamental guarantees. Yet very often, small special interest groups get away with attempting to curb other citizens' civil rights with nary an eyebrow raised in opposition. Those who attempt to take away what the Founding Fathers saw as our "God-given" rights are no less dangerous simply because they are not the Federal government.

Quoting the U.S. Commission on Obscenity and Pornography: "Empirical research designed to clarify the question has found no evidence to date that exposure to explicit sexual material plays a significant role in the causation of a delinquent or criminal behavior among youth or adults." This finding has been affirmed and reaffirmed by studies even more thorough than the Commission's, yet some people continue to believe not what is proven to them, but what their uninformed minds want to believe.

Also, the legal aspect of the pornography issue is not exactly as the advertisement has stated. According to the Supreme Court's new ruling, only the following fall under the jurisdiction of legal systems: "works, when taken as a whole, appeal to the prurient interest in sex, which portray sexual conduct in a patently offensive way, and which do not have serious literary, artistic, political or scientific value." The key here, as the majority opinion goes on to clarify, is "patently offensive." Very few magazines on Victoria newsstands, when taken as a whole, are "patently offensive" to anyone with a reasonably healthy mind. In the ad, the continual reference to these magazines as "pornographic" is legally unfounded, and likely to remain so as long as rational minds prevail.

Finally, I would like to comment on the moral aspect of the pornography issue. Man was born naked. It is not animal nature—or God's intention, depending upon your affiliation—that has made nudity and human sexuality something disgusting. Man has done that himself. Many people today are striving to free society from the stigma that has grown around sex and nudity, and I think this is a good thing. It is one more step toward man's freedom and total acceptance of himself. If some people abuse this noble endeavor along the way, well, they must be tolerated. So-called "victimless crimes" are receiving much leniency in our society. This is only fair, since personal freedom is vital to our aspirations.

William Blake said, "You never know what is enough unless you know what is more than enough." Let us, then, put society's newly acquired permissiveness to practical use in the arts and in our lives, rather than attempting to associate it with legality and morality, where clearly it has no place in Constitutional America.

BOB MARTIN

MARTIN'S LETTER DRAWS CHALLENGE

Editor,

In the January 1, 1974 issue, you published a letter from Bob Martin on the subject of pornography. I am sure that letter pleased the smut peddlers. The lack of truth and logic was typical of pornographer's propaganda. The heading read: "Morality Group Here Challenged on Ad." In response to that, you might call this "A Challenge to the Challenger." As I write this letter, I am not representing a morality organization; however, as a concerned father and citizen, I am submitting these words to meet Wertin's challenge.

I agree with Mr. Wertin when he says, "Both sides of

the issue must be aired in order for the citizenry to make a just decision in this important matter." I am glad he considers it an important matter. For the most part, however, the pornographer's side has been heard, so I am ready to air the issue with Mr. Martin or anyone who is like-minded.

Since I am not acquainted with Mr. Martin, this is not to be taken as an attack upon him. I am attacking the inane ideas he has presented to the public.

Mr. Martin wants "to compare the pornography issue with other recent trends in our society." I, too, want to make a comparison. Look at the recent trend in Victoria's crime rate, especially forcible rape. The city's Police Department statistics show a 400 per cent increase of forcible rape cases in just one year, 1972 to 1973. How can we account for this, when other cities of comparable size had very slight increases? In *Paris Adult Theater I* v. *Slaton*, the United States Supreme Court decision cited the Hill-Link report which indicated that there was at least "an arguable correlation between obscene material and crime."

When Mr. Martin criticizes "small special interest groups" who are "attempting to curb other citizens' civil rights," he seems to be affirming that it is a pornographer's civil right to present filth to our children. By the same logic, one could uphold the dope peddler's right to sell LSD to little boys and girls. Mr. Martin is afraid that someone will "take away what the Founding Fathers saw as our 'God-given' rights." Such rights will not be taken away by decent people; they will be taken away by smut peddlers and their filthy friends.

Mr. Martin quotes the U.S. Commission on Obscenity and Pornography in an attempt to show that "exposure to explicit sexual material" has no significant relation to criminal behavior. Such a statement is an insult to people with common sense. In essence, it declares that words and pictures do not influence behavior. But fathers and mothers have enough common sense to know that children and adults alike are taught and influenced by pictures and words. It is really a shame that some people have been duped by the conclusions of a few Washington politicians. But like Mr. Martin says, "some people continue to believe not what is proven to them, but what their uninformed minds want to believe." That is so true, and informed minds know that the conclusions of the quoted commission were rejected by the Senate and the President. By a 60 to 5 vote, the Senate declared that

"(1) generally the findings and recommendations are not supported by the evidence considered by or available to the Commission and (2) the Commission has not properly performed its duties nor has it complied with the mandates of Congress." The President said: "The Commission has performed a disservice and I totally reject its report."

In regard to "the legal aspect of the pornography issue," the United States Supreme Court decision of June 21, in *Miller* v. *California*, said: "This much has been categorically settled by the Court, that obscene material is unprotected by the First Amendment."

When Mr. Martin speaks about the "magazines on newsstands," he at least admits that some are "patently offensive." Since that is the truth, the law is being violated, and people with "rational minds" want something done about it.

Mr. Martin's "comment on the moral aspect of the pornography issue" is ridiculous. In an illogical attempt to justify adult nudity, he says: "Man was born naked." Mr. Martin failed to add that when man realized he was naked, he clothed himself (Gen. 3:7, 21).

Mr. Martin expresses his concern about man's freedom. He should know that society has the right to limit freedoms that threaten public safety. A dope peddler wants freedom to sell marijuana and heroin; the rapist wants to be as free as a rooster in a barnyard; members of the "gay liberation" want to marry each other (Rom. 1:27); and smut peddlers want to perform their "noble endeavor" and "free society from the stigma that has grown around sex and nudity." Decent families, who opposed all of this—"well, they must be tolerated."

Mr. Martin quotes a verse from William Blake's "Proverbs of Hell," and that is interesting. He said: "You never know what is enough unless you know what is more than enough." The very next verse says: "Listen to the fool's reproach!"

Finally, in answering Mr. Martin's challenge, I will affirm that pornography has "no place in Constitutional America." In *Roth* v. *U.S.*, the U.S. Supreme Court said: "We hold that obscenity is not within the area of constitutionally protected speech or press." In *Kaplan* v. *California*, the Court said: "Obscenity is not protected by the Constitution."

With this challenge met, you can be assured that I will not remain a silent citizen.

JIM SANDER

OPPOSES GROUP HERE

Editor,

Until this time, I could not take the self-righteous group who call themselves Christians for Decency in Media, etc., seriously enough to warrant a response. However, a letter by Miss Paulson, who is a long-time friend, prompted this response.

Initially, I think the title this group has imposed on itself is totally incorrect. I feel a title such as "Communists for Decency," etc., would be much more appropriate. I base this opinion on the definition of communism. Also, I feel that a Christian would not be so anxious to stick his nose into a person's private affairs.

Secondly, Miss Paulson insists that the pornographic material is soiling the minds of our children. I wonder if she truly believes that the flow of such material can possibly be prevented from reaching a curious child. I just hope that when my children are at an impressionable age and come across such "treacherous" material, they will not have the fear and guilt feelings that will prevent them from coming to me and discussing the matter and SEX openly.

I am convinced there are many more people with mental problems resulting from the needless ignorance, fear, and guilt of sex than from the "great problem" of someone viewing a *Playboy* or *Penthouse* openly. The fear, ignorance, and guilt usually result from the attitudes imposed on them by parents with much the same problem. I would not care to speculate the number of people who may belong to this Decency Group who may fit into this category.

Also, the last time my wife and I were attending the local theater showing these "perverted movies," I certainly cannot recall seeing any children who had driven out to corrupt their minds.

Lastly, I would like to challenge Mr. C. O. Darmer, since he seems to be challenging the local law enforcement agencies, to publicly advertise that anyone who views pornographic material would not be welcomed in his stores because surely he would not care to profit from their filthy money.

I cannot ever recall being forced to view pornographic material or any other material and for this I thank God every day. Also a Christian,

NORRIS NYLAND

MINISTER RAPS MISSIVE

Editor,

I suppose it is impossible to respond to every letter published in *The Advocate* concerning decency, but Mr. Norris Nyland's letter is more degenerate than some of the films advertised in *The Advocate*. Inasmuch as Mr. Nyland is of the judgment that "Christians for Decency" might better be called "Communists for Decency," one does not have to wonder about his use or understanding of the term "Christian," when he closed with the incredible line, "Also a Christian." Since it is obvious that he doesn't know what a "Christian" is, one could not expect him to recognize a "Communist." I would suggest to the reading public that being a communist for decency is much to be preferred over Mr. Nyland's idea of a "Christian for indecency."

The statement of fact that Mr. Nyland is convinced that "there are many more people with mental problems resulting from needless ignorance, fear and guilt of sex" is surely not to suggest that such things as these are faced and solved by promoting subscriptions to pornographic magazines. "Christians for Decency" are opposed to ignorance, fear and neurotic guilt, as well as being opposed to pornographic magazines.

"Christians for Decency" are not opposed to art, beauty or sex. If everyone found as much joy in decency as "Christians for Decency" find in sex, neither the psychologists nor the police would be overworked. Some of the letters published may make a few wonder if it would be best if ministers in the future referred the desperate parents, whose unmarried daughter is pregnant, to Mr. Carlson, Mr. Martin, Mr. Nyland and their colleagues. What about it? Please advise us whether or not you think this city and the future of this country would be better secured if we refer, for counseling, to our pornographic promoters the man who confides in us that he covets his neighbor's wife? Do you honestly believe that our libertine friends are interested in, and can help the young rapist with whom we've been working, now on probation from prison?

I would write more, but I just received a call from a mother of several small children. Their utilities have been turned off, being unable to pay the bill. They are cold, hungry, deserted—lacking the warmth of security of love. You see, they are "children of passion," victims of a marriage of sex without love. We do not know where the father is. We've tried to reach him, but he doesn't spend much time in church. However, it is reported that he does frequent adult movie houses and pornographic book shops. Do you suppose Mr. Martin, Mr. Carlson, Mr. Nyland or one of their colleagues just might bump into him, and help him to be a better husband and father?

"He who has mud in mind is worse than ostrich with head in sand." Neither,

GEORGE CASH
Minister of Men

MINISTER RAPS 'DECENCY' UNIT

Editor,

The current group of self-righteous protectors of public decency have espoused two of the basic tactics of those who would destroy the God-given freedom of people from coercion.

First, the so-called decency group has chosen a negative issue to proclaim and defend. It is easy to be against something, for the issue and defense of that issue lie in the simple and destructive ability to say no. A negative stand requires only blind devotion to destruction of ideas and people who would choose to be in opposition to it. At the same time, defense of a negative position requires no debate with people, no listening to divergent views, and no compassionate concern for others; but only a slavish and negative legalism.

The so-called decency group has also adopted the ancient and despicable tactic of asserting that their viewpoint alone is the epitome of righteousness, while any who oppose them are by definition evil. Such shabby, cowardly and underhanded tactics speak poorly for those who would proclaim Jesus the Christ as Lord and Savior.

This so-called decency group behaves as if the totality of the gospel is narrow, negative legalism. In reality, the key to life in the Spirit of Jesus the Christ is the great good news of His good victory over evil, His victory of life over death, and the victory of His YES over man's selfish, narrow, and legalistic no. The decency vigilantes seem to have forgotten that Jesus came to save, rather than to destroy sinners. I am confident that Jesus has not forgotten.

THE REV. MR. DON MARK OLSON
Presbyterian Church, U.S.

REV. OLSON'S VIEW ATTACKED BY MINISTER

Editor,

The people are well acquainted with the "Decency in Media and Literature" group. I fully support the aim of this group in their fight to improve the moral climate of our community. I know we have "filth and obscene" literature and movies being openly paraded. It is a literal fact that the public distribution and sale of such things is illegal. It is further a fact that such materials have mind-warping effect upon both youth and adult. In spite of both of these facts the sales and distribution continue.

There have been numerous charges hurled against the "decency" group. Some of these charges are utterly false and many others are caused by misunderstanding and misinformation. But the charge that compelled me to write was a matter written by Rev. Don Mark Olson, Presbyterian Church. His opening paragraph reads: "The current group of self-righteous protectors of public decency have espoused two of the basic tactics of those who would destroy the God-given freedom of people from coercion."

In his article Mr. Olson glibly uses the name of Jesus and the Gospel in his tirade against those who seek to uphold morality and the "law of the land." He uses far worse tactics himself than those he castigates. He calls us (I'm a member of the group) a group of "self-righteous protectors." That charge is a lie. It is a charge he cannot prove and shows judgmentalism in his own mind. He further condemns us for being "cowardly, shabby and underhanded" in our tactics which (he says) speaks poorly of those who would proclaim Jesus as Lord and Saviour. I ask, "What is shabby, underhanded and cowardly about council?" "What is cowardly in a public challenge to anyone for a debate on this issue?" If such things are cowardly, then either he or I flunked English. But I further ask, "What is more cowardly than making public accusations of unchristian tactics on a group of people while such accusations are totally unsupported by fact, logic or inference?"

Mr. Olson's article is public proof of the fruits of religious liberalism. The modernistic view of "Taking Jesus' YES over evil which (they say) negates man's NO" actually means nothing to the average man. To liberal theologians it means a man can "say Yes to Jesus in his heart and then live as he well pleases."

The religious liberalistic view (which seems to be his) completely denies the Word of God. If someone cannot stand up and fight immorality, then he must censure the apostle Paul for demanding the disfellowship from the church the man who was living in a perverted sexual situation (1 Cor. 5:1). Further, Paul was wrong when he told the Ephesians to "stand, fight and uphold" the truth of God (Eph. 6:10-17). Certainly, we wouldn't want anyone so fanatical as to refuse to be "conformed to the world" (Rom. 12:2). The problem lies in the fact that liberals and modernists do not believe the Bible.

And please, Mr. Olson, most of us have enough trouble "seeking to live right" without some preachers going around saying "wrong is right." While we certainly praise God for His salvation through Jesus, we still need to get a "cord of ropes" and drive sin-peddlers from the "temple of our community."

ANDY ELGIN, Minister

Check it out for yourself. Do the letters educate or do they merely boast, rage, and insult?

When you write: (1) nail down the issues; (2) write clear, tight, and tough; and (3) re-write it and re-write it until you get it right.

Notes for Chapter 1

1. Jeremiah 23:27 says, "If they [leaders] were mine, they would try to turn my people from their evil ways."
2. Not the same as George Orwell's distinguished novel.
3. UPI Release, October, 1975.
4. "The Dirty Business of Kid Pornography," Joseph Mancini, *New York Post*, April 30, 1977.
5. "Child's Garden of Perversity," *Time*, April 4, 1977.
6. Densen-Gerber citation.
7. Bantam Books, 1970, N.Y., pp. 640-650.
8. *Cleveland Plain Dealer*, 11-25-75.
9. Cited in *Nashville Tennesseean*, October 2, 1975.
10. George Denison, "Sultan of Smut: The Life and Times of Mike Thevis, Operator of America's Largest Network," *Reader's Digest*, November, 1975, pp. 107-108.
11. *New York Times*, April 21, 1972, p. 20.
12. Artificial vaginas and penises, life-size (5'4") rubber dolls of women "anatomically complete" with mouths spread open.
13. *The Minneapolis Star*, November 17, 1975, p. 1ff.

Notes for Chapter 2

1. *Texas Police Journal*, March, 1974, pp. 1, 2.

Notes for Chapter 3

1. There is a difference between nakedness and nudity. See Question and Answer Section, chapter 9.

Notes for Chapter 4

1. Sometimes, to "punish" a retailer, a wholesaler will discontinue all magazines. But the wholesaler can't keep that up—especially if *all* retailers refuse to handle porno.
2. Jack Exum, "I Can't Believe I'm That Powerful," *World Radio News*, Fall, 1973.
3. In Rhode Island we do and we make it stick.
4. The "dangerous citizen" label was yelled in my face by a police chief who threatened to lock me up. His city was loaded with porno and he refused to move. I kept on complaining and picketing. Eventually, the shelves and screens were cleaned.
5. In the past three years, you've been in hundreds and hundreds and hundreds of supermarkets, drugstores, quick-stop stores, book-stores, airport/motel lobbies, too. Did you look at the magazine racks? Did you complain?
6. And kids also buy them. I once asked a clerk how he checked ID's to be sure that he wasn't breaking the law by selling to kids.

He said, "Oh, are you supposed to check ID's? Are there some people who are not supposed to read this?"

7. "Times Square Getting Moral Boost," *The National Courier,* October 21, 1975, p. 4.

8. You can start by writing a letter of thanks to: Kenneth A. Macke, President, Target Stores, 777 Nicollet Mall, Minneapolis, Minn. 55402 (Target is a discount chain in the midwest and southwest); W. Harrison, Sr., Taylor Drug Stores, Box 1884, Louisville, KY 40201 (drugstore chain in Ky.); and President, First National Stores, Somerville, Mass. 02143 (Supermarket chain in New England).

All three chains, though suffering financial loss, refuse to sell any porno magazines, including the long pin, *Playboy.* Don't just write. Shop at these stores and tell these managers *why* you're shopping there.

9. See pp. 134-136.

10. In that particular city, three letters to the editor and news items were in the paper each day for several weeks straight. It was the hottest news item of the year. People who wanted to sell and read porno bristled with hate in their letters.

11. William Barclay, *The Letter to the Romans.* Philadelphia: The Westminster Press, 1957, p. 240.

12. Courtesy, *Morality in Media,* 487 Park Avenue, N.Y., N.Y., pp. 24, 25.

13. *Rochester Democrat and Chronicle,* Rochester, N.Y., April 19, 1975.

14. "Censoring the Obscene: A Place for Common Sense," *Times-Union,* April 29, 1975, p. 14A.

15. "Mike the Porno Fighter," *Rochester Magazine,* Rochester, N.Y., April 1974, pp. 33-39.

16. "The Man Who Took a Stand for Decency," *Guideposts,* May, 1974, pp. 22, 23.

17. "MM Man of the Month , Robin Tellor," *Morality in Media,* December, 1976, p. 4.

18. *Palo Alto Times,* December 1, 1976, p. 11.

19. Jimmy Carter, *Why Not the Best,* Bantam Books, p. 31.

20. *National Decency Reporter,* November-December, 1976, p. 2.

21. The 1976 Presidential elections dramatized the importance of *personal* visits. Beginning in New Hampshire, Jimmy Carter and his (then) small group of supporters knocked on doors, talking to people—one at a time.

22. Volume XIII, No. 6, p. 2.

23. *Newsweek,* February 28, 1977.

Notes for Chapter 5

1. *Why We Can't Wait,* New America Library, 1964, p. 42.

2. In several places in the decision, the Court used "community" interchangeably with "state," suggesting that "community standards" are, at least, statewide standards. At least several states

have so interpreted it and so have written it into their obscenity codes.

3. Areola is the shaded portion encircling the nipple.

4. If interested in further information, see *State of Rhode Island* v. *Normand J. Cardin* (IND. No. 72-269) and *State of Rhode Island* v. *Joseph Markovitz* (IND. No. 72-281) in Appendix, pp. 214, 215.

5. *Boston Herald Traveler—Record American*, "Renewed Drive Against Smut," July 18, 1972, p. 20.

6. The law was challenged in Nashville and *upheld* in Court.

7. Neither of which are necessary under this law.

8. Court decision in Appendix.

9. See steps outlined on pp. 86-101.

10. Or they'll be forced to clean up their magazines, making their pages vehicles for ideas rather than flesh.

11. *The Evening Bulletin*, Prov., R.I., Thursday, April 7, 1977.

12. *Ginsberg* v. *New York*, supra, 640.

13. *Ginsberg* v. *New York*, supra, 638.

14. *The Providence Journal*, Providence, R.I., May 9, 1975, p. A13.

15. *Providence Journal Evening Bulletin*, Prov., R.I. 2/9/77, p. A4.

16. *Christian Life*, January, 1977, p. 15.

17. *The Weekly Journal*, Anaheim, California, November 20, 1975, pp. 1, 5.

18. Taken from *Kisley* v. *City of Falls Church*, 187 S.E. 2d 168 (Sup. of Va., 1972), *cert.* denied, 40 L.W. 2616 U.S. Supr. Crt., 8/3/72.

Notes for Chapter 6

1. *Bearded God of Histiaia*, Attic, c. 470 B.C., Athens.

2. *Detail of David*, Michelangelo, Florence.

3. *Samson Defeating Philistines*, After Michelangelo. Casa Buonarroti, Florence.

4. *Mercury*, Giambologna, Borgello, Florence.

5. *Soldier's Gravestone*, Greco-Roman. Capitoline, Rome.

6. *Crucifixion*, Michelangelo. Louvre.

7. *Muscular Legs*, Leonardo da Vinci. Royal Library. Windsor.

8. *Creation of Adam*, Michelangelo. Sistine Chapel, Vatican.

9. A prostitute is anyone selling his or her body for sexual purposes.

10. From *The Prosecutor*, 1970, by William Cahn, District Attorney of Nassau County, New York, and president, National District Attorney's Association.

Notes for Chapter 7

1. Ronald J. Snider, "Evangelism or Social Justice: Eliminating the Options," *Christianity Today*, October 8, 1976, pp. 26-29.

2. Dr. Stanley Mooneyham, *What Do You Say to a Hungry World*, 1975, p. 241.

3. "Times Square Getting Moral Boost," William Proctor, *National Courier,* Oct. 21, 1975, p. 4.

4. T. W. Wilson, Chapel address, Southwestern Baptist Theological Seminary, September 23, 1971. Fort Worth, Texas.

5. *National Decency Reporter*, January-February, 1977, pp. 1, 4.

Notes for Chapter 8

1. American Library Association, Intellectual Newsletter, September, 1973, p. 122.

2. *Texas Police Journal*, March, 1974, p. 1.

3. *New York Daily News*, November 6, 1976.

4. Quality of judges, however, rapidly increases with public pressure.

5. Reinhold Niebuhr said: "Man's capacity for good makes democracy possible; but man's capacity for evil makes democracy necessary."

6. Frederick Douglass, 4th of July, 1852.

7. *The Boston Herald American,* November 17, 1976, p. 1. (One month later, Populo died.)

8. *Providence Journal Evening Bulletin*, November 30, 1976, p. A-3.

Notes for Chapter 9

1. Simon Leis, District Attorney for Hamilton County (Cincinnati, Ohio), won the landmark conviction against *Hustler* magazine.

Notes for Chapter 11

1. *The Cedar Rapids Gazette*, December 24, 1975, p. 7.

2. *Christianity Today,* January 7, 1977, p. 39.

3. *Morality in Media,* June-July, 1976.

4. *The Evening Bulletin*, March 25, 1976, p. A-10.

5. *Christianity Today,* November 5, 1976, p. 89.

Notes for Appendix 3

1. Robert K. Dornan is now a United States Representative.

Notes for Appendix 4

1. James Clancy is a constitutional attorney who has argued many obscenity cases before the Supreme Court.

2. James Clancy, speech at Salt Palace, Salt Lake City, Utah, October 16, 1976.